THE **BIG** **BOOK** OF
CURRIES

SUNIL VIJAYAKAR

THE **BIG** BOOK OF **CURRIES**

365 MOUTHWATERING RECIPES FROM AROUND THE WORLD

DUNCAN BAIRD PUBLISHERS
LONDON

For Finn and Geraldine, with love and thanks.

The Big Book of Curries
Sunil Vijayakar

Distributed in the USA and Canada by
Sterling Publishing Co., Inc.
387 Park Avenue South
New York, NY 10016-8810

This edition first published in the UK and USA in 2010 by
Duncan Baird Publishers Ltd
Sixth Floor, Castle House
75–76 Wells Street
London W1T 3QH

Managing Editor: Grace Cheetham
Editor: Nicole Bator
Managing Designer: Suzanne Tuhrim
Commissioned photography: William Lingwood
Photography Assistant: Isobel Wield
Food Stylist: Sunil Vijayakar
Assistant Food Stylist: Aya Nishimura
Prop Stylist: Rachel Jukes

Library of Congress Cataloging-in-Publication Data

Vijayakar, Sunil.
  The big book of curries : 365 mouthwatering recipes from around the world / Sunil Vijayakar.
    p. cm.
  Includes bibliographical references and index.
  ISBN 978-1-84483-958-2 (alk. paper)
  1. Cookery (Curry) 2. Cookery, Southeast Asian. I. Title.
  TX819.C9V546 2010
  641.5959--dc22

                        2010007297

ISBN: 978-1-84483-958-2

10 9 8 7 6 5 4 3 2 1

Typeset in Frutiger
Color reproduction by Scanhouse, Singapore
Printed in China by Imago

For information about custom editions, special sales, premium and corporate purchases, please contact Sterling Special Sales Department at 800-805-5489 or specialsales@sterlingpub.com.

Publisher's Note: While every care has been taken in compiling the recipes for this book, Duncan Baird Publishers, or any other persons who have been involved in working on this publication, cannot accept responsibility for any errors or omissions, inadvertent or not, that may be found in the recipes or text, nor for any problems that may arise as a result of preparing one of these recipes. If you are pregnant or breastfeeding or have any special dietary requirements or medical conditions, it is advisable to consult a medical professional before following any of the recipes contained in this book. Ill or elderly people, babies, young children and women who are pregnant or breastfeeding should avoid the recipes containing uncooked eggs or raw meat or fish.

Notes on the recipes
Unless otherwise stated:
• Use large eggs, fruit, and vegetables
• Use fresh ingredients, including herbs and chilies
• 1 tsp. = 5ml 1 tbsp. = 15ml 1 cup = 240ml

Author's acknowledgments: Many thanks to Nicole for her meticulous editing and delicious cookies, to Suzanne for being a terrific designer of this book, to William for his beautiful photography and to Grace for commissioning this book.

CONTENTS

INTRODUCTION

Curry. The word alone awakens the senses, invoking visions of vibrantly colored spices piled high, their aromatic fragrances filling the air of far-away bustling markets. The word also sets a certain expectation—of a hot and piquant dish that sets the palette on fire in a dizzying melody of spice and heat. Yes, you can eat a curry that will blow your socks off, but on the whole, most curry recipes are a balanced blend of various spices and herbs, used with delicacy and intended to appeal to highly sophisticated tastes.

ORIGINS OF THE CURRY

Stemming from the South Indian Tamil word "kari," which means "sauce" or "gravy," the word curry in India refers to the spice blend used to flavor a dish. The term in English has evolved to describe any of a general variety of spiced, saucy dishes, which use as their base fresh and dried herbs and spices. Curries are best known in the cuisines of South and Southeast Asia, but foreign trade, invasions, and immigration have all helped to spread these traditional dishes around the world, influencing a diverse range of other cuisines, from Jamaica to Japan.

In our modern life, we take culinary diversity for granted. With supermarkets, restaurants, greengrocers, farmers' markets, and speciality stores catering for every possible cuisine and taste, we are fortunate enough to be able to enjoy food from all over the world. During the European Age of Discovery, though, when exotic spices were first exported around the world, they were seen as rare and valuable commodities, sometimes fetching prices greater than those for precious stones and gold. As trade from merchant ships flourished during the eighteenth century, a greater variety of exotic spices was available to many more countries, each of which worked these ingredients into their own cuisines.

The concept of curry was brought to the West in the eighteenth century by British colonists in India. Civil servants and officers in the British Raj acquired a taste for the spicy dishes found throughout the subcontinent, and they soon brought these newly discovered recipes home and to other parts of their empire. In the process, the British adapted these recipes to suit their own tastes. Mulligatawny soup, for example, is a mild version of its fiery Indian forebear, which was a type of South Indian sauce.

This culinary exchange also worked in reverse. From the British in India, Malaysia, and Burma; the French and Chinese in Vietnam; the Dutch in Indonesia; the Spanish in the Philippines; and the Portuguese in the Goa, colonial powers brought new ingredients and new ways of life with them, leaving their mark on recipes, too. In the sixteenth century, for example, the Portuguese introduced meats such as pork and beef into Indian cuisine; the famous Goan pork vindaloo remains popular today.

HOW TO EAT A CURRY

Curries are almost always served with a simple rice dish or bread. Other accompaniments are used to add refreshing flavors or to temper a curry's spiciness. Crunchy salads, such as Kachumber, and cooling relishes, such as yogurt-based raitas, are some of the most common accompaniments.

In general, a "wet" curry (one that is saucy) is usually served on or with rice and can be accompanied by the pickles and chutneys of your choice. 'Dry' curries, kebabs, and many vegetable curries are usually served with bread, such as naan, paratha, and roti, and are usually eaten by scooping the food with your fingers into pieces of the bread. These, too, can be served with small quantities of pickles, chutneys, and relishes to add an extra kick to the meal.

CURRYING Flavor
A Glossary of Ingredients

The recipes in this book use many familiar ingredients, such as cinnamon, cayenne pepper, and garlic. Other ingredients, such as curry leaves, star anise, and kaffir lime leaves, might be new to you. This section introduces some of these more "exotic" ingredients. You can buy most of them in any large supermarket or specialty food store, or order them online and have them delivered to your door.

Fresh Aromatics and Wet Spices

Fresh herbs and aromatics, such as Thai basil, lemongrass, and cilantro, and "wet" spices, such as galangal, coconut, and shallots, play an essential role in curries of all kinds. Always buy the freshest ingredients you can find.

Chilies: Fresh green and red chilies are used in many curries to provide heat and flavor. The intensity of their heat depends largely on the variety of chili. Red chilies, especially bird's-eye chilies, tend to be hotter than green chilies, but there are exceptions. Much of the heat resides in the pith and seeds, so if you want the chili flavor but with less heat, slit the chilies in half lengthwise and remove the pith and seeds before slicing or chopping.

Cilantro: The "parsley" of the East, fresh cilantro is used widely in Asian cooking. Often the delicate leaves are used to flavor dishes, but the stems and roots are also occasionally used, especially in Thai curry pastes.

Curry leaves: These highly aromatic leaves are used fresh in Indian and Southeast Asian cooking. They come attached to stems in sprays—simply pull the leaves off the stems to use and freeze any leftovers. Frozen curry leaves can be used straight from the freezer. If fresh curry leaves are not available, many supermarkets sell dried ones.

Curry paste: A blend of dry and wet aromatics, curry paste is often used as the base for a curry. The paste is often fried in a small amount of oil at the start of cooking to release the flavors. See pages 13 to 15 for a selection of the curry pastes used in this book.

Galangal: Like its cousin ginger, galangal is a common ingredient in curries and other savory dishes. It is peeled and cut into very fine slivers or finely chopped. You can substitute ginger for it if needed.

Kaffir lime leaves: These leaves come from the knobbly kaffir lime tree and are highly aromatic. They are usually finely shredded or sliced when used in a curry, but they can sometimes be left whole. They freeze very well and can be used straight from the freezer.

Lemongrass: Widely used in Southeast Asia, this green grass is used for its citrus flavor and aroma. It can be used by bruising the base of the stem and then adding it whole to a sauce and leaving it to infuse; or it can be sliced finely or chopped. Make sure to remove the outer layer of leaves before using.

Shallots: These sweet, pungent members of the onion family are widely used in Southeast Asian cooking. The easiest way to peel them is to slice them in half and remove the outer skin. Thai shallots are smaller than regular shallots and usually pinkish-purple in color; use small regular shallots if these are unavailable.

Sugar cane: This tropical grass is the source of cane sugar. The hard, fibrous stalks, or sticks, are available in some Asian and Caribbean speciality shops. Sugar cane is used in beverages, juiced, or distilled. The sticks can also be used as skewer for grilling, broiling, or frying foods.

Thai basil: Found in Asian food stores, this delicate herb is usually used to garnish and flavor a Thai curry. You can substitute regular basil if Thai basil is unavailable.

Dry Spices and Other Ingredients

Dried spices and other cupboard ingredients are as integral to a successful curry as fresh ingredients. Use dried herbs and spices within six months, as they lose their flavor over time.

Amchoor: Also known as dried mango powder, this spice is used as a souring agent in Indian curries. Substitute with a little lemon juice or tamarind paste if amchoor is unavailable.

Asafetida: Sold in ground or lump form, this plant resin is extremely strong and pungent in flavor. It is used only in very tiny amounts, usually in lentil preparations. It is believed to counteract flatulence.

Cardamom: This spice is usually used whole, in its pod, as an aromatic addition to rice and curries, but you can also use the black seeds inside the pods by crushing the pods to release them. Cardamom is a common component of spice mixtures such as garam masala and curry powders, which might use whole cardamom pods or just the seeds.

Cassia: Also known as Chinese cinnamon, cassia has a coarser texture and stronger flavor than cinnamon.

Chapati flour: Also known as atta, this blend of wholewheat and all-purpose flours is used to make various kinds of Indian flatbreads. It can be found easily in any good Asian supermarket or specialty food store.

Coconut cream: Used in smaller quantities than coconut milk (see below), coconut cream is thicker than coconut milk because it contains less water.

Coconut milk: Indispensable in the cuisines of many Asian countries, canned coconut milk imparts a rich, creamy texture. You can make your own coconut milk from the grated flesh of fresh coconuts, but this is a time-consuming job, as the coconut has to be mixed with water, blended, and then strained. Good-quality canned coconut milk, used throughout this book, is sold in supermarkets.

Coriander seeds: These small, pale brown seeds of the coriander plant form the base of many curry pastes and mixes. They are available whole or ground.

Crispy fried onions: These can be bought already fried from any good Asian supermarket. If you want to make your own from scratch, however, slowly fry thinly sliced onions in a large skillet with a little sunflower oil over low heat 15 to 20 minutes until golden. Drain on paper towels until crisp and dried.

Cumin seeds: Essential in Asian cooking, these small brown seeds are used whole or ground. They have a distinctive, warm, pungent aroma. Whole seeds can be dry-roasted and sprinkled over a curry or dish just before serving.

Curry powder: A blend of different spices, curry powder is a frequent addition to, but not always a requirement for, curry dishes. See pages 11 to 12 for a selection of the curry powders used in this book. Prepared curry powders are widely available in many different varieties.

Dried bean curd skins: Also called bean curd skins or Chinese yuba, these are made from the skin that forms on soy milk when it is heated. Dried bean curd comes in many shapes—the sheets and sticks are two of the more common ones. Normally, dried bean curd is reconstituted by dipping it in warm water before using, unless it is being simmered or the dish is meant to be very crisp. If kept in a cool, dry place, bean curd skins will keep indefinitely.

Fenugreek seeds: These shiny yellow seeds are usually square in shape. They are used widely in pickles and ground into spice mixes for curries.

Fish sauce: Also widely known as nam pla, this sauce is one of the main ingredients in Thai and Vietnamese cooking. It is made from the liquid extracted from salted, fermented fish. It should be refrigerated after opening.

Garam masala: This classic spice mix is usually added to a dish at the end of cooking. A classic mix comprises ground cardamom, cloves, cumin, peppercorns, cinnamon, and nutmeg. See the recipe on page 11.

Ghee: Also known as clarified butter, ghee is butter that has been heated to remove the milk solids, then left to cool and solidify again. The removal of the milk solids means ghee can withstand high temperatures without burning as easily as regular butter. It can be found in supermarkets and Asian shops.

Gram flour: Also known as besan or chickpea flour, this pale yellow flour is used widely in Indian cuisine for thickening and binding. It is also the main ingredient in many savory batters and breads.

Kecap asin/kecap manis: Kecap is the Indonesian word for soy sauce. There are many varieties, but the two used in this book are kecap asin, a slightly thick, salty sauce, and kecap manis, a thick, sweet sauce. They are available in Asian speciality shops.

Legumes: Widely used in many cuisines, legumes are an excellent low-fat source of protein and fiber. When using dried legumes, pick through them carefully to remove any stones that might have slipped through during packaging and rinse them well. Soaking legumes prior to cooking helps shorten the cooking time. The most common pulses used in curries are split red lentils (masoor) and yellow split lentils (chana dal), neither of which requires soaking.

Mustard seeds: Black, brown, or yellow, these tiny round seeds are a common flavoring in many dishes and impart a mellow, nutty flavor. They are usually fried in oil until they "pop," then cooked with other ingredients or drizzled over a finished dish just before serving.

Nigella seeds: Also known as black onion seeds or kalonji, these tiny matt black seeds are most frequently used to flavor the breads and pickles that are served alongside curries.

Noodles: In many Asian countries, noodles are a popular accompaniment to curries. They can be made from ingredients such as rice, wheat, beans, or eggs, and some types require soaking prior to cooking.

Palm sugar: Known as jaggery in India and nam tan peep in Thailand, this sugar comes from the sap of various kinds of palm trees. Sold in cakes or cans, the sugar has a deep caramel flavor and is light brown in color. It is usually grated or ground and then used in curries to balance the spices.

Paneer: This cheese, made from whole milk that's been curdled and strained, is used widely in savory curries in India and Southeast Asia.

Panko: These dried, white breadcrumbs are slightly coarser in texture than regular dried breadcrumbs. They are used in Japan to coat and fry food.

Rice: The staple food in every country where curries are part of the traditional diet, rice is the basic accompaniment to any curry and makes a perfect buffer against saucy spices. There are many different varieties available, many of which are typical to specific regions. Basmati rice is used throughout India, while jasmine and sticky rice are more common in Southeast Asia.

Saffron: These deep-orange strands are the dried stamens of the saffron crocus. They are usually soaked in warm milk or water and then added to rice dishes or desserts, but they can also be used dried. Saffron imparts a musky fragrance, golden color, and distinct flavor to the dishes in which it is used.

Sambal oelek: A spicy chili sauce from Indonesia, sambal oelek is available in Asian specialty shops and some supermarkets.

Shrimp paste: This pungent preserve used in Asian cooking is made by pounding shrimp with salt and leaving the mixture to ferment. It is sold in small jars and has a very powerful aroma, which disappears when cooked. It should be refrigerated after opening.

Star anise: A flower-shaped collection of seed pods from a Chinese evergreen tree, star anise is dark brown in color with a strong aniseed flavor.

Sweet chili sauce: This is a relatively sweet and mild sauce made from red chilies, sugar, garlic, and vinegar. It is usually served as an accompaniment to appetizers, such as egg rolls, and in some other Asian preparations.

Tamarind paste: Used as a souring agent in curries, the paste from this pod can be used straight from the jar. You can also buy it in semidried pulp form, which needs to be soaked in warm water and strained before use.

Turmeric: This orange-yellow spice is related to ginger, but has a musky flavor. Usually used in powdered form, it is added to dishes in small quantities.

White poppy seeds: Also known as khus, these tiny white poppy seeds are used in Indian cooking, mainly to thicken sauces and curries.

TECHNIQUES

Cooking Rice Perfectly

There are many techniques for cooking rice and using rice in dishes. Adding hot, just-boiled water to rice at the beginning of cooking will result in lighter, separate grains, while adding cold water will yield a stickier texture. As a general rule, serve mild rice dishes with very spicy curries and more substantial, flavorful rice dishes with mild curries.

For most everyday meals, you can get good results without soaking your rice. If using older rice that's been in the cupboard for a while, soak it in cold water for 15 to 30 minutes, which makes the grains less brittle and prone to breakage. Soaking is also traditional for basmati rice, as it helps the rice expand to its maximum length.

The simplest method for cooking rice is the absorption method. In this method, the rice is cooked in a measured amount of water so that by the time it is cooked, all the water has been absorbed. As this happens, trapped steam finishes the cooking.

The key to this method is figuring out the correct amount of water. As a general rule, for 1 part basmati or long-grain white rice use 1½ to 1¾ parts water. You might need to experiment a little to find the amount you like best. Brown rices require more water, while shorter-grain rices require less. Keep in mind that more water gives you softer, stickier rice and less water results in firmer rice.

All you need, in terms of equipment, is a good, heavy-bottomed saucepan with a tight-fitting lid and perhaps a heat diffuser (see page 10).

The Absorption Method: Follow these simple steps for perfect rice every time.

Step One: Put the rice in a strainer and rinse it under cold, running water until the water is clear. This removes loose starch, making the rice less sticky.

Make sure you drain the rice thoroughly or you'll be using more water in cooking than you intended.

Step Two: Put the rice in a heavy-bottomed saucepan. Measure the amount of cold water needed for your quantity of rice and add it to the pan.

Step Three: Bring the rice and water to a boil over high heat. Cover tightly and lower the heat to low. After 12 to 15 minutes, the liquid should be absorbed and the rice just tender.

If you served the rice at once, you'd find the top layer drier and fluffier than the bottom, which can be very moist and fragile. Here's where you need patience: remove the pan from the heat and leave it to stand, undisturbed, covered, at least 5 minutes and for as long as 30 minutes. This lets the moisture redistribute, resulting in a more uniform texture, with the bottom layers as fluffy as the top.

The Stir-Frying Method

For perfect fried rice, with loose, separate grains, it's important to use cold, cooked rice and a very hot wok or skillet. Cook your rice ahead of time and, after it has cooled completely, store it in the refrigerator until ready to make your fried rice. This makes sure the rice remains firm during cooking. The high cooking temperature used for stir-frying prevents the rice from sticking to the pan.

Sterilizing Jars for Chutneys and Pickles

When making preserves, such as chutneys or pickles, you will need to store them in clean, sterilized jars. Make sure you use rubber-lined canning lids on your jars, as these are noncorrosive and won't react with vinegar or other acids.

Step One: Put the pickling jars and lids in a large saucepan of boiling water and boil 10 minutes. You can also sterilize jars by running them through the regular wash cycle of your dishwasher, but without adding soap.

Step Two: Carefully remove the jars from the heat, using tongs, and wipe dry with a clean dish towel.

Step Three: Fill the warm jars with the pickle or chutney, cover with the lids, and seal tightly.

Storage: Fresh pickles and chutneys can usually be stored in the refrigerator up to 1 week. Preserves and pickles with a high salt and vinegar (acid) content can be stored for longer, either in a cool, dry cupboard or in the refrigerator. See individual recipes for specific storage instructions.

ESSENTIAL EQUIPMENT

Cooking curries does not require any expensive or complicated equipment, but a few essential items will help you prepare them easily and efficiently.

Skillets, saucepans, and woks: A heavy bottom makes sure food will be heated evenly during cooking, without burning or sticking to the bottom of the pan. This is especially important when a recipe requires slow cooking over low heat for a long period. Make sure saucepans have tight-fitting lids that keep the steam in. If a lid fits loosely, you can put a clean dish towel between the lid and the pan to keep the steam in—but be very careful if you have a gas stovetop.

Heat diffuser: This is a flat disk made of perforated metal, usually with a removable handle. It sits on top of your heat source and you place the pan on it. Diffusers are especially great when an even, low, well-distributed heat is required (for example, for slow-cooked curries and rice). Available from any good kitchenware store, they are inexpensive and last for years, so worth buying.

Idli pans: Idlis, or steamed rice cakes, are a popular accompaniment to curries in South India. For these, you'll need an idli pan, fitted with stackable molds for steaming the idlis. The pans look a bit like the molds for poaching eggs and they are available from Indian kitchen are suppliers.

Spice grinders: The secret of any good curry is the base: the curry powder or paste, which is made up of a number of dry and wet spices and herbs. A mortar and pestle is the traditional method of combining these ingredients, but it does involve quite a lot of elbow grease. An electric coffee grinder or spice mill is especially handy for grinding "dry" spices. These are available widely and are inexpensive, but make sure to devote one exclusively to grinding spices—otherwise your coffee will end up tasting pretty strange! A mini food processor or blender is invaluable for blending ingredients into smooth pastes.

BASIC RECIPES: CURRY POWDERS & PASTES

Curry Powder

PREPARATION TIME 5 minutes   COOKING TIME 3 minutes   MAKES about/½ cup

6 to 8 dried curry leaves
5 or 6 cloves
4 dried red chilies, roughly broken
  (for mild Curry Powder, use
  2 chilies; for hot Curry Powder,
  use 6 chilies)
1 cinnamon stick or cassia bark stick
2 tbsp. cumin seeds

2 tbsp. ground coriander
2 tsp. turmeric
1 tsp. whole black peppercorns
1 tsp. cardamom seeds
½ tsp. black mustard seeds
¼ tsp. fenugreek seeds
¼ tsp. ground ginger

1 Put all of the ingredients in a dry, nonstick skillet and heat over low heat, stirring continuously, 2 to 3 minutes until fragrant. Remove from the heat and leave to cool completely.
2 Transfer to a small blender or spice grinder and grind 2 minutes until the mixture forms a fine powder (or use a mortar and pestle). Use immediately or store in an airtight jar up to 1 month or in the refrigerator up to 3 months.

Garam Masala

PREPARATION TIME 5 minutes   COOKING TIME 5 minutes   MAKES about ⅔ cup

4 cardamom pods, crushed
3 dried bay leaves
2 cinnamon sticks
6 tbsp. cumin seeds

4 tbsp. coriander seeds
1 tsp. cloves
1 tsp. whole black peppercorns
1 tsp. ground mace or nutmeg

1 Put all of the ingredients in a large dry, nonstick skillet and heat over low heat, stirring continuously, 4 to 5 minutes until fragrant. Remove from the heat and leave to cool.
2 Transfer to a small blender or spice grinder and grind 2 minutes until the mixture forms a fine powder (or use a mortar and pestle). Use immediately or store in an airtight jar up to 1 month or in the refrigerator up to 3 months.

Nonya Curry Powder

PREPARATION TIME 5 minutes   COOKING TIME 4 minutes   MAKES about 1¼ cups

1¼ cups coriander seeds
½ cup cumin seeds
1 star anise
1¾in. cinnamon stick

4 tsp. crushed dried red chilies
2 tsp. whole black peppercorns
2 cloves
2 tsp. turmeric

1 Put all of the ingredients, except the turmeric, in a large dry, nonstick skillet and heat over low heat, stirring continuously, 3 to 4 minutes until fragrant. Remove from the heat and leave to cool.
2 Transfer to a small blender or spice grinder (or use a mortar and pestle) and grind 2 minutes until the mixture forms a fine powder, then mix in the turmeric. Use immediately or store in an airtight jar up to 2 weeks.

Madras Curry Powder

PREPARATION TIME 5 minutes   **COOKING TIME** 5 minutes   **MAKES** about ½ cup

4 to 6 dried red chilies
4 dried curry leaves
3 tbsp. coriander seeds
2 tbsp. cumin seeds

1 tbsp. whole black peppercorns
1 tsp. black mustard seeds
1 tsp. turmeric

1   Put all of the ingredients in a large dry, nonstick skillet and heat over
    medium-low heat, stirring continuously, 4 to 5 minutes until fragrant. Remove
    from the heat and leave to cool.
2   Transfer to a small blender or spice grinder and grind 2 minutes until the mixture
    forms a fine powder (or use a mortar and pestle). Store in an airtight jar up to
    1 month or in the refrigerator up to 3 months.

Sri Lankan Curry Powder

PREPARATION TIME 5 minutes   **COOKING TIME** 3 minutes   **MAKES** about 1 cup

12 dried curry leaves
6 cloves
2 cinnamon sticks
4 tbsp. coriander seeds
2 tbsp. cumin seeds

2 tbsp. fennel seeds
1 tbsp. cayenne pepper
2 tsp. turmeric
1 tsp. fenugreek seeds
1 tsp. ground cardamom

1   Put all of the ingredients in a large dry, nonstick skillet and heat over medium-low
    heat, stirring continuously, 2 to 3 minutes until fragrant. Remove from the heat
    and leave to cool.
2   Transfer to a small blender or spice grinder and grind 2 minutes until the mixture
    forms a fine powder (or use a mortar and pestle). Use immediately or store
    in an airtight jar up to 1 month or in the refrigerator up to 3 months.

Japanese Curry Sauce

PREPARATION TIME 5 minutes, plus making the curry powder and garam masala
COOKING TIME 30 minutes   **MAKES** about 3 cups

2 tbsp. butter
1 onion, thinly sliced
1 tsp. grated garlic
1 tsp. peeled and grated gingerroot
2 tbsp. all-purpose flour

1 tbsp. mild Curry Powder
 (see page 11)
3 cups vegetable stock
½ tsp. Garam Masala (see page 11)

1   Melt half of the butter in a skillet over low heat. Add the onion and cook, stirring
    frequently, 12 to 15 minutes until brown. Add the garlic and ginger and cook,
    stirring, 2 to 3 minutes longer, then set aside.
2   Melt the remaining butter in a medium saucepan over low heat. Add the flour
    and cook, stirring, 1 to 2 minutes until the mixture forms a paste. Add the curry
    powder and mix well, then stir in the stock a little at a time, mixing well.
3   Stir in the onion mixture and simmer, stirring occasionally, 10 minutes, or until the
    sauce thickens. Remove from the heat, sprinkle the garam masala over, and mix
    well. Use immediately or store in an airtight jar in the refrigerator up to 2 days.

Massaman Curry Paste

PREPARATION TIME 10 minutes   **MAKES** about 2 cups

3 Thai or small shallots, sliced
5 garlic cloves
2 red chilies, finely chopped
2 kaffir lime leaves, thinly sliced
2 tbsp. finely chopped lemongrass
1 tbsp. ground coriander
1 tbsp. ground cumin
1 tbsp. peeled and finely grated gingerroot

1 tbsp. fish sauce or dark soy sauce (optional)
1 tsp. ground cardamom
1 tsp. cinnamon
1 tsp. shrimp paste (optional)
½ tsp. ground nutmeg
¼ tsp. ground cloves
scant 1 cup coconut milk

1   Put all of the ingredients in a blender or food processor and blend 1 to 2 minutes until the mixture forms a smooth paste. Use immediately or store in an airtight jar in the refrigerator up to 1 week.

Burmese Curry Paste

PREPARATION TIME 5 minutes, plus 30 minutes soaking   **MAKES** about 1¼ cups

6 dried red chilies
¾in. piece fresh or dried galangal or gingerroot, peeled and finely chopped
2 tbsp. finely chopped fresh or dried lemongrass
8 Thai or small shallots, finely chopped

10 to 12 garlic cloves, finely chopped
1 tbsp. coarsely ground coriander seeds
2 tsp. coarsely ground cumin seeds
1 tsp. turmeric
1 tsp. shrimp paste (optional)

1   Crumble the chilies into a bowl, along with the galangal and lemongrass. Cover with 1 cup plus 2 tablespoons water and leave to soak 30 minutes.
2   Transfer the chilies and soaking liquid to a blender or small food processor. Add all the remaining ingredients and blend 1 to 2 minutes until the mixture forms a smooth paste. Use immediately or store in an airtight jar in the refrigerator up to 1 week.

Penang Red Curry Paste

PREPARATION TIME 10 minutes   **MAKES** about 2 cups

1 small onion, quartered
3 garlic cloves, coarsely chopped
2 kaffir lime leaves
1 to 2 red chilies, coarsely chopped
4 tbsp. tomato paste
2 tbsp. soy sauce
2 tbsp. fish sauce or dark soy sauce (optional)
2 tbsp. cayenne pepper
2 tbsp. ground coriander
1 tbsp. ground cumin

1 tbsp. paprika
1 tbsp. peeled and finely grated gingerroot
1 tsp. shrimp paste (optional)
½ tsp. cinnamon
½ tsp. turmeric
¼ tsp. ground cloves
¼ tsp. ground nutmeg
1¾ cups coconut milk
juice of ½ lime

1   Put all of the ingredients in a blender or food processor and blend 2 to 3 minutes until the mixture forms a smooth paste. Use immediately or store in an airtight jar in the refrigerator up to 3 days.

Green Masala Paste

PREPARATION TIME 10 minutes   MAKES about 1¾ cups

6 garlic cloves, chopped
2 green chilies, sliced
2 cloves
1in. piece gingerroot, peeled
  and chopped
2 tbsp. malt or white wine vinegar
1 tbsp. shredded coconut or 2 tbsp.
  freshly grated coconut

2 tsp. cumin seeds
1 tsp. turmeric
1 tsp. cardamom seeds
1 bunch cilantro leaves, coarsely
  chopped
juice of 1 lime
½ cup sunflower oil

1 Put all of the ingredients in a food processor or blender and blend 2 to 3 minutes until the mixture forms a smooth paste. Use immediately or store in an airtight jar in the refrigerator up to 1 week.

Red Masala Paste

PREPARATION TIME 10 minutes, plus 30 minutes soaking   MAKES about 1 cup

12 to 14 dried red chilies
4 garlic cloves, chopped
1in. piece gingerroot, peeled
  and chopped
8 whole black peppercorns
5 cloves
1 cinnamon stick

3 tbsp. malt or white wine vinegar
1 tbsp. shredded coconut or 2 tbsp.
  freshly grated coconut
1 tsp. ground cardamom
¼ tsp. freshly grated nutmeg
½ cup sunflower oil

1 Put the chilies in a small bowl, cover with hot water, and leave to soak 30 minutes, then drain and transfer to a blender or small food processor.
2 Add all of the remaining ingredients and blend 2 to 3 minutes until the mixture forms a fine paste. Use immediately or store in an airtight jar in the refrigerator up to 1 week.

Tandoori Curry Paste

PREPARATION TIME 10 minutes, plus making the garam masala   COOKING TIME 3 minutes
MAKES about 1 cup

2 tsp. cumin seeds
2 tsp. coriander seeds
6 garlic cloves, crushed
4 tbsp. tomato paste
4 tbsp. paprika
2 tbsp. peeled and finely grated
  gingerroot

2 tsp. Garam Masala (see page 11)
2 tsp. cayenne pepper
2 tsp. salt
1 tsp. turmeric
juice of 2 lemons
½ cup sunflower oil

1 Put the cumin and coriander seeds in a nonstick skillet and dry-roast over low heat, stirring continuously, 2 to 3 minutes until fragrant. Transfer to a small blender or spice grinder (or use a mortar and pestle) and grind to a fine powder.
2 Transfer to a bowl and add all of the remaining ingredients. Stir well until the mixture forms a smooth paste. Use immediately or store in an airtight jar in the refrigerator up to 3 days.

Thai Green Curry Paste

PREPARATION TIME 10 minutes   MAKES about ¾ cup

4 to 6 long green chilies, chopped
4 shallots, finely chopped
2 tbsp. chopped garlic
2 tbsp. chopped lemongrass
1 tbsp. peeled and finely chopped
   galangal or gingerroot

2 tsp. chopped kaffir lime leaves
2 tsp. ground coriander
2 tsp. ground cumin
2 tsp. shrimp paste (optional)
1 tsp. whole white peppercorns
1 tbsp. sunflower oil

1   Put all of the ingredients in a blender or food processor and blend 2 minutes until the mixture forms a smooth paste (or use a mortar and pestle). Use immediately or store in an airtight jar in the refrigerator up to 1 month.

Thai Red Curry Paste

PREPARATION TIME 10 minutes   MAKES about ⅔ cup

2 tsp. ground coriander
1 tsp. ground cumin
1 tsp. whole white peppercorns
8 long dried red chilies, seeded and
   finely chopped
2 tbsp. finely grated garlic
2 tbsp. finely chopped lemongrass

1 tbsp. peeled and finely chopped
   galangal or gingerroot
3 cilantro roots, finely chopped
2 tsp. chopped kaffir lime leaves
2 tsp. shrimp paste (optional)
2 tbsp. sunflower oil

1   Put all of the ingredients in a blender or food processor and blend 2 minutes until the mixture forms a smooth paste (or use a mortar and pestle). Use immediately or store in an airtight jar in the refrigerator up to 1 month.

Korma Curry Paste

PREPARATION TIME 10 minutes, plus making the garam masala   COOKING TIME 3 minutes
MAKES about 1½ cups

1 cinnamon stick
2 tsp. cumin seeds
2 tsp. coriander seeds
1 tsp. cardamom seeds
2 tsp. Garam Masala (see page 11)
2 tsp. cayenne pepper
2 tsp. salt

1 tsp. turmeric
6 garlic cloves, crushed
2 tbsp. peeled and finely grated
   gingerroot
2 cups very finely ground almonds
½ cup sunflower oil

1   Put the cinnamon stick and the cumin and cardamom seeds in a nonstick skillet and dry-roast over low heat, stirring continuously, 2 to 3 minutes until fragrant. Transfer to a small blender or spice grinder (or use a mortar and pestle) and grind to a fine powder.
2   Transfer the mixture to a food processor and add all of the remaining ingredients. Blend 2 to 3 minutes until the mixture forms a fine paste. Use immediately or store in an airtight jar in the refrigerator up to 3 days.

CHAPTER 1

APPETIZERS

Spices and herbs can add a terrific twist to any first-course dish, including soups, salads, and appetizers, and to snacks. Their complex flavors tease the tastebuds, preparing you for the meal ahead. When I was growing up in India, seeing streets lined with stalls selling all kinds of such tantalizing foods always fascinated me. Many of the recipes in this chapter are my versions of the popular street foods I enjoyed then, and others are dishes I have discovered from other corners of the globe. From zesty Aloo Chat to steamed Malaysian Spiced Fish Mousse, these dishes let you experience the different ways spices are used to stimulate the palette. Try crisp-fried Onion Bhajiyas, Steamed Pork & Mushroom Rice Balls, or Moroccan Spiced Fish Cakes, for example, and see how the careful use of ingredients can kick off a meal with sensational flavors.

Many of the dishes in this chapter, such as Chicken Samosas, Thai Green Curry Chicken Soup, or Lemon, Soy & Chili Roasted Drumsticks, also make great options for a light meal or snack. Just serve them with a crisp green salad for a delightfully satisfying meal.

BABY SPINACH & COCONUT SALAD (SEE PAGE 41)

001 Marinated Lamb Skewers

PREPARATION TIME 20 minutes, plus at least 24 hours marinating, 1 hour standing, and making the curry powder, bread, and accompaniments **COOKING TIME** 15 minutes **SERVES** 4

1lb. 12oz. lamb tenderloin, cut into
   bite-size pieces
1 recipe quantity Papaya & Chili Raita
   (see page 212), to serve
1 recipe quantity Mint Chutney
   (see page 204), to serve
1 recipe quantity Naan
   (see page 190), to serve

MARINADE
1 onion, finely chopped
2 tsp. garlic salt

2 tsp. ground ginger
1 tbsp. ground cumin
1 tbsp. mild Curry Powder
   (see page 11)
1 tbsp. cayenne pepper
1 tbsp. fennel seeds
6 tbsp. chopped cilantro leaves
2 tbsp. finely chopped mint leaves
1 cup plus 2 tbsp. plain yogurt
½ tsp. sugar
juice of 2 limes
salt and freshly ground black pepper

1 Put the lamb in a large dish. Put all of the ingredients for the marinade in a blender and blend 2 minutes, or until smooth. Season with salt and pepper, pour it over the lamb, cover, and leave to marinate in the refrigerator 24 to 48 hours.
2 Remove the lamb from the refrigerator and leave it to come to room temperature 1 hour. If using wooden skewers, soak them in warm water 30 minutes.
3 Preheat the oven to 400°F and line a baking sheet with parchment paper. Thread the lamb onto 8 skewers and put them on the baking sheet. Bake 12 to 15 minutes until tender and cooked through. Serve hot with raita, chutney, and warm bread.

002 Malaysian Bean Curd Rolls

PREPARATION TIME 20 minutes, plus 1 hour standing **COOKING TIME** 20 minutes
SERVES 4 to 6

9oz. ground pork
1 small carrot, coarsely grated
6 canned water chestnuts, drained
   and chopped
2 scallions, finely chopped
4 tbsp. chopped cilantro leaves
1 tsp. Chinese five-spice powder
1 tbsp. light soy sauce

1 tsp. sesame oil
1 egg, lightly beaten
1 tbsp. all-purpose flour
7oz. large dried bean curd skins
1 tsp. cornstarch
3 cups canola oil, for deep-frying,
   or more as needed
plum sauce, to serve

1 Put the pork, carrot, water chestnuts, scallions, cilantro, five-spice powder, soy sauce, sesame oil, and egg in a bowl and mix well, using your hands. Add the flour and mix well. Cover and leave to stand at room temperature 1 hour.
2 Cut the bean curd skins into 6 rectangles, each about 8 x 6 inches, then soak them in water 3 to 5 minutes until soft. Meanwhile, put the cornstarch and 1 tablespoon cold water in a small bowl and mix well until it forms a paste, then set the mixture aside.
3 Put 2 tablespoons of the pork mixture in the middle of 1 bean curd rectangle. Fold the bottom of the rectangle over the filling and roll up tightly, tucking in the sides as you roll. Seal the edges with the cornstarch paste and transfer to a plate or sheet of parchment paper. Repeat with the remaining bean curd skins and filling, arranging them in a single layer on the plate.
4 Put the plate in a steamer and steam, covered, 12 minutes over boiling water until the bean curd skins become lighter in color. Remove the rolls from the steamer and pat away any excess moisture with paper towels.
5 Fill a large wok or saucepan one-third full with oil over medium-high heat and heat it to 350°F, or until a small piece of bread dropped into the oil browns in 15 seconds. Working in batches to avoid overcrowding the wok, carefully drop the rolls into the oil and deep-fry 1 to 2 minutes until golden brown. Remove the rolls from the pan, using a slotted spoon, and drain on paper towels. Slice each roll diagonally into 3 or 4 pieces and serve hot with plum sauce for dipping.

Vietnamese Beef Pho

PREPARATION TIME 35 minutes   **COOKING TIME** 30 minutes   **SERVES** 4

5oz. dried rice noodles
heaped ½ cup bean sprouts
6 scallions, thinly sliced
1 small handful mint leaves
1 small handful cilantro leaves,
   coarsely chopped
1 red chili, sliced
2 limes, cut into wedges
9oz. beef tenderloin, very thinly
   sliced

BEEF PHO BROTH
4 cups beef stock
6 cloves
10 whole black peppercorns
1¼in. piece gingerroot, peeled
   and sliced
3 cinnamon sticks
3 star anise
6 green cardamom pods
2 tbsp. fish sauce, plus extra to serve

1 Put all of the ingredients for the broth in a large saucepan and simmer gently over low heat 20 to 30 minutes.
2 While the broth is simmering, put the rice noodles in a large bowl, cover well with boiling water, and leave to soak 15 minutes, then drain and divide into four serving bowls. Put the bean sprouts, scallions, mint and cilantro leaves, chili, lime wedges, and fish sauce in small individual bowls.
3 Bring the broth to a boil over high heat. Fill a large soup ladle with some of the steak slices, dip it into a boiling broth 5 to 10 seconds until the beef turns pale pink, then pour it over the noodles in one of the bowls. Top up the bowl with extra broth to cover the noodles. Repeat for each of the bowls and serve immediately, allowing guests to help themselves to the garnishes.

004 Vietnamese Spicy Steak Salad

PREPARATION TIME 30 minutes, plus 1 hour marinating and making the rice
COOKING TIME 8 minutes   **SERVES** 4

4 thick strip steaks
5 garlic cloves, crushed
1 tsp. fish sauce
½ tsp. sugar
½ tsp. salt
3 tsp. olive oil
4 scallions, finely chopped
2 tsp. rice wine vinegar

2oz. watercress, thick stems
  removed
1 small bunch cilantro leaves,
  coarsely chopped
1 small bunch mint leaves
1 recipe quantity Bamboo Steamed
  Sticky Rice (see page 184), to serve

1   Rub the steaks all over with 4 of the garlic cloves and put the steaks in a glass
    or ceramic dish. Sprinkle the fish sauce, sugar, salt, and olive oil over and rub
    the steaks again. Cover and leave to marinate in the refrigerator at least 1 hour.
2   Preheat the broiler to medium-high. Put the scallions, vinegar, and remaining
    garlic clove in a small bowl and set aside.
3   Broil the steaks 3 to 4 minutes on each side, or until cooked to your liking, then
    transfer to a plate, cover, and leave to rest 10 minutes.
4   Thinly slice the steaks and put them in a large bowl. Toss in the marinated scallion
    mixture, watercress, cilantro, and mint. Serve with rice.

005 Curry Puffs

PREPARATION TIME 20 minutes, plus making the curry powder and chutney
COOKING TIME 10 minutes   **SERVES** 4

1 large potato, peeled and chopped
1 tbsp. sunflower oil
½ small onion, finely chopped
3 garlic cloves, crushed
1 tsp. peeled and finely grated
  gingerroot
1 red chili, seeded and finely chopped
2 tbsp. hot Curry Powder
  (see page 11)
2 to 3oz. ground pork

4 tbsp. chopped cilantro leaves
2 sheets ready-rolled puff pastry
  dough, about 9oz. each
1 egg, lightly beaten
3 cups canola oil, for deep-frying,
  or more as needed
salt and freshly ground black pepper
1 recipe quantity Mint & Cilantro
  Chutney (see page 201), to serve

1   Bring a saucepan of lightly salted water to a boil. Add the potato and boil
    12 to 15 minutes until tender. Drain, then return to the pan and mash well.
    Leave to cool, then chill, covered.
2   Heat the sunflower oil in a wok or skillet over low heat. When it is hot, add the
    onion, garlic, ginger, and chili and cook, stirring, 2 to 3 minutes until starting
    to become soft. Add the curry powder and pork, increase the heat to high, and
    stir-fry 4 to 5 minutes until the meat is brown and just cooked through. Transfer
    the mixture to a bowl and mix in the mashed potato and cilantro. Season with
    salt and pepper, then set aside to cool slightly.
3   Using a 3-inch cookie cutter, cut 8 circles from the puff pastry dough. Put a large
    spoonful of the pork mixture in the middle of each dough circle. Brush the edges
    of the dough with the beaten egg and fold the dough over to enclose the filling.
    Press the edges with the tines of a fork to seal.
4   Fill a large wok or saucepan one-third full with canola oil and heat it over high
    heat until it reaches 350°F, or until a small piece of bread dropped into the oil
    browns in 15 seconds. Working in batches to avoid overcrowding the wok,
    carefully drop the puffs into the oil and deep-fry 2 to 3 minutes until puffed and
    golden. Remove from the pan, using a slotted spoon, and drain on paper towels.
    Serve immediately with chutney for dipping. Alternatively, preheat the oven to
    425°F and put the uncooked puffs on a baking sheet. Bake 15 to 20 minutes until
    golden, then serve hot with chutney.

006 Steamed Pork & Mushroom Rice Balls

PREPARATION TIME 15 minutes, plus at least 3 hours chilling   **COOKING TIME** 1 hour 20 minutes
SERVES 4

2 tbsp. sunflower oil
3 cups finely chopped shiitake
 mushrooms
14oz. ground pork
4 scallions, finely chopped
2 garlic cloves, crushed
1 tbsp. Fish sauce
1 tbsp. soy sauce
1 tsp. peeled and finely grated
 gingerroot
4 tbsp. finely chopped
 cilantro leaves

1 egg
1 cup jasmine rice
salt and freshly ground
 black pepper

DIPPING SAUCE
½ cup sweet chili sauce
7 tbsp. soy sauce
1 tbsp. Chinese rice wine
1 to 2 tsp. chili oil

1   Heat the oil in a large wok or skillet over high heat. Add the mushrooms and
    stir-fry 2 to 3 minutes until light brown. Transfer to a food processor and add
    the pork, scallions, garlic, fish sauce, soy sauce, ginger, cilantro, and egg. Process
    30 to 40 seconds until just combined (be careful not to overwork it into a paste).
    Transfer to a bowl and mix well, using your hands. Cover and chill in the
    refrigerator 3 to 4 hours, or overnight.
2   Put the rice in a bowl. With wet hands, divide the pork mixture into 20 equal
    portions and roll each one into a firm ball. Roll each ball in the rice to coat evenly.
    Arrange the balls, spaced well apart, in a double bamboo steamer lined with
    parchment paper. Cover and steam over a wok of simmering water 1 hour
    15 minutes, or until the rice turns opaque and soft. Top up with extra boiling
    water as needed to prevent the steamer from drying out.
3   Meanwhile, put all of the ingredients for the dipping sauce in a small bowl.
    Mix well and set aside.
4   Remove the rice balls from the steamer and serve warm or at room temperature
    with the dipping sauce.

007 Seekh Kebabs

PREPARATION TIME 15 minutes, plus at least 6 hours marinating and making the bread
COOKING TIME 20 minutes   **SERVES** 4

1 tsp. roasted cumin seeds
1 green chili, seeded and finely
 chopped
2 tsp. ground ginger
5 garlic cloves, very finely chopped
2 tbsp. finely chopped cilantro leaves
1 tsp. cinnamon
1 tsp. ground cardamom
1lb. 2oz. ground beef

2 tbsp. very finely chopped onion
1 tsp. cayenne pepper
1 egg, beaten
1¼ cups fresh breadcrumbs
2 tsp. salt
sunflower oil, for brushing
1 recipe quantity Naan
 (see page 190), to serve
1 lemon, cut into wedges, to serve

1   Put the cumin seeds in a small skillet and dry-roast over medium-low heat
    2 to 3 minutes until fragrant, then transfer to a large bowl. Add the chili,
    ginger, garlic, cilantro leaves, cinnamon, cardamom, beef, onion, cayenne,
    egg, breadcrumbs, and salt and mix well, using your hands. Cover and leave
    to marinate in the refrigerator 6 to 8 hours, or overnight.
2   Preheat the oven to 375°F and line a baking sheet with parchment paper. If using
    wooden skewers, soak them in warm water 30 minutes. Divide the mixture into
    12 equal portions and shape each one around a metal or bamboo skewer to
    make a 4-inch-long oval. Put the kebabs on the baking sheet and brush lightly
    with oil. Bake 15 to 20 minutes, turning once halfway through. Serve immediately
    with warm bread and lemon wedges for squeezing over.

008 Spiced Meat & Phyllo Rolls

PREPARATION TIME 30 minutes   COOKING TIME 50 minutes   SERVES 4 to 6

4 tbsp. sunflower oil
1 onion, finely chopped
1lb. 2oz. ground beef or lamb
2 tsp. cinnamon
½ tsp. ground ginger
1 bunch flat-leaf parsley, chopped
1 bunch cilantro leaves, chopped
3 eggs, lightly beaten

10oz. phyllo pastry dough sheets
⅔ cup (1¼ sticks) butter, melted,
    or 7 tbsp. sunflower oil, plus extra
    for greasing
salt
freshly ground black pepper,
    or a generous pinch cayenne
    pepper

1   Heat the oil in a large skillet over low heat. Add the onion and cook, stirring occasionally, 5 minutes, or until soft. Add the ground meat, cinnamon, and ginger and season with salt and pepper. Cook 10 minutes, or until the meat is brown, breaking it up with a fork and turning it over occasionally.

2   Stir in the parsley, cilantro, and eggs and cook over low heat 30 to 40 seconds, stirring continuously, until the eggs set to a creamy consistency; be careful not to overcook them, as residual heat will continue cooking the eggs even after the pan is removed from the heat. Set aside and leave to cool completely. Taste and adjust the spices, if desired.

3   Preheat the oven to 350°F and grease a baking sheet with butter. Using large scissors, cut all of the sheets of phyllo dough together, without separating them, into 3 strips, each about 12 x 6 inches, or about 30 pieces. Stack the 3 piles together so they do not dry out and brush the top layer of dough very lightly with some of the melted butter.

4   Put 1 tablespoon of filling in a line along one of the short ends of the top layer of phyllo, about ¾ inch in from the edges. Roll the phyllo up into a log, folding in the long sides at the halfway point so the filling does not fall out. Repeat with the remaining dough and filling.

5   Put the rolls on the baking sheet, brush the tops with the remaining melted butter, and bake 30 minutes, or until golden. Serve hot.

009 Vietnamese Chicken Noodle Soup

PREPARATION TIME 20 minutes, plus making the dipping sauce   COOKING TIME 30 minutes
SERVES 4

6½ cups chicken stock
1 tbsp. Nuoc Cham Dipping Sauce
    (see page 204)
5 tbsp. peeled and finely chopped
    galangal or gingerroot
3 star anise
2 cinnamon sticks
1 tsp. palm sugar
9oz. boneless, skinless chicken breasts
1 tbsp. sunflower oil

2 shallots, thinly sliced
9oz. thin dried rice noodles
salt and freshly ground black pepper

TO SERVE
6 scallions, diagonally sliced
4 small red chilies, finely chopped
crushed skinless roasted peanuts
cilantro leaves
2 limes, cut into wedges

1   Put the stock, nuoc cham, galangal, star anise, cinnamon, and sugar in a large saucepan and season with salt and pepper. Bring to a boil over high heat, then lower the heat to low and simmer 10 minutes. Add the chicken and simmer, stirring occasionally, 20 minutes longer, or until cooked through.

2   Meanwhile, heat the oil in a small skillet over medium-high heat. Add the shallots and fry 3 to 4 minutes until crisp, then drain on paper towels and set aside.

3   Transfer the chicken to a plate, using a slotted spoon. Strain the stock into a clean pan and cover to keep warm. Shred the chicken into a bowl.

4   Meanwhile, cook the rice noodles according to the package directions and drain.

5   Divide the noodles into four large bowls. Divide the chicken and then the strained stock over each portion of noodles. Serve immediately with the fried shallots, scallions, chilies, peanuts, and cilantro in separate bowls so everyone can help themselves, and with the limes for squeezing over.

Thai Green Curry Chicken Soup

PREPARATION TIME 15 minutes, plus making the curry paste   **COOKING TIME** 30 minutes
SERVES 4

2 boneless, skinless chicken breast
  halves
1 tsp. Thai Green Curry Paste
  (see page 15)
4 kaffir lime leaves, finely shredded
2 tbsp. very finely chopped
  lemongrass
1 tsp. peeled and very finely grated
  galangal
5 cups chicken stock

juice of 1 lime
6 tbsp. very finely chopped cilantro
  leaves
2 tsp. fish sauce
1 red chili, seeded and very thinly
  sliced, plus extra to serve
scant ½ cup coconut milk
4 scallions, very thinly sliced
salt and freshly ground black pepper
Thai basil leaves, to serve

1   Put the chicken, curry paste, lime leaves, lemongrass, galangal, and stock in
    a medium saucepan and bring to a boil over high heat. Lower the heat to low
    and simmer, covered, 20 to 25 minutes until the chicken is cooked through, then
    remove from the heat. Transfer the chicken to a plate, using a slotted spoon, and
    when cool enough to handle, tear it into bite-size shreds using your fingers.
2   Return the chicken to the pan. Add the lime juice, cilantro, fish sauce, chili,
    coconut milk, and most of the scallions. Season with salt and pepper and heat
    over low heat 4 to 5 minutes until warm. Serve immediately, sprinkled with the
    remaining scallions and chili and basil leaves.

011 Creamy Tandoori Chicken Kebabs

PREPARATION TIME 15 minutes, plus at least 24 hours marinating and making the garam masala, curry paste, and rice **COOKING TIME** 8 minutes **SERVES** 4

1lb. 5oz. boneless, skinless chicken thighs, cut into bite-size pieces
sunflower oil, for brushing
1 recipe quantity Mushroom Pulao (see page 183), to serve

MARINADE
½ cup plain yogurt
½ cup light cream
4 garlic cloves, finely chopped
juice of 1 lemon

1 tbsp. peeled and finely grated gingerroot
2 tsp. paprika
1 tsp. turmeric
1 tbsp. ground cumin
1 tbsp. ground coriander
1 tsp. Garam Masala (see page 11)
1 tsp. ground cardamom
2 tbsp. tomato paste
2 tbsp. Tandoori Curry Paste (see page 14)
salt and freshly ground black pepper

1 Put the chicken in a wide, shallow glass or ceramic dish. Mix together all of the ingredients for the marinade and season well with salt and pepper. Pour the mixture over the chicken, cover, and leave to marinate in the refrigerator 24 to 48 hours.
2 Preheat the broiler to medium-high. Thread the pieces of chicken onto 8 metal skewers and put them in a single layer on a lightly greased broiler rack. Lightly brush with sunflower oil and broil 3 to 4 minutes on each side until cooked through. Serve hot with rice.

012 Green Masala Kebabs

PREPARATION TIME 15 minutes, plus at least 6 hours marinating or overnight and making the masala paste and bread **COOKING TIME** 8 minutes **SERVES** 4

1lb. 5oz. boneless, skinless chicken breast halves, cut into bite-size pieces
juice of 1 lime
6 tbsp. plain yogurt
1 tsp. peeled and finely grated gingerroot
1 garlic clove, crushed
1 green chili, seeded and chopped

1 small handful mint leaves, chopped
1 small handful cilantro leaves, chopped
4 tbsp. Green Masala Paste (see page 14)
salt
1 recipe quantity Roomali Roti (see page 194), to serve
1 lime, cut into wedges, to serve

1 Put the chicken in a large glass or ceramic bowl. Put the lime juice, yogurt, ginger, garlic, chili, mint, cilantro, and masala paste in a food processor. Season with salt and blend 2 to 3 minutes until smooth, adding a little water if the mixture is too thick or coarse. Pour the mixture over the chicken and mix well. Cover and leave to marinate in the refrigerator 6 to 8 hours, or overnight.
2 If using wooden skewers, soak them in water for 30 minutes. Preheat the broiler or a barbecue to high (if using a charcoal barbecue, make sure any flames die down first). Thread the chicken onto 8 skewers and grill or barbecue 6 to 8 minutes, turning once or twice, until the chicken is cooked through. Serve immediately with bread and lime wedges for squeezing over.

013 Broiled Ginger Chicken Wings

PREPARATION TIME 10 minutes, plus at least 6 hours marinating and making the curry powder
COOKING TIME 15 minutes   **SERVES** 4

12 large chicken wings, skin removed
2 tsp. peeled and finely grated
   gingerroot
2 tsp. salt
1 tbsp. Curry Powder (see page 11)
2 tsp. hot chili sauce

2 garlic cloves, very finely chopped
juice of 2 lemons
2 tsp. palm sugar
4 tbsp. plain yogurt
1 to 2 tbsp. sunflower oil
mixed salad leaves, to serve

1   Put the chicken wings in a large glass or ceramic bowl. Mix the ginger, salt, curry powder, chili sauce, garlic, lemon juice, sugar, and yogurt together well, then pour it over the chicken. Toss well, then cover and leave to marinate in the refrigerator 6 to 8 hours, or overnight.
2   When ready to cook, preheat the broiler to medium. Remove the wings from the marinade, put them on the broiler rack and brush lightly with the oil. Broil 12 to 15 minutes, turning once or twice, until the wings are cooked through and light brown. Serve hot on a bed of mixed salad leaves.

014 Lemon, Soy & Chili Roasted Chicken Drumsticks

PREPARATION TIME 10 minutes, plus making the rice   **COOKING TIME** 30 minutes
SERVES 4

12 large chicken drumsticks
2 tbsp. dried chili flakes
4 tbsp. sweet chili sauce
6 tbsp. light soy sauce
4 tbsp. honey

finely grated zest and juice
   of 2 lemons
2 tbsp. olive oil, to drizzle
salt and freshly ground black pepper
1 recipe quantity Classic Egg-Fried
   Rice (see page 178), to serve

1   Preheat the oven to 350°F. Using a sharp knife, make several deep slashes on the sides of each drumstick and arrange them in a layer in a nonstick roasting pan.
2   In a bowl, mix together the chili flakes, chili sauce, soy sauce, honey, and lemon zest and juice. Spread the mixture onto the chicken, working it into the slashes in the flesh. Season well with salt and pepper and drizzle with a little olive oil.
3   Roast 25 to 30 minutes, turning occasionally, until cooked through and tender. Serve warm or at room temperature with rice.

015 Mulligatawny Soup

PREPARATION TIME 15 minutes, plus making the curry powder   **COOKING TIME** 35 minutes
SERVES 4

2 tbsp. sunflower oil
1 large onion, finely chopped
2 large carrots, diced
2 potatoes, peeled and diced
¼ cup basmati rice
4oz. lamb tenderloin, diced

2 tbsp. Madras Curry Powder
   (see page 12)
5 cups vegetable stock
1 small bunch cilantro leaves,
   chopped, plus extra leaves, to serve
salt and freshly ground black pepper

1   Heat the oil in a large saucepan over low heat. Add the onion and fry, stirring occasionally, 3 to 4 minutes until soft. Stir in the carrots, potatoes, rice, and lamb and cook 1 minute longer. Stir in the curry powder, then add the stock and mix well and season with salt and pepper. Bring to a boil, then lower the heat and simmer, covered, 30 minutes, or until the vegetables are tender.
2   Using an immersion blender, pulse the soup a few times to puree it slightly, then stir in the cilantro. Serve immediately, sprinkled with cilantro leaves.

016 Chicken Samosas

PREPARATION TIME 20 minutes, plus making the curry powder and chutney
COOKING TIME 40 minutes **SERVES** 4 to 6

2oz. potato, peeled
2 tbsp. sunflower
10oz. ground chicken
1 onion, chopped
1 tbsp. Curry Powder (see page 11)
⅓ cup frozen peas
4 tbsp. chopped cilantro leaves

4 tbsp. chopped mint leaves
5 large sheets phyllo pastry dough
1 egg, beaten
salt and freshly ground black pepper
1 recipe quantity Mint Chutney
(see page 204), to serve

1   Bring a saucepan of water to a boil. Add the potato and cook 12 to 15 minutes until tender. Drain and leave to cool, then cut into ½-inch cubes and set aside. Meanwhile, heat the oil in a skillet over low heat. Add the chicken, onion, and curry powder and season with salt and pepper. Fry, stirring occasionally, 10 minutes, or until the chicken is just cooked and the juices evaporate from the pan. Mix in the potatoes and peas, then remove the pan from the heat and add the cilantro and mint. Set aside to cool.
2   Lay out the phyllo dough on a clean cutting board. Cut in half lengthwise, then in half once more widthways to make 4 rectangles from each whole sheet. Cover the pieces with a clean, barely damp dish towel to prevent them drying out.
3   Preheat the oven to 425°F. Put one phyllo rectangle on the work surface with one of the short sides closest to you. Put a heaped teaspoon of the chicken mixture onto the end closest to you, leaving a little space between the edges of the dough and the filling. Fold the top-left corner of the dough down over the filling to form a triangle, then fold the lower left-hand corner over toward the center to create another triangle. Continue folding, keeping the triangular shape, until you reach the end of the dough and the filling is enclosed. Brush the finishing edge with a little of the beaten egg to seal, then transfer to a baking sheet and brush again with the egg. Repeat with the remaining dough and filling to make 20 samosas.
4   Bake 10 to 12 minutes until golden brown. Serve warm with chutney.

017 Savory Stuffed Vietnamese Crêpes

PREPARATION TIME 15 minutes, plus making the dipping sauce   **COOKING TIME** 55 minutes
SERVES 4–6

1½ cups rice flour
1 tbsp. canola oil, plus extra
for brushing
12 raw jumbo shrimp, shelled
and deveined
3oz. ground pork
1 shallot, finely chopped

3oz. bean sprouts
1 iceberg lettuce, leaves separated
1 small handful mint leaves
1 small handful cilantro leaves
1 recipe quantity Nuoc Cham Dipping
Sauce (see page 204), to serve

1   Put the flour and 1½ cups plus 2 tablespoons water in a bowl and whisk well, then leave to stand while you prepare the filling.
2   Heat the oil in a wok or skillet over high heat. Add the shrimp, pork, shallot, and bean sprouts and stir-fry 3 minutes, or until the shrimp are pink and cooked through.
3   Brush an 8-inch skillet with a little oil and heat over high heat. Pour in enough of the batter to evenly cover the bottom of the pan, tipping any excess back into the bowl. Spread a thin layer of the pork mixture over half of the crêpe, fold the other half over it, and cook 5 minutes, or until the underside is crisp. Using a wide spatula or pancake turner, turn the crêpe over and continue cooking 1 to 2 minutes longer until the underside is crisp. Transfer to a plate and repeat with the remaining batter and filling to make 8 crêpes.
4   Cut each crêpe into 4 or 5 pieces. Wrap each piece in 1 lettuce leaf with some of the mint and cilantro. Serve with the dipping sauce.

Vietnamese Spring Rolls

PREPARATION TIME 20 minutes   **COOKING TIME** 5 minutes   **SERVES** 4

2oz. rice vermicelli
8 rice-paper wrappers
8 large cooked shrimp, shelled,
  deveined, and halved
3 tbsp. chopped Thai sweet
  basil leaves
3 tbsp. chopped mint leaves
3 tbsp. chopped cilantro leaves
2 lettuce leaves, chopped

2 tbsp. lime juice
2 tbsp. sugar
4 tsp. fish sauce
1 tsp. garlic chili sauce
1 garlic clove, very finely chopped
3 tbsp. hoisin sauce
2 tsp. finely chopped skinless roasted
  peanuts, plus extra for sprinkling

1   Bring a medium saucepan of water to a boil. Add the rice vermicelli and boil
    3 to 5 minutes, or according to the package directions, until al dente. Drain, then
    rinse well under cold running water to prevent them sticking together.

2   Fill a large bowl with warm water. Working with 1 wrapper at a time, dip
    a wrapper into the water 3 to 4 seconds to soften. Put the wrapper on a board or
    clean, slightly damp dish towel and put 2 shrimp halves, a handful of the noodles,
    and some of the basil, mint, cilantro, and lettuce in the center, leaving a 2-inch
    gap on each side. Fold the sides over the filling, then roll tightly into a log and set
    aside. Repeat with the remaining wrappers and fillings to make 8 rolls.

3   In a small bowl, mix together the lime juice, sugar, fish sauce, garlic chili sauce,
    garlic, and 4 tablespoons water. In another small bowl, mix together the hoisin
    sauce and peanuts. Sprinkle the spring rolls with peanuts and serve with the
    sauces for dipping.

019 Warm Shrimp & Lemongrass Salad

PREPARATION TIME 10 minutes, plus making the curry powder   COOKING TIME 5 minutes
SERVES 4

scant 1 cup fish stock
2 tbsp. fish sauce
2 tsp. mild Curry Powder (see page 11)
24 raw jumbo shrimp, shelled and
  deveined
3 Thai or small shallots, very finely
  chopped
2 tbsp. finely chopped lemongrass

2 tbsp. lemon juice
1 tsp. palm sugar
2 scallions, trimmed and
  finely chopped
1 small cucumber, cut into thin
  ribbons with a vegetable peeler
1 carrot, cut into thin shreds with
  a vegetable peeler

1   Put the stock, fish sauce, and curry powder in a saucepan and bring to a boil
    over high heat. Add the shrimp and cook 3 to 4 minutes until pink and cooked
    through. Stir in all of the remaining ingredients and cook 1 minute longer until
    hot, then remove from the heat.
2   Divide the warm salad into four bowls and serve hot.

020 Ground Shrimp on Sugar Cane

PREPARATION TIME 20 minutes, plus 1 hour soaking   COOKING TIME 15 minutes   SERVES 4

1 cup dried shrimp
1lb. 2oz. raw jumbo shrimp, shelled
  and deveined
2oz. pork fat
⅓ cup finely chopped shallots
1 tbsp. fish sauce, plus extra
  for dipping (optional)
1 red chili, finely chopped

1 tsp. freshly ground black pepper
12 sticks sugar cane or lemongrass,
  trimmed into 6in.-long sticks
sesame seeds for coating
3¼ cups canola oil, for deep-frying,
  or more as needed
mixed salad leaves, to serve

1   Put the dried shrimp in a bowl, cover with hot water, and leave to soak 1 hour,
    then drain.
2   Put the raw shrimp and pork fat in a food processor and blend 2 to 3 minutes
    until the mixture forms a coarse paste. Add the dried shrimp, shallots, fish sauce,
    chili, and black pepper and blend again to combine. Be careful not to overwork.
3   With wet hands, mold a ball of the shrimp mixture around one end of one of the
    sticks of sugar cane. Smooth out the mixture so it is egg-shaped, then roll it in the
    sesame seeds to coat. Repeat to make 11 more balls.
4   Fill a large wok or saucepan one-third full with oil over medium-high heat
    and heat it to 350°F, or until a small piece of bread dropped into the oil browns
    in 15 seconds. Working in batches to avoid overcrowding the wok, carefully drop
    the shrimp sticks into the oil and deep-fry 5 minutes, or until golden. Serve
    immediately on a bed of salad leaves with extra fish sauce for dipping, if desired.

021 Moroccan Spiced Fish Cakes

PREPARATION TIME 15 minutes   **COOKING TIME** 20 minutes   **MAKES** 15 small cakes

1lb. 2oz. boneless white fish, skinned
and cut into chunks
1½ tsp. ground cumin
¼ tsp. dried chili flakes
3 garlic cloves, crushed
1 handful flat-leaf parsley or cilantro
leaves, or a mix of both, chopped
1 egg, lightly beaten

finely chopped zest of ½ to
1 preserved lemon (optional)
5 tbsp. all-purpose flour
1 cup sunflower oil, as needed,
for frying
salt
1 lemon, cut into wedges, to serve

1 Put the fish, cumin, chili flakes, garlic, parsley, egg, and preserved lemon, if using,
in a food processor and season with salt. Process 5 seconds only, until finely
chopped and well mixed. Be careful not to overprocess into a paste.

2 Sprinkle the flour onto a plate. With wet hands, shape the mixture into 15 balls
of equal size and flatten slightly. Turn the fish cakes in the flour to coat all over.

3 In a heavy-bottomed skillet over medium-high heat, heat enough oil to cover the
fish cakes half-way. Working in batches, add the cakes to the pan and fry
2 to 3 minutes on each side until golden brown. Remove them from the pan,
using a metal spatula or pancake turner, and drain on paper towels. Serve hot
or cold with the lemon wedges for squeezing over.

022 Burmese Curried Fish Soup

PREPARATION TIME 15 minutes   **COOKING TIME** 45 minutes   **SERVES** 4

4 tbsp. rice flour
3 tbsp. sunflower oil
1 onion, grated
4 garlic cloves, very finely chopped
1in. piece gingerroot, peeled and
finely grated
1 lemongrass stalk, very finely
chopped (remove tough outer
leaves first)

1 tsp. cayenne pepper
1 tsp. turmeric
6 tbsp. Fish sauce
4 shallots, peeled but left whole
14oz. firm white fish fillet, cut
into chunks
7oz. fine rice noodles

1 Put the flour in a small bowl. Add 1 to 2 tablespoons cold water and mix well,
then set aside.

2 Heat the oil in a large saucepan over low heat. Add the onion, garlic, ginger,
lemongrass, cayenne, and turmeric and fry, stirring, 1 to 2 minutes until fragrant.
Add 6½ cups water, then add the fish sauce, shallots, and rice flour paste.
Mix well and bring to a boil, stirring well to prevent any lumps forming. Boil
10 minutes, or until slightly thickened, then lower the heat to low and simmer
20 minutes, or until thick. Stir in the fish and continue cooking 10 minutes longer,
or until hot.

3 Meanwhile, bring a separate large saucepan of water to a boil. Add the noodles
and cook 5 minutes, or until tender, then drain well. Divide the noodles into four
soup bowls, top with the soup, and serve hot.

023 Mauritian Salmon Croquettes

PREPARATION TIME 15 minutes, plus 30 minutes chilling   COOKING TIME 40 minutes   SERVES 4

1lb. 2oz. potatoes
14oz. cooked salmon, skinned
  and boned
3 tbsp. milk
1 tsp. finely grated lemon zest
2 tbsp. finely chopped parsley

4 scallions, green part only,
  thinly sliced
1 egg white
1 cup dried breadcrumbs
1 cup sunflower oil, as needed,
  for frying
1 lemon, cut into wedges, to serve

1 Bring a saucepan of lightly salted water to a boil. Add the potatoes and boil
   12 to 15 minutes until tender. Drain, then return to the pan and mash well. Leave
   to cool, then chill, covered.
2 Finely flake the salmon into a bowl. Add the mashed potato, milk, lemon zest,
   parsley, scallions, and egg white. Mix well, then divide the mixture evenly into
   8 to 12 balls and flatten slightly into oval croquettes or round patties.
3 Spread the breadcrumbs on a plate and coat the croquettes all over. Put them
   on a plate and chill 30 minutes, or until firm and set.
4 In a large skillet over medium-high heat, heat enough oil to cover the croquettes
   half-way. Working in batches, add the croquettes to the pan, and fry
   3 to 4 minutes on each side until golden brown. Drain on paper towels, then
   serve immediately with lemon wedges for squeezing over.

024 Malaysian Shrimp Fritters

PREPARATION TIME 10 minutes   COOKING TIME 30 minutes   SERVES 4 to 6

2 eggs, beaten
scant 1¼ cups all-purpose flour
1 onion, finely chopped
1 red chili, thinly sliced
30 shelled and deveined cooked
  jumbo shrimp, coarsely chopped

3 cups canola oil, for deep-frying,
  or more as needed
1oz. bean sprouts, coarsely chopped
salt and freshly ground black pepper

1 Put the eggs and ½ cup water in a small bowl. Season with salt and pepper and
   whisk together. Sift the flour into a separate large bowl. Make a well in the
   center, then pour in the egg mixture and mix well to form a smooth batter. Mix
   in the onion, chili, and shrimp.
2 Fill a large wok or saucepan one-third full with oil and heat it to 350°F, or until
   a small piece of bread dropped into the oil browns in 15 seconds. Working
   in batches to avoid overcrowding the wok, fill a small metal ladle half-way with
   some of the shrimp mixture, add some bean sprouts, and then top up with little
   more of the mixture. Immerse the ladle in the hot oil and fry 1 to 2 minutes until
   the batter becomes firm and separates from the ladle. Continue frying
   1 to 2 minutes longer until golden brown, then remove the fritter from the ladle
   and drain on paper towels. Repeat with the remaining shrimp mixture and bean
   sprouts to make about 16 fritters. Serve immediately.

025 Caribbean Curried Salt Cod Fritters

PREPARATION TIME 25 minutes, plus at least 24 hours soaking and making the curry powder
COOKING TIME 30 minutes   **SERVES** 4

7oz. salt cod
1 tbsp. Curry Powder (see page 11)
1 large onion, finely chopped
1 Scotch bonnet or habanero chili,
   finely chopped
2 tsp. thyme leaves
2 tbsp. finely chopped parsley

2 cups all-purpose flour
2 tsp. baking powder
1¼ cups light cream
1 egg, lightly beaten
3 cups canola oil, for deep-frying,
   or more as needed

1   Soak the salt cod in cold water at least 24 hours before cooking, changing
    the water at least 6 times. When ready to cook, drain and rinse the salt cod
    thoroughly, then put it in a saucepan and cover with cold water. Bring to a boil
    over high heat, then lower the heat to medium and simmer 15 minutes, or until
    tender. Remove the fish from the pan, using a slotted spoon, and immerse
    it in a bowl of fresh cold water. Drain immediately and, when cool enough to
    handle, remove and discard any skin and bones, then flake the flesh in small
    pieces into a large bowl.
2   Mix in the curry powder, onion, chili, thyme, parsley, flour, and baking powder.
    Add the cream and egg and stir until the mixture forms a doughlike mixture,
    loose enough to just fall off the spoon. Add a little water if needed.
3   Fill a large wok or saucepan one-third full with oil and heat it to 350°F, or until
    a small piece of bread dropped into the oil browns in 15 seconds. Dip the head
    of a metal tablespoon into the oil, then use it to scoop up spoonfuls of the salt
    cod mixture (the oil prevents the mixture from sticking to the spoon). Carefully
    drop it into the oil and fry 1 to 2 minutes until golden and crisp. Work in batches
    to avoid overcrowding the pan.
4   Remove the fritters from the pan, using a slotted spoon, and drain on paper
    towels. Serve immediately while hot and crisp.

026 Burmese Jumbo Shrimp Salad

PREPARATION TIME 10 minutes   **COOKING TIME** 4 minutes   **SERVES** 4

2 tbsp. sesame oil
12 raw jumbo shrimp, shelled and
   deveined
4 scallions, thinly sliced diagonally
2 red chilies, finely chopped

1 tsp. fish sauce
14in. piece cucumber, cut into
   2in.-long julienne pieces
1 tbsp. finely chopped cilantro leaves
juice of 1 lemon

1   Heat the oil in a wok or skillet over medium-high heat. When it is very hot,
    add the shrimp and stir-fry 3 to 4 minutes until they turn pink and are cooked
    through. Remove the shrimp from the wok, using a slotted spoon, and thinly slice
    them diagonally.
2   Put the shrimp in a bowl, add all of the remaining ingredients, and toss well.
    Serve immediately.

027 Curried Panko Shrimp

PREPARATION TIME 15 minutes, plus making the curry powder   **COOKING TIME** 5 minutes
SERVES 4

20 raw jumbo shrimp, peeled and
   deveined, but tails left intact
2 tbsp. cornstarch
3 extra-large eggs, lightly beaten
1 cup panko breadcrumbs
1 tbsp. Curry Powder (see page 11)

3 cups canola oil, for deep-frying,
   or more as needed
salt
sweet chili sauce, to serve
1 lime, cut into wedges, to serve

1   Using a small, sharp knife, cut down the back of each shrimp and gently press
   down to "butterfly" them. Put them on a plate and season well with salt.
2   Put the cornstarch, eggs, and panko in three separate bowls. Add half of the
   curry powder to the panko and the other half to the eggs and mix well. Dip each
   shrimp first in the cornstarch, then in the eggs, and then in the panko to coat
   evenly all over. Put the coated shrimp on a plate.
3   Fill a wok or saucepan one-third full with oil and heat it over medium-high heat
   to 350°F, or until a piece of bread dropped into the oil browns in 15 seconds.
   Working in batches to avoid overcrowding the wok, carefully drop the shrimp into
   the oil and deep-fry 1 minute, or until light golden and crisp. Remove from the
   pan, using a slotted spoon, and drain on paper towels. Serve hot with sweet chili
   sauce for dipping and lime wedges for squeezing over.

028 Curried Shrimp Poppadoms

PREPARATION TIME 15 minutes, plus making the curry powder COOKING TIME 8 minutes
SERVES 4

1 tbsp. sunflower oil
1 small onion, finely diced
4 garlic cloves, finely chopped
1 tsp. peeled and finely chopped
  gingerroot
1 or 2 mild red chilies, seeded and
  thinly sliced, plus extra to serve
  (optional)
1 to 2 tsp. nigella seeds

1 tbsp. mild Curry Powder
  (see page 11)
20 raw jumbo shrimp
1 plum tomato, finely diced
juice of 1 lime
1 small handful cilantro leaves,
  chopped
8 cooked poppadoms
salt and freshly ground black pepper

1   Heat the oil in a large, nonstick wok or skillet over medium-low heat. Add the
    onion, garlic, ginger, chilies, nigella seeds, and curry powder and cook, stirring
    occasionally, 3 to 4 minutes until soft and fragrant. Increase the heat to high and
    add the shrimp and tomato. Stir-fry 3 to 4 minutes until the shrimp turn pink and
    are just cooked through.
2   Remove the wok from the heat and stir in the lime juice. Season well with salt
    and pepper and stir in the cilantro leaves.
3   Divide the poppadoms onto four plates and divide the shrimp mixture over them.
    Sprinkle with a little extra sliced red chili, if using, and serve immediately.

029 Spiced Shrimp Rolls

PREPARATION TIME 15 minutes, plus making the curry powder and kachumber
COOKING TIME 40 minutes SERVES 4

5oz. potatoes, peeled
1 tbsp. sunflower oil
1 onion, finely chopped
1 tsp. finely chopped garlic
1 tsp. peeled and finely grated
  gingerroot
2 tsp. cumin seeds
1 tbsp. Madras Curry Powder
  (see page 12)
12 raw jumbo shrimp, shelled,
  deveined, and coarsely chopped

4 tbsp. finely chopped cilantro leaves
juice of ½ lime
1 to 2 tbsp. all-purpose flour
8 uncooked poppadoms
3 cups canola oil, for deep-frying,
  or more as needed
salt and freshly ground black pepper
mixed salad leaves, to serve
1 recipe quantity Kachumber
  (see page 200), to serve

1   Bring a saucepan of water to a boil. Add the potatoes and cook 15 to
    20 minutes until tender, then drain. When cool enough to handle, chop
    coarsely and set aside.
2   Heat the oil in a large skillet over low heat. Add the onion and cook, stirring
    occasionally, 6 to 8 minutes until soft. Add the garlic, ginger, cumin seeds, and
    curry powder and cook, stirring, 1 to 2 minutes until fragrant. Add the shrimp
    and potatoes and mix well. Season with salt and pepper, then stir in the cilantro
    and lime juice. Remove from the heat and set aside to cool.
3   Meanwhile, put the flour in a small bowl and add just enough cold water to make
    a smooth, thick paste. Soak the poppadoms in warm water 3 to 4 minutes until
    just soft. Pat dry with paper towels and arrange side by side on a clean work
    surface. Divide the shrimp mixture evenly onto the poppadoms and carefully roll
    each one into a log, folding in the sides to enclose the filling. Spread a little of the
    flour paste along the edge and press to seal.
4   Fill a large wok or saucepan one-third full with oil over medium-high heat
    and heat it to 325°F, or until a small piece of bread dropped into the oil browns
    in 20 seconds. Working in batches to avoid overcrowding the wok, carefully drop
    the rolls into the oil and deep-fry 2 minutes, or until golden and crisp. Remove
    from the wok, using a slotted spoon, and drain on paper towels. Serve hot with
    salad leaves and kachumber.

030 Malaysian Spiced Fish Mousse

PREPARATION TIME 15 minutes, plus 1 hour soaking   **COOKING TIME** 10 minutes   **SERVES** 4

3 dried red chilies
1lb. 2oz. white fish fillet, coarsely
   chopped
5 candlenuts or macadamia nuts
1 onion, grated
1 tbsp. shrimp paste
1 tsp. turmeric

1 egg, beaten
2 tbsp. coconut milk
1 tbsp. palm sugar
1 tsp. salt
4 banana leaves
sunflower oil, for brushing

1   Put the dried chilies in a small bowl, cover with hot water, and leave to soak 1 hour. Drain well and set aside.
2   Put the fish in a blender or food processor and blend 2 to 3 minutes until it forms a paste. Transfer to a bowl and add 4 tablespoons water, a spoonful at a time, and beat with a wooden spoon until the mixture is light and fluffy.
3   Put the drained chilies, nuts, onion, shrimp paste, and turmeric in a mortar and pestle and pound to make a coarse paste. Mix the paste into the fish mixture, then add the egg and beat well. Stir in the coconut milk, sugar, and salt.
4   Cut the banana leaves into 12 squares, each about 6 inches square. Put them in a heatproof bowl, cover with boiling water, and leave to soak 2 minutes, or until soft, then drain and pat dry with paper towels. Put 2 tablespoons of the fish mixture in the center of each square and roll up to form open-ended tubes. Fasten each end with a toothpick.
5   Preheat the broiler to high, or a charcoal barbecue until very hot (waiting until any flames die down). Brush the banana leaves lightly with oil and broil 5 minutes on each side, or until the leaves are slightly charred and the filling is firm when pressed. Serve immediately.

031 Spicy Squid

PREPARATION TIME 10 minutes, plus 30 minutes marinating   **COOKING TIME** 1 minute
SERVES 4

1lb. 2oz. fresh squid, dressed
2 garlic cloves, very finely chopped
1 tsp. finely grated gingerroot
1 tbsp. fish sauce
2 tbsp. sunflower oil

2 scallions, finely shredded
3 red chilies, seeded and sliced
salt and freshly ground black pepper
cilantro leaves, to garnish

1   Cut open the squid bodies and cut a crisscross pattern over the inside of the flesh, using a sharp knife, then cut into small bite-size pieces.
2   Bring a saucepan of water to a boil. Add the squid pieces and tentacles and boil 1 minute, then drain and pat dry with paper towels.
3   Put the garlic, ginger, and fish sauce in a bowl and mix well. Season well with salt and pepper, then toss in the squid and leave to marinate in the refrigerator, covered, 25 to 30 minutes.
4   Meanwhile, heat the oil in a small saucepan over medium-high heat until hot but not smoking. Remove the pan from the heat, add the scallions and chilies and set aside to infuse 15 to 20 minutes.
5   Put the squid and marinade on a plate and pour the infused oil, scallions, and chili over. Sprinkle with cilantro leaves and serve at room temperature.

032 Vietnamese Vegetable Salad

PREPARATION TIME 15 minutes   **COOKING TIME** 6 minutes   **SERVES** 4

1 tbsp. sunflower oil
4 tbsp. chopped skinless raw peanuts
2 shallots, thinly sliced
1 head Chinese leaves, torn into
  bite-size pieces
2 carrots, coarsely grated
6 scallions, thinly sliced lengthwise
4 tbsp. chopped mint leaves
1 small bunch cilantro leaves

SPICED DRESSING
3 red chilies, seeded and chopped
3 garlic cloves, crushed
2 tbsp. palm sugar
1 tbsp. rice wine vinegar
juice of 2 limes
1 tbsp. fish sauce
3 tbsp. sunflower oil

1   To make the dressing, put all of the ingredients in a bowl, whisk until well combined and then set aside.
2   Heat the oil in a small pan over low heat. Add the peanuts and cook, stirring, 1 to 2 minutes until golden. Remove from the pan, using a slotted spoon, and drain on paper towels, then set aside.
3   Add the shallots to the oil in the pan and cook, stirring, 3 to 4 minutes over low heat until golden and crisp. Remove from the pan, using a slotted spoon, and drain on paper towels.
4   Put the Chinese leaves, carrots, scallions, and mint in a large bowl and toss well. Drizzle the dressing over and toss again, then serve, sprinkled with the cilantro, reserved peanuts, and shallots.

033 Sprouted Bean Salad

PREPARATION TIME 10 minutes   **COOKING TIME** 3 minutes   **SERVES** 4

4 tbsp. sunflower oil
1 tsp. black mustard seeds
1 tsp. cumin seeds
1 tsp. peeled and finely grated
  gingerroot
1 red chili, seeded and finely chopped
  or sliced

14oz. mixed sprouted beans
1 tsp. cayenne pepper
juice of 2 limes
4 scallions, thinly sliced
7oz. cherry tomatoes, halved
salt
Belgian endive leaves, to serve

1   Heat the oil in a large skillet over low heat. Add the mustard and cumin seeds. When the mustard seeds start to pop, add the ginger, chili, and sprouted beans and cook, stirring, 2 to 3 minutes until slightly softened. Mix in the cayenne, then remove from the heat and squeeze the lime juice over.
2   Stir in the scallions and cherry tomatoes and season well with salt. Serve immediately on a bed of Belgian endive leaves.

034 Spiced Cabbage Salad

PREPARATION TIME 20 minutes   **COOKING TIME** 7 minutes   **SERVES** 4

2 to 3 tbsp. freshly grated or
  shredded coconut
2 tbsp. sunflower oil
2 tsp. black mustard seeds
1 tbsp. peeled and finely grated
  gingerroot

10 to 12 curry leaves
2 large carrots, coarsely grated
5 cups halved, cored, and finely
  shredded white cabbage
salt and freshly ground black pepper

1   If using shredded coconut, soak it in warm water 20 minutes, then drain.
2   Heat the oil in a large wok or skillet over high heat. Add the mustard seeds and when they start to pop after a few seconds, add the ginger, curry leaves, carrots, and cabbage. Stir-fry 4 to 5 minutes until the cabbage just wilts. Add the coconut and stir-fry 1 to 2 minutes until hot.
3   Season with salt and pepper and serve immediately.

035 Spiced Eggplant Dip with Crudités

PREPARATION TIME 25 minutes, plus chilling   COOKING TIME 45 minutes   SERVES 4

3 eggplants
4 garlic cloves, crushed
4 tbsp. light cream
3 tbsp. olive oil, plus extra
   for drizzling
2 tbsp. tahini
juice of 1 large lemon
1 tsp. ground cumin
½ tsp. paprika

3 tbsp. finely chopped flat-leaf
   parsley leaves, plus extra to serve
1 tbsp. very finely chopped mint
   leaves
salt and freshly ground black pepper
vegetable crudités, such as radishes,
   cucumber sticks, and baby carrots,
   to serve
toasted slices of baguette, to serve

1   Preheat the oven to 400°F. Prick the eggplants all over with a fork and put them in a roasting pan. Bake 40 to 45 minutes until soft and wrinkled, then set aside to cool slightly.
2   When the eggplants are cool enough to handle, peel off and discard the skins over a large bowl, saving any juices. Roughly chop the flesh and put it in a food processor with the reserved juices and the garlic, cream, oil, tahini, lemon juice, cumin, paprika, parsley, and mint. Blend 1 to 2 minutes until creamy and smooth. Season well with salt and pepper, then transfer to a serving bowl and chill, covered, until ready to serve.
3   Just before serving, drizzle the dip with a little oil and sprinkle with extra parsley. Serve with crudités and bread.

036 Thai-Style Deep-Fried Eggs

PREPARATION TIME 20 minutes   COOKING TIME 20 minutes   SERVES 4

6 extra-large eggs
3 cups canola oil, for deep-frying,
   or more as needed
½ cup palm sugar
6 tbsp. tamarind juice
5 tbsp. fish sauce
2 tbsp. sweet chili sauce

6 shallots, thinly sliced
4 garlic cloves, thinly sliced
2 red chilies, seeded and
   thinly sliced
3oz. mixed salad leaves
1 small handful cilantro leaves
1oz. bean sprouts

1   Put the eggs in a pan and cover with cold water. Bring to a boil over high heat and cook 4 minutes. Drain and rinse in cold water, then carefully peel off and discard the shells.
2   Fill a large wok or saucepan one-third full with oil and heat it to 350°F, or until a small piece of bread dropped into the oil browns in 15 seconds. Working in batches to avoid overcrowding the wok, carefully lower the eggs into the oil, lowering them, one at a time, in a slotted spoon. Deep-fry 2 to 3 minutes until lightly golden. Remove and drain on paper towels and cover to keep warm.
3   Put the palm sugar, tamarind juice, fish sauce, and 2 tablespoons water in a small saucepan and bring to a boil over high heat, stirring until the sugar dissolves. Lower the heat to low and simmer 3 to 4 minutes until slightly thickened. Transfer to a heatproof bowl and stir in the sweet chili sauce.
4   Heat 2 tablespoons of the oil in a nonstick skillet over low heat. Add the shallots, garlic, and chilies and fry, stirring occasionally, 4 to 5 minutes until light brown. Remove from the heat and set aside, draining on paper towels if desired.
5   Put the salad leaves, cilantro, and bean sprouts in a bowl and toss in the tamarind mixture. Divide the salad evenly onto four plates. Cut the deep-fried eggs in half and arrange 3 halves on top of each portion of salad. Sprinkle the shallot mixture over and serve immediately.

37 Spiced Eggplant Fritters

PREPARATION TIME 15 minutes, plus making the raita **COOKING TIME** 10 minutes
SERVES 4

1 cup gram flour
1 tsp. baking powder
½ tsp. turmeric
2 tsp. ground coriander
1 tsp. ground cumin
1 tsp. cayenne pepper
1 cup plus 2 tbsp. chilled soda water

3 cups canola oil, for deep-frying,
   or more as needed
2 large eggplants, cut into
   ½in.-thick batons
salt
1 recipe quantity Corn Raita
   (see page 212), to serve

1. Sift the gram flour, baking powder, turmeric, coriander, cumin, and cayenne together into a large bowl. Season with salt and make a well in the center. Gradually add the soda water, incorporating the flour as you do, to make a thick batter. Be careful not to overmix.
2. Fill a large wok or saucepan one-third full with oil and heat it to 350°F, or until a small piece of bread dropped into the oil browns in 15 seconds. Working in batches to avoid overcrowding the wok, dip the eggplant batons in the batter and carefully drop them into the oil. Deep-fry 1 to 2 minutes until crisp and golden, then remove the fritters from the oil, using a slotted spoon, and drain on paper towels. Serve immediately with raita.

038 Singharas

PREPARATION TIME 25 minutes, plus 30 minutes cooling and making the chutney
COOKING TIME 30 minutes **SERVES** 6 to 8

2 garlic cloves, chopped
½ tsp. cayenne pepper
1 tsp. cumin seeds
½ tsp. black mustard seeds
½ tsp. fenugreek seeds
¼ tsp. fennel seeds
3 cups canola oil, for deep-frying,
   or more as needed
1 small onion, chopped

8oz. potatoes, peeled and finely
   chopped
1 tbsp. lemon juice
12 egg roll skins
salt and freshly ground black pepper
1 recipe quantity Mint Chutney
   (see page 204) or plain yogurt,
   to serve

1. Put the garlic, cayenne, and the cumin, mustard, fenugreek, and fennel seeds in a small food processor or mortar and pestle and blend until roughly crushed.
2. Heat 1 tablespoon of the oil in a heavy-bottomed saucepan over low heat. Add the garlic mixture and cook, stirring occasionally, 2 minutes, or until aromatic. Add the onion and potatoes and cook, stirring, 2 minutes longer, or until the onions are soft. Add 7 tablespoons water and cook, covered, 8 to 10 minutes until the potatoes are soft. Add the lemon juice and season with salt and pepper, then set aside to cool 30 minutes.
3. Working with one egg roll skin at a time and keeping the rest covered with a clean, damp dish towel, cut each skin in half into rectangles and moisten the edges with water. Put 2 teaspoons of the cool potato filling at one end of the skin, leaving a small border around the edges. Fold the end of the skin over to form a triangle and then continue folding, keeping the triangular shape. Press the edges to seal and put the package on a baking sheet. Repeat with the remaining filling and skins to make 24 singharas.
4. Fill a large wok or saucepan one-third full with oil over medium-high heat and heat it to 350°F, or until a small piece of bread dropped into the oil browns in 15 seconds. Working in batches to avoid overcrowding the wok, carefully drop the singharas into the oil and deep-fry 2 to 3 minutes until golden brown. Remove from the pan, using a slotted spoon, and drain on paper towels. Serve hot with chutney or yogurt.

039 Spiced Carrot, Cilantro & Ginger Soup

PREPARATION TIME 15 minutes, plus making the curry powder **COOKING TIME** 25 minutes
SERVES 4

2 tbsp. sunflower oil
1 onion, finely chopped
2 garlic cloves, finely chopped
1 tbsp. mild Curry Powder
  (see page 11)
2 tsp. peeled and finely grated
  gingerroot

4 cups vegetable stock
1lb. 4oz. carrots, coarsely chopped
½ cup finely chopped
  cilantro leaves
4 tbsp. plain yogurt,
  lightly whisked

1 Heat the oil in a large saucepan over low heat. Add the onion, garlic, curry powder, and ginger and cook, stirring occasionally, 2 to 3 minutes until the onion is soft and translucent.
2 Add the stock and carrots and bring to a boil over high heat. Lower the heat to medium and simmer 20 minutes, or until the carrots are tender.
3 Using an immersion blender, blend the soup until smooth. Remove from the heat, stir in the cilantro, and serve immediately, drizzled with the yogurt.

040 Spicy Crisp Noodle Pancakes

PREPARATION TIME 20 minutes   **COOKING TIME** 15 minutes   **SERVES** 4

5oz. rice vermicelli
1 red chili, finely chopped
¼ small red onion, finely chopped
1 tsp. very finely chopped lemongrass
2 tsp. garlic salt
1 tsp. ground ginger

1 tsp. ground cumin
1 tsp. ground coriander
large pinch of turmeric
4 tbsp. canola oil, plus extra
  as needed
salt and freshly ground black pepper

1 Roughly break up the noodles and put them in a large heatproof bowl. Cover with boiling water and leave to soak 4 to 5 minutes, then drain and rinse under cold running water. Dry thoroughly on paper towels.
2 Put the noodles in a bowl and add the chili, red onion, lemongrass, garlic salt, ginger, cumin, coriander, and turmeric. Toss well and season with salt and pepper.
3 Heat the oil in a large, nonstick skillet over medium-high heat until hot. Working in batches, carefully drop large tablespoons of the noodle mixture into the oil. Using a spatula, flatten the pancakes while they are cooking and fry 1 to 2 minutes on each side until crisp and golden, then drain on paper towels. Repeat with the remaining mixture, adding more oil to the pan as needed. Serve immediately.

041 Spiced Mixed Fruit Salad

PREPARATION TIME 10 minutes, plus 30 minutes chilling and making the chaat masala
SERVES 4

2 pomegranates
7oz. black seedless grapes
1 pink grapefruit, peeled and
  segmented
1 ripe guava, halved, seeded, and cut
  into small bite-size pieces

2 large oranges, peeled
  and segmented
2 tbsp. Chaat Masala
  (see Aloo Chaat, page 45)
1 handful mint leaves

1 Firmly tap the pomegranates all over with a wooden spoon, then cut each one in half. Hold each half over a bowl and continue tapping with the wooden spoon until the seeds fall out. Add the remaining fruit to the bowl and mix well, then sprinkle the chaat masala over. Cover and chill 30 minutes.
2 Add the mint leaves, toss well to combine, and serve immediately.

Onion Bhajiyas

PREPARATION TIME 10 minutes, plus making the chutney   **COOKING TIME** 10 minutes
SERVES 4

3 or 4 onions, halved and thinly sliced
1 tsp. cayenne pepper
1 tsp. turmeric
2 tsp. cumin seeds
1 tbsp. crushed coriander seeds
2½ cups gram flour

3 cups canola oil, for deep-frying,
   or more if needed
salt
cilantro leaves, to serve
1 recipe quantity Mint & Cilantro
   Chutney (see page 201), to serve

1   Separate the onion slices and put them in a large bowl. Add the cayenne, turmeric, and cumin and coriander seeds, then season with salt and mix well.
2   Add the gram flour, a little at a time, stirring to coat the onions. Gradually sprinkle ⅔ cup cold water over, adding just enough to make a very sticky batter that coats the onions. Use your fingers to mix thoroughly.
3   Fill a large saucepan one-quarter full with oil and heat it over medium-high heat to 350°F, or until a small piece of bread dropped into the oil browns in 15 seconds. Working in batches to avoid overcrowding the pan, drop spoonfuls of the mixture into the oil and deep-fry 1 to 2 minutes until golden brown and crisp. Remove the bhajiyas from the pan, using a slotted spoon, and drain on paper towels. Serve immediately with cilantro leaves and chutney.

043 Quail Eggs with Masala-Spiced Sea Salt

PREPARATION TIME 10 minutes, plus making the curry powder **COOKING TIME** 10 minutes
SERVES 4

1 tbsp. coriander seeds
1 tbsp. cumin seeds
1 tbsp. fennel seeds
24 quail eggs

½ cup sea salt
1 tsp. cayenne pepper
1 tsp. Madras Curry Powder
(see page 12)

1 Put the coriander, cumin, and fennel seeds in a small skillet and dry-roast over
   low heat 2 to 3 minutes until fragrant, then crush lightly using a mortar and
   pestle and set aside
2 Put the eggs in a saucepan of cold water and bring to a boil over high heat.
   Lower the heat to low and simmer 5 to 6 minutes, then drain. Cover the
   eggs in cold water, then drain again. Carefully peel away the shells, arrange
   the eggs on a plate, and leave to cool.
3 Meanwhile, mix together the toasted seeds, salt, cayenne pepper, and curry
   powder and put the mixture in a small dipping bowl. Serve the eggs with the
   salt mixture for dipping or sprinkle the salt mixture over the eggs.

044 Gujarati Carrot Salad

PREPARATION TIME 10 minutes   **COOKING TIME** 1 minute   **SERVES** 4

1lb. 4oz. carrots, coarsely chopped
juice of 2 limes
1 tsp. sugar

3 tbsp. sunflower oil
1 tbsp. black mustard seeds
salt and freshly ground black pepper

1   Put the carrots in a large bowl. Mix together the lime juice and sugar until the
    sugar dissolves, then stir the mixture into the carrots. Toss well and set aside.
2   Heat the oil in a small skillet over low heat. Add the mustard seeds and when
    they start to pop after a few seconds, pour them and the oil over the carrot
    mixture. Toss well, season with salt and pepper, and serve.

045 Minted Daikon Salad

PREPARATION TIME 10 minutes, plus 30 minutes chilling   **SERVES** 4

⅔ cup plain yogurt
¼ tsp. ground cumin
1 tbsp. finely chopped mint leaves
1 small red onion, very thinly sliced

1lb. daikon (white radish),
   coarsely grated
salt and freshly ground black pepper

1   Put the yogurt in a bowl and whisk until smooth, then season well with salt and
    pepper. Stir in the cumin, mint, and red onion and mix well.
2   Add the daikon and mix well. Cover and chill 30 minutes before serving.

046 Burmese Lentil Soup

PREPARATION TIME 10 minutes, plus making the curry powder   **COOKING TIME** 25 minutes
SERVES 4

1¼ cups split red lentils, rinsed
   and drained
1 tbsp. Curry Powder (see page 11)
½ cup finely chopped cilantro leaves
salt and freshly ground black pepper

2 green chilies, thinly sliced, to serve
2 tbsp. crispy fried onions, to serve
2 tomatoes, finely chopped,
   to serve

1   Put the lentils, curry powder, and 2½ cups water in a large saucepan and bring
    to a boil over high heat. Lower the heat to medium and simmer, partially covered,
    20 to 30 minutes until the lentils break apart and the mixture thickens into the
    consistency of a thick oatmeal.
2   Stir in the cilantro and season with salt and pepper. Ladle the soup into bowls
    and serve with the chilies, onions, and tomatoes in separate bowls for topping.

047 Baby Spinach & Coconut Salad

PREPARATION TIME 20 minutes   **COOKING TIME** 1 minute   **SERVES** 4

⅓ cup freshly grated or shredded
   coconut
10oz. baby spinach leaves, finely
   chopped
1 small carrot, coarsely grated

4 tbsp. sunflower oil
1 tsp. black mustard seeds
1 tsp. cumin seeds
juice of 1 lime
salt and freshly ground black pepper

1   If using shredded coconut, soak it in warm water 20 minutes, then drain.
2   Put the spinach, carrot, and coconut in a large bowl and toss lightly.
3   Heat the oil a small skillet over low heat. Add the mustard and cumin seeds and
    cook, stirring, 20 to 30 seconds until the mustard seeds start to pop. Pour the
    mixture over the salad, drizzle the lime juice over, and season with salt and
    pepper. Toss well and serve.

048 Spiced Middle Eastern Bulgur Salad

PREPARATION TIME 50 minutes   COOKING TIME 2 minutes   SERVES 4

1¼ cups bulgur
1 tbsp. tomato paste
juice of 1½ lemons
⅓ cup olive oil
½ to 1 red or green chili,
  finely chopped
5 to 7 scallions,
  thinly sliced

2 cups diced tomatoes
1⅔ cups chopped parsley leaves
½ cup chopped mint leaves
salt
2 baby romaine or hearts of
  lettuces, leaves separated,
  to serve

1   Put the bulgur in a large heatproof bowl and cover with 2½ cups boiling water. Stir and leave to stand 15 to 20 minutes until the bulgur is tender. Don't be tempted to add more water, as the juice from the lemons and tomatoes will soften the bulgur more.

2   Mix in the tomato paste, lemon juice, olive oil and chili and season with salt. Add the scallions, tomatoes, parsley, and mint and mix well.

3   Arrange the lettuce leaves around the edges of the bowl and serve. Alternatively, roll the bulgur mixture into balls the size of a small egg, put each one in the hollow of a lettuce leaf and serve.

049 Turkish Spiced Tomato Soup

PREPARATION TIME 5 minutes, plus at least 3 hours chilling and making the curry powder
SERVES 4

1lb. 12oz. canned chopped tomatoes
2 tbsp. olive oil
juice of ½ lemon
1 tbsp. white wine vinegar
½ tsp. Curry Powder (see page 11)

1 cup plain yogurt
salt and freshly ground black pepper
chopped flat-leaved parsley leaves,
  to serve

1   Put the tomatoes, oil, lemon juice, vinegar, curry powder, and yogurt in a food processor and blend 1 to 2 minutes until smooth. Season well with salt and pepper, then transfer to a bowl, cover, and chill 3 to 4 hours.

2   Divide the chilled soup into bowls, sprinkle with parsley, and serve.

050 Broiled Chili & Lime Corn-on-the-Cob

PREPARATION TIME 10 minutes   COOKING TIME 8 minutes   SERVES 4

4 corn-on-the-cobs, husks stripped
  and reserved
2 tbsp. salt

4 tsp. cayenne pepper
1 tsp. ground cumin
2 limes, halved

1   Preheat the broiler or a barbecue to high. Hold each corn cob under cold running water to remove any silken threads, then drain and pat dry with paper towel. In a small bowl, mix together the salt, cayenne, and cumin, then set aside.

2   Broil or grill the corn 6 to 8 minutes, turning often to cook evenly, until lightly charred in a few places and cooked through. Transfer to a plate.

3   Dip the cut side of 1 lime half in the salt and chili mixture and rub it all over one of the corn cobs, squeezing the lime juice onto the corn. Repeat with the remaining corn and lime halves. Serve hot on the reserved husks of corn.

051 Crunchy Curry Leaf, Cucumber & Peanut Salad

PREPARATION TIME 10 minutes   COOKING TIME 2 minutes   SERVES 4

1 large cucumber, peeled and
   finely chopped
juice of 1 lemon
4 tbsp. sunflower oil
1 tsp. yellow mustard seeds
2 tsp. black mustard seeds

8 to 10 curry leaves
1 to 2 red chilies, seeded and
   finely chopped
4 tbsp. finely chopped skinless
   roasted peanuts
salt

1   Put the cucumber in a large bowl, sprinkle the lemon juice over, and season with
    salt. Mix well and set aside.
2   Heat the oil in a small skillet over low heat. Add the yellow and black mustard
    seeds, curry leaves, and chilies and cook, stirring, 1 to 2 minutes until fragrant
    and the mustard seeds start to pop, then pour the mixture over the cucumber.
    Mix well, sprinkle the peanuts over, and serve immediately.

052 Chilled Spinach & Buttermilk Shorba

PREPARATION TIME 10 minutes   SERVES 4

10oz. frozen spinach, thawed
1 garlic clove, crushed
½ tsp. peeled and finely grated
   gingerroot
2 cups plus 2 tbsp. buttermilk

3 tbsp. finely chopped mint leaves,
   plus extra to serve
salt and freshly ground black pepper
8 ice cubes, to serve

1   Put the spinach in a colander and squeeze out the excess water, then chop it very
    finely. Put the spinach in a blender and add the garlic, ginger, and buttermilk.
2   Season well with salt and pepper, then stir in the mint. Add 1½ cups very cold
    water and blend 2 to 3 minutes until smooth.
3   Divide the ice cubes into four bowls and ladle over the shorba. Sprinkle with mint
    leaves and serve immediately.

053 Zucchini Fritters

PREPARATION TIME 15 minutes   COOKING TIME 10 minutes   SERVES 4

1 cup gram flour
1 tsp. baking powder
1 tsp. cayenne pepper
½ tsp. turmeric
2 tsp. crushed coriander seeds
1 tsp. cumin seeds
1 tsp. mustard seeds

3 cups canola oil, for deep-frying,
   or more as needed
4 zucchini, cut into ½in.-thick batons
salt
1 lime, cut into wedges,
   to serve

1   Put the gram flour, baking powder, cayenne, turmeric, and coriander, cumin, and
    mustard seeds into a large bowl and season with salt. Gradually add 1 cup plus
    2 tablespoons cold water and mix until the ingredients come together in a thick
    batter—be careful not to overmix.
2   Fill a large wok or saucepan one-third full with oil over medium-high heat and
    heat it to 350°F, or until a small piece of bread dropped into the oil browns
    in 15 seconds. Working in batches to avoid overcrowding the wok, dip the
    zucchini batons in the batter and carefully drop them into the oil. Deep-fry
    1 to 2 minutes until crisp and golden. Remove the fritters from the pan, using
    a slotted spoon, and drain on paper towels. Serve immediately, with lime wedges
    for squeezing over.

054 Cumin-Spiced Moroccan Carrot Salad

PREPARATION TIME 10 minutes **COOKING TIME** 15 minutes **SERVES** 4

5 carrots, cut into ½in.-thick batons
6 tbsp. olive oil
4 garlic cloves, finely chopped
1 tsp. ground cumin

juice of 1 lemon
4 tbsp. finely chopped cilantro leaves
salt and freshly ground black pepper

1   Put the carrots in a saucepan of lightly salted water and bring to a boil. Boil
    10 to 12 minutes until tender but still with a little bite, then drain.
2   Heat the oil in a large skillet over medium-high heat. Add the carrots, garlic,
    and cumin and season with salt and pepper. Cook, stirring, 1 minute, or until the
    garlic just begins to color. Remove from the heat and stir in the lemon juice and
    cilantro. Serve at room temperature.

055 Spiced Potato & Pea Fritters

PREPARATION TIME 20 minutes, plus at least 2 hours chilling and making the chutney
COOKING TIME 30 minutes **SERVES** 4 to 6

1lb. 4oz. potatoes, peeled and diced
1 tbsp. sunflower oil
4 tsp. cumin seeds
1 tsp. black mustard seeds
1 small onion, finely chopped
2 tsp. peeled and finely grated
   gingerroot
2 green chilies, seeded and chopped
heaped 1¼ cups shelled fresh peas
juice of 1 lemon
6 tbsp. chopped cilantro leaves

1 cup gram flour
⅔ cup all-purpose flour
1 tsp. baking soda
¼ tsp. turmeric
2 tsp. crushed coriander seeds
3 cups canola oil, for deep-frying,
   or more as needed
salt and freshly ground black pepper
1 recipe quantity Mint & Cilantro
   Chutney (see page 201), to serve

1   Bring a large pan of lightly salted water to a boil. Add the potatoes and cook
    6 to 8 minutes until just tender. Drain in a colander, then set aside to dry and
    leave to cool slightly.
2   Heat the oil in a large skillet over low heat. When it is hot, add the cumin
    and mustard seeds and cook, stirring, 1 to 2 minutes. Add the onion, ginger,
    and chilies and cook, stirring, 3 to 4 minutes until soft and fragrant.
3   Add the potatoes and peas and cook, stirring occasionally, 3 to 4 minutes. Season
    with salt and pepper, then stir in the lemon juice and cilantro leaves. Remove
    from the heat and set aside. When cool enough to handle, divide the mixture into
    20 portions and shape each one into a ball. Put the balls on a baking sheet, cover,
    and chill 2 to 3 hours.
4   Meanwhile, sift the flours and baking soda into a bowl and season with salt and
    pepper. Stir in the turmeric and coriander seeds, then gradually whisk in 1½ cups
    water and whisk until it is fairly smooth and thick.
5   Fill a large wok or saucepan one-third full with oil over medium-high heat
    and heat it to 350°F, or until a teaspoon of batter dropped into the oil sizzles
    immediately. Working in batches to avoid overcrowding the wok, dip the potato
    balls in the batter, carefully drop them into the oil and deep-fry 1 to 2 minutes
    until crisp and golden. Drain on paper towels, then serve hot with chutney.

Aloo Chaat

PREPARATION TIME 20 minutes, plus 30 minutes cooling and 30 minutes chilling
COOKING TIME 25 minutes   **SERVES** 4

1lb. waxy potatoes, peeled
1 red apple, peeled, cored, and cut
   into small cubes
1 small cucumber, cut into small cubes
juice of 2 limes
1 handful freshly chopped cilantro
   and mint leaves

CHAAT MASALA
1 tbsp. cumin seeds
1 tbsp. freshly ground black pepper
2 tbsp. salt
1 tbsp. amchoor (dried mango
   powder)
1 tsp. cayenne pepper

1 Bring a large saucepan of water to a boil. Add the potatoes and cook
   15 to 20 minutes until tender, then drain and set aside to cool completely.
2 Meanwhile, make the chaat masala. Put the cumin seeds in a small skillet over
   medium-low heat and heat, stirring continuously, 2 to 3 minutes until fragrant.
   Remove from the heat and leave to cool, then transfer to a spice grinder and
   grind for a few seconds until coarse. Transfer to a small bowl and mix in the black
   pepper, salt, amchoor, and cayenne. If not using immediately, store the chaat
   masala in an airtight container up to 3 months.
3 Cut the potatoes into small cubes and put them in a bowl. Add the apple,
   cucumber, and lime juice and sprinkle 4 teaspoons of the chaat masala over. Toss
   well, then cover with plastic wrap and chill 30 minutes to let the flavors develop.
4 Toss in the cilantro and mint and serve immediately.

CHAPTER 2

MEAT

Wherever curries are a popular part of the cuisine, you'll find an impressive variety of meat dishes that reflect every possible flavor, texture, and degree of spiciness imaginable.

For me, nothing can beat the bold flavor and meltingly tender texture of a slow-cooked meat curry. Kashmiri Saffron, Almond & Lamb Curry, for example, is an aromatic dish designed to comfort and satisfy. Equally irresistible are dishes such as Bangkok Sour Pork Curry, Middle Eastern Spiced Lamb Meatballs, and Japanese Beef Curry, which burst with complex flavors—sometimes sweet and pungent, sometimes sharp and bright, and always deeply satisfying.

Many meat curries taste even better the day after they're made—once the spices have had time to infuse the dish fully. So, if you can resist the temptation to eat it immediately, it will be worth the wait. This also makes entertaining a breeze because you can cook many of the recipes here in advance, or leave them to cook slowly. They basically look after themselves, leaving you more time to spend with your guests.

BANGKOK SOUR PORK CURRY (*SEE PAGE 76*)

057 Thai Red Beef Curry with Bamboo Shoots

PREPARATION TIME 20 minutes, plus making the curry paste and rice
COOKING TIME 50 minutes   **SERVES** 4

1lb. 12oz. beef filet mignon steaks
1 tbsp. sunflower oil
2 tbsp. Thai Red Curry Paste
   (see page 15)
1¾ cups coconut milk
scant 1 cup beef stock
2 tbsp. fish sauce

1 tbsp. lime juice
6 kaffir lime leaves, finely shredded
8oz. canned bamboo shoots, rinsed
   and drained
1 small handful Thai basil leaves
jasmine rice, to serve

1 Put a sheet of plastic wrap on a clean work surface, arrange the steaks in single
   layer on top, and cover with a second sheet of plastic wrap. Using a meat mallet
   or a rolling pin, pound the steaks until evenly flattened and about ½ inch thick.
   Remove the plastic wrap and cut the beef into thin strips.
2 Heat the oil in a large, heavy-bottomed saucepan over medium-high heat. Add
   the beef in batches and stir-fry 2 to 3 minutes until brown. Transfer to a plate,
   using a slotted spoon, and set aside.
3 Add the curry paste to the saucepan and stir-fry 2 to 3 minutes over low heat.
   Stir in the coconut milk and stock, then add the fish sauce, lime juice, lime leaves,
   and beef. Bring to a boil, then lower the heat to low and simmer, uncovered,
   30 minutes, or until thicker.
4 Add the bamboo shoots and continue simmering 10 minutes until hot. Season
   with salt and pepper and remove from the heat. Stir in the basil leaves just
   before serving hot with steamed jasmine rice.

058 Burmese Beef & Potato Curry

PREPARATION TIME 10 minutes, plus making the curry paste and bread
COOKING TIME 55 minutes   SERVES 4

1 tbsp. sesame oil
7 tbsp. sunflower oil
3 tbsp. Burmese Curry Paste
 (see page 13)
1 tsp. ground cumin
2 tsp. ground coriander
1lb. 12oz. beef tenderloin, cut into
 bite-size pieces

1lb. potatoes, peeled and cut
 into quarters
2 cups plus 2 tbsp. beef stock
salt and freshly ground black pepper
1 recipe quantity Burmese Paratha
 (see page 191), to serve

1   Heat the oils in a deep-sided skillet over medium-high heat. Carefully stir in
 the curry paste (it will splutter), then lower the heat to low and cook, stirring
 occasionally, 10 minutes, or until the paste is golden brown and has a little oil
 around the edge. If the mixture starts to burn during cooking, add a little water.
2   Stir in the cumin and coriander and stir-fry 30 seconds, then add the beef and
 stir-fry 3 to 4 minutes longer until light brown. Season well with salt and pepper.
3   Add the potatoes and stock and simmer 35 to 40 minutes until the meat is
 tender and potatoes are cooked through. Serve hot with bread.

059 Burmese Beef & Pumpkin Curry

PREPARATION TIME 10 minutes, plus making the curry paste and rice
COOKING TIME 35 minutes   SERVES 4

½ cup sunflower oil
2 tbsp. Burmese Curry Paste
 (see page 13)
1lb. 12oz. beef, such as strip steak
 or filet mignon, cut into bite-size
 chunks

1lb. pumpkin, peeled, seeded,
 and cut into 2in. cubes
salt and freshly ground black pepper
1 recipe quantity Burmese Golden
 Rice (see page 185), to serve

1   Heat the oil in a deep skillet with a lid over medium-high heat. Carefully stir in the
 curry paste (it will splutter), then lower the heat to low and cook 10 minutes, or
 until the paste is golden brown and has a little oil around the edge. If the mixture
 starts to burn during cooking, add a little water. Add the beef and pumpkin and
 cook, stirring, over low heat 2 to 3 minutes until coated.
2   Stir in 2 cups plus 2 tablespoons water and simmer, covered, 20 minutes until the
 meat and pumpkin are tender. Season with salt and pepper. Serve hot with rice.

060 Massaman Beef & Butternut Squash Curry

PREPARATION TIME 15 minutes, plus making the curry paste and rice
COOKING TIME 2 hours 25 minutes   SERVES 4

1lb. 12oz. stewing beef, cut into large
 bite-size pieces
2¼ cups beef stock
3 tbsp. Massaman Curry Paste
 (see page 13)
2 tbsp. tamarind paste
3½ cups coconut milk
2 lemongrass stalks, lightly crushed

16 shallots, peeled but left whole
12oz. butternut squash, peeled,
 seeded, and cut into
 bite-size pieces
finely chopped scallions, to serve
1 recipe quantity Thai Fried Rice
 (see page 189), to serve

1   Put the beef, stock, curry paste, tamarind, coconut milk, and lemongrass in a
 large, heavy-bottomed saucepan and bring to a boil over high heat. Lower the
 heat to low and simmer, uncovered, 2 hours, stirring occasionally, until tender.
2   Add the shallots and butternut squash and cook 20 to 25 minutes longer until
 the squash is tender. Sprinkle with scallions and serve hot with rice.

061 Beef Madras

PREPARATION TIME 15 minutes, plus 24 hours marinating and making the curry powder, garam masala, and rice   COOKING TIME 1 hour 20 minutes   SERVES 4

1lb. 12oz. beef tenderloin, cut
  into large bite-size pieces
5 tbsp. plain yogurt
5 tbsp. Madras Curry Powder
  (see page 12)
2 tbsp. sunflower oil
1 large onion, halved and thinly sliced
3 garlic cloves, finely chopped

1 tsp. peeled and finely grated
  gingerroot
7oz. canned crushed tomatoes
2 cups coconut milk
¼ tsp. Garam Masala (see page 11)
salt
chopped cilantro leaves, to serve
1 recipe quantity Lemon Rice
  (see page 182), to serve

1   Put the beef in a stainless-steel or other nonreactive bowl. Mix together the yogurt and curry powder and pour it over the meat. Season with salt, cover, and leave to marinate in the refrigerator 24 hours.
2   Heat the oil in a large, nonstick wok or skillet with a lid over low heat. Add the onion and stir-fry 4 to 5 minutes until soft. Add the garlic and ginger and stir-fry 30 seconds. Lower the heat to low, add the beef and marinade, and stir-fry 10 to 15 minutes.
3   Stir in the tomatoes and coconut milk and bring to a boil. Lower the heat to low, cover the pan tightly, and simmer gently 1 hour, stirring occasionally, until the meat is meltingly tender. Check the seasoning and adjust as needed. Remove from the heat, sprinkle with cilantro, and serve hot with rice.

062 Antiguan Curried Beef & Bean Stew

PREPARATION TIME 15 minutes, plus making the curry powder and rice
COOKING TIME 55 minutes   SERVES 4

1lb. 12oz. beef strip steak, cut into
  bite-size pieces
3 tbsp. sunflower oil
6 cloves
1 onion, finely chopped
2 tbsp. Curry Powder (see page 11)
2 carrots, coarsely chopped
2 celery sticks, diced
1 tbsp. thyme leaves

2 garlic cloves, crushed
4 tbsp. tomato paste
3½ cups beef stock
1 large potato, peeled and diced
7oz. canned black-eyed peas,
  rinsed and drained
salt and freshly ground black pepper
1 recipe quantity Jamaican Plantain
  Rice (see page 179), to serve

1   Season the beef with salt and pepper. Heat the oil in a large saucepan over medium-high heat. Add the beef and cook, turning occasionally, 5 to 6 minutes until brown all over.
2   Add the cloves, onion, and curry powder and stir-fry 2 to 3 minutes until the onions start to soften and turn translucent, then stir in the carrots, celery, thyme, and garlic. Cook, stirring, for 2 minutes longer.
3   Stir in the tomato paste and add enough stock to just cover the meat, then add the potato and beans. Bring the stew to a slow boil, then lower the heat to low and simmer 35 to 40 minutes until the beef is tender. Serve hot with rice.

063 Aromatic Vietnamese Beef Curry

PREPARATION TIME 15 minutes, plus making the rice   **COOKING TIME** 20 minutes
SERVES 4

3 tbsp. sunflower oil
1lb. 12oz. beef minute steak,
  cut into thin strips
1 onion, thinly sliced
4 garlic cloves, finely chopped
1 red chili, thinly sliced
2 star anise
1 tsp. crushed cardamom seeds
1 cinnamon stick

10oz. green beans, trimmed
1 carrot, cut into thin ¼in.-thick batons
2 tbsp. fish sauce
2 tbsp. oyster sauce
1 small handful cilantro leaves,
  finely chopped
1 small handful mint leaves,
  finely chopped
jasmine rice, to serve

1   Heat half of the oil in a large, nonstick skillet over low heat. When it is hot, add
    the beef, working in batches if necessary, and stir-fry 1 to 2 minutes until brown.
    Transfer to a plate with a slotted spoon and cover to keep warm.
2   Heat the remaining oil in the skillet. Add the onion and stir-fry 5 minutes, or until
    soft. Add the garlic, chili, star anise, cardamom seeds, cinnamon, green beans,
    and carrot and stir-fry 6 to 8 minutes.
3   Return the beef to the pan and add the fish and oyster sauces. Stir-fry 3 to 4
    minutes until heated through. Remove from the heat, sprinkle the cilantro and
    mint over, and serve hot with rice.

064 Spiced Liver Curry

PREPARATION TIME 15 minutes, plus making the rice   **COOKING TIME** 50 minutes   **SERVES** 4

1lb. 5oz. calf's liver, trimmed,
  outer membrane discarded,
  and thinly sliced
10 whole black peppercorns
1 tbsp. ghee or butter
1 onion, finely chopped
3 garlic cloves, finely chopped
1 tsp. peeled and finely chopped
  gingerroot
1 lemongrass stalk

¼ tsp. ground cloves
1 tsp. freshly ground black pepper
½ tsp. cinnamon
10 curry leaves
3 tbsp. white wine vinegar
2 cups coconut milk
2 tbsp. chopped dill
1 recipe quantity Lemon Rice
  (see page 182), to serve

1   Wash the liver, put it in a small saucepan, and add enough water to cover. Add
    the peppercorns, season with salt, and cook over low heat about 15 minutes until
    the liver is just firm but still pink inside. (It is important not to overcook it,
    otherwise it will be tough.) Remove the pan from the heat and drain. When the
    liver is cool enough to handle, cut it into small cubes.
2   Meanwhile, melt the ghee in a large skillet over low heat. Add the onion, garlic,
    and ginger and cook, stirring occasionally, 12 to 15 minutes until soft. Add all the
    remaining ingredients and the liver and simmer slowly, uncovered, over low heat
    20 minutes, or until the sauce is thick. Serve hot with rice.

065 Burmese Lamb & Yogurt Skewers

PREPARATION TIME 15 minutes, plus at least 24 hours marinating and making the rice
COOKING TIME 8 minutes   **SERVES** 4

1lb. 2oz. lamb tenderloin,
  cut into bite-size pieces
1 red onion, very thinly sliced
juice of 1 lemon
salt
sunflower oil, for brushing
  and greasing
chopped cilantro leaves,
  to serve
rice, to serve

MARINADE
scant 1 cup plain yogurt, lightly whisked
4 garlic cloves, crushed
1 tbsp. ground cumin
1 tbsp. ground coriander
2 tsp. paprika
1 tsp. turmeric
¼ tsp. ground cloves
¼ tsp. ground nutmeg
2 tbsp. tomato paste
juice of 1 lemon
salt and freshly ground black pepper

1 Put the lamb in a wide, shallow dish. Put all of the ingredients for the marinade in a bowl and mix well. Season well with salt and pepper, then pour the mixture over the lamb. Cover and leave to marinate in the refrigerator 24 to 48 hours.

2 If using wooden skewers, soak them in warm water for 30 minutes. Put the onion and lemon juice in a small bowl, season with salt and mix well, then set aside.

3 Preheat the broiler to medium-high. Thread the lamb onto 8 skewers and arrange them in a single layer on a lightly greased broiler rack. Lightly brush with sunflower oil, then broil 3 to 4 minutes on each side until cooked through. Sprinkle with cilantro and serve warm with the onion and rice.

066 South African Curried Beef Pie

PREPARATION TIME 15 minutes, plus making the curry powder, chutney, and salad
COOKING TIME 50 minutes **SERVES** 4

1lb. 5oz. ground beef
1 large onion, finely chopped
2 garlic cloves, crushed
2 tbsp. Curry Powder (see page 11)
3 tbsp. Sweet Mango Chutney
  (see page 213)
⅓ cup golden raisins

1½ cups light cream
2 slices of white bread, crusts
  removed
3 extra-large eggs
salt and freshly ground black pepper
green salad, to serve

1 Preheat the oven to 350°F. Heat a large, nonstick skillet over medium heat. Add the beef and fry 2 to 3 minutes, stirring continuously, until brown. Add the onion and cook 4 to 5 minutes longer, stirring occasionally, until the onion starts to become soft and the beef is light brown.
2 Add the garlic and curry powder and fry 1 to 2 minutes to let the spices cook. Remove the pan from the heat and stir in the chutney and golden raisins.
3 Put scant 1 cup of the cream into a small bowl. Tear the bread into small pieces and add them to the cream. Leave to soften 1 minute, then stir the mixture into the beef.
4 Transfer the mixture into a shallow 2-quart baking dish and press down well with the back of a spoon. Whisk the remaining cream with the eggs and season well with salt and pepper, then pour it over the beef.
5 Bake 30 to 40 minutes until piping hot and the top is set and golden brown. Serve hot with a crisp green salad.

067 Calcutta Beef Curry

PREPARATION TIME 20 minutes, plus 24 hours marinating and making the curry powder, garam masala, rice, and chutney **COOKING TIME** 1 hour 25 minutes **SERVES** 4

1lb. 12oz. stewing beef, cut into
  bite-size pieces
⅓ cup plain yogurt
3 tbsp. Curry Powder (see page 11)
2 tbsp. mustard or sunflower oil
1 dried bay leaf
1 cinnamon stick
3 cloves
4 green cardamom pods, crushed
1 large onion, halved and thinly sliced

3 garlic cloves, very finely chopped
1 tsp. peeled and finely grated
  gingerroot
2½ cups beef stock
¼ tsp. Garam Masala (see page 11)
salt
1 recipe quantity Mushroom Pulao
  (see page 183), to serve
1 recipe quantity Spiced Tomato
  Chutney (see page 210), to serve

1 Put the meat in a stainless steel or other nonreactive bowl. In a small bowl, mix together the yogurt and curry powder, then add it to the meat and mix well. Season with salt, cover with plastic wrap, and leave to marinate in the refrigerator 24 hours.
2 Heat the oil in a large, nonstick wok or skillet over low heat. Add the bay leaf, cinnamon, cloves, and cardamom and stir-fry 1 minute, or until fragrant. Add the onion and stir-fry 4 to 5 minutes until soft, then add the garlic and ginger and stir-fry 1 minute longer. Lower the heat to low, add the beef and marinade, and stir-fry 10 to 15 minutes.
3 Add the beef stock and bring to a boil over high heat, then lower the heat again to low, cover tightly, and simmer, stirring occasionally, 1 hour, or until the meat is meltingly tender. Adjust the seasoning if necessary and serve hot with rice and chutney.

068 Caribbean Curried Oxtail Stew

PREPARATION TIME 20 minutes, plus making the curry powder and rice
COOKING TIME 3 hours 20 minutes   SERVES 4

3lb. beef oxtail, cut into large pieces
2 tbsp. sunflower oil
2 tsp. ground allspice
2 tsp. Curry Powder
  (see page 11)
6½ cups beef stock
4 carrots, sliced
2 onions, finely chopped
3 garlic cloves, finely chopped
2 thyme sprigs

1 Scotch bonnet or habanero chili,
  coarsely chopped
15oz .canned crushed tomatoes
4 tbsp. cornstarch
15oz. canned butter beans, rinsed
  and drained
salt and freshly ground black pepper
1 recipe quantity Vegetable Jollof
  Rice (see page 188), to serve

1 Bring a large saucepan of water to a boil. Add the oxtail, then bring back to a boil. Lower the heat to medium-low and simmer 10 to 12 minutes. Remove from the pan, using a slotted spoon, and drain well on paper towels.

2 Heat the oil in a heavy flameproof casserole over medium-high heat, add the oxtail, and season with salt and pepper. Cook 6 to 8 minutes on each side until brown. Stir in the allspice, curry powder, stock, carrots, onions, garlic, thyme, chili, tomatoes, and cornstarch. Bring to a boil, then cover and simmer slowly 2½ hours, or until the oxtail is meltingly tender. Stir in the beans and cook 15 minutes longer, or until tender. Serve hot with rice.

069 Turkish-Style Stuffed Spiced Eggplants

PREPARATION TIME 25 minutes, plus 30 minutes soaking and making the bread
COOKING TIME about 1 hour 10 minutes   SERVES 6

6 long, thin eggplants, caps trimmed,
  but stems left on
1 tbsp. salt, plus extra to season
½ cup plus 2 tbsp. sunflower oil,
  for frying, or more as needed
2 large tomatoes
2 onions, chopped
14oz. ground lamb or beef
1 tbsp. tomato paste

1 tsp. ground cinnamon
1 tsp. ground allspice
1 large handful flat-leaf parsley
  leaves, chopped
1 cup plus 2 tbsp. tomato juice
freshly ground black pepper
1 recipe quantity Turkish Pide Bread
  (see page 190), to serve

1 Using a vegetable peeler, peel lengthwise strips of skin off of the eggplants, leaving ½-inch strips of skin in between so the eggplants have a striped appearance. Fill a shallow bowl with water and add the salt. Soak the eggplants in the salted water 30 minutes, then drain. Pat them dry with paper towels.

2 Preheat the oven to 350°F. Heat ½ cup of the oil in a skillet over medium-high heat. Working in batches of two or three at a time, fry the eggplants very briefly in the oil, turning to brown them lightly all over. Drain them on paper towels.

3 To make the filling, skin and chop one of the tomatoes and cut the other into slices. Set aside. Heat the remaining 2 tablespoons oil in a clean pan over low heat. Add the onions and fry, stirring occasionally, 5 minutes, or until soft. Add the lamb and cook 10 minutes, crushing it with a fork and turning it over until it changes color. Add the tomato paste, chopped tomato, cinnamon, and allspice and season with salt and pepper. Stir well and simmer about 10 minutes until the liquid reduce and cooks away.

4 Put the eggplants in a single layer in a baking dish. Using a sharp knife, make a slit in each one lengthwise, along one of the bare strips on the top until about 1 inch from each end. Carefully open the slits and, using a teaspoon, press against the flesh on the insides to make a hollow pocket. Fill each eggplant with some of the filling and top with a slice of the remaining tomato. Pour the tomato juice into the dish, cover with foil, and bake 40 minutes, or until soft. Leave to stand 5 minutes, then serve warm with bread.

070 Spiced Ground Beef with Peas

PREPARATION TIME 20 minutes, plus making the curry paste, rice and pickle
COOKING TIME 2 hours **SERVES 4**

2 tbsp. sunflower oil
1 large onion, finely chopped
4 garlic cloves, finely chopped
1 tsp. peeled and finely grated
  gingerroot
1 or 2 green chilies, seeded and
  thinly sliced
1 tbsp. cumin seeds
3 tbsp. Tandoori Curry Paste
  (see page 14)
1lb. 10oz. ground beef
15oz. canned crushed tomatoes

4 tbsp. tomato paste
1 tsp. sugar
1⅔ cups fresh or frozen peas
1 large handful cilantro leaves,
  chopped
salt and freshly ground black pepper
1 recipe quantity Curry Leaf
  & Coconut Rice (see page 186),
  to serve
1 recipe quantity Beet Pickle
  (see page 199), to serve

1 Heat the oil in a large, heavy-bottomed saucepan over low heat. Add the
onion and cook, stirring occasionally, 15 to 20 minutes until soft and just turning
lightly golden. Add the garlic, ginger, chilies, cumin seeds, and curry paste and
stir-fry over high heat 1 to 2 minutes until fragrant. Add the beef and stir-fry
3 to 4 minutes, pressing down on it with a fork to break it up.

2 Stir in the tomatoes, tomato paste, and sugar and bring to a boil. Season with salt
and pepper, lower the heat to low, and cook, covered, 1½ hours, or until thick.
Ten minutes before the end of cooking, stir in the peas. Sprinkle with the cilantro
and serve hot with rice and pickle.

071 Japanese Beef Curry

PREPARATION TIME 10 minutes, plus making the curry powder, garam masala, and rice
COOKING TIME 35 minutes **SERVES 4**

2 tbsp. butter
1lb. 12oz. ground beef
1 onion, thinly sliced
2 tsp. peeled and grated gingerroot
2 tsp. grated garlic
3 tbsp. all-purpose flour

3 tbsp. mild Curry Powder
  (see page 11)
3½ cups beef stock
½ tsp. Garam Masala (see page 11)
rice, to serve

1 Melt half the butter in a skillet over high heat. Add the beef and cook, stirring
occasionally, 5 to 6 minutes, pressing down with a fork to break it up, until light
brown. Add the onion and continue stir-frying 6 to 8 minutes until soft. Stir
in the ginger and garlic, remove from the heat, and set aside.

2 Melt the remaining butter in a separate pan over low heat. Add the flour and
cook, stirring, 3 to 4 minutes until thick. Sprinkle in the curry powder and mix
well. Gradually add the stock, whisking until smooth.

3 Add the beef and onion mixture to the sauce and simmer, stirring occasionally,
10 to 15 minutes until thick. Stir in the garam masala and serve hot with rice.

072 Kofta Curry

PREPARATION TIME 15 minutes, plus making the curry powder and rice
COOKING TIME 25 minutes **SERVES** 4

1lb. 12oz. ground beef or lamb
2 tsp. peeled and finely grated
  gingerroot
2 garlic cloves, very finely chopped
2 tsp. crushed fennel seeds
1 tsp. cinnamon
1 tsp. cayenne pepper, plus a pinch,
  to serve
2 cups passata (bottled strained
  pureed tomatoes)

1 tsp. turmeric
2 tbsp. Curry Powder (see page 11)
1 tsp. sugar
salt and freshly ground black pepper
⅓ cup plain yogurt, whisked, to serve
chopped mint leaves, to serve
1 recipe quantity Lemon Rice
  (see page 182), to serve

1   Put the ground meat, ginger, garlic, fennel seeds, cinnamon, and cayenne
    in a bowl and season with salt and pepper. Mix well, using your hands, then
    shape the mixture into small balls, about 1½ inches in diameter, and set aside.
2   Pour the passata into a medium saucepan and add the turmeric, curry powder,
    and sugar. Bring to a boil. Lower the heat to a simmer, season well with salt and
    pepper, and carefully place the meatballs in the sauce. Cover and cook slowly
    15 to 20 minutes, turning the meatballs occasionally, until cooked through.
3   Drizzle with the yogurt, sprinkle the cayenne and mint leaves over, and serve
    immediately with rice.

073 Malaysian Beef Rendang

PREPARATION TIME 15 minutes, plus making the rice and sambal   **COOKING TIME** 1 hour
SERVES 4

1 large onion, chopped
2 garlic cloves, chopped
1 tbsp. peeled and finely grated
   gingerroot
3 red chilies, halved lengthwise
   and seeded
1 tsp. turmeric
2 tbsp. peanut oil

1lb. 12oz. stewing beef, diced
2 bay leaves
1¾ cups coconut milk
rice, to serve
1 recipe quantity
   Malaysian Star Fruit Sambal
   (see page 199), to serve

1   Put the onion, garlic, ginger, chilies, and turmeric in a blender or food processor
    and blend 2 to 3 minutes until smooth.
2   Heat the oil in a large saucepan over medium-high heat. Add the paste and
    stir-fry 2 minutes, or until fragrant. Add the beef and continue frying, turning
    occasionally, 5 to 6 minutes until the meat is light brown.
3   Add the bay leaves and 1 cup plus 2 tablespoons water and bring to a boil. Lower
    the heat to low, cover tightly, and simmer 45 minutes, or until the meat is tender.
    The mixture should be relatively dry, but if the sauce dries out too much, add a
    little more water as needed. Stir in the coconut milk and bring to a boil again,
    then remove from the heat immediately. Serve hot with rice and sambal.

074 Srinagar Saffron Lamb Curry

PREPARATION TIME 20 minutes, plus 24 hours marinating, 1 hour standing, and making
the bread and chutney   **COOKING TIME** 2 hours 10 minutes   **SERVES** 4

1lb. 12oz. lamb neck tenderloin,
   cut into bite-size pieces
½ cup plain yogurt, lightly whisked
7oz. light cream
1 tbsp. saffron threads
1 tbsp. finely grated garlic
2 tsp. peeled and finely grated
   gingerroot
2 tsp. cayenne pepper
1 tbsp. ground coriander
2 tbsp. ghee or butter

1 tbsp. crushed fennel seeds
2 onions, halved and sliced
15oz. canned crushed tomatoes
1 bay leaf
1¼ cups good-quality lamb stock
salt and freshly ground black pepper
chopped cilantro leaves, to serve
1 recipe quantity Besan Roti
   (see page 193), to serve
1 recipe quantity Mint Chutney
   (see page 204), to serve

1   In a large stainless steel or other nonreactive bowl, mix together the yogurt,
    cream, saffron, garlic, ginger, cayenne, and coriander. Season well with salt
    and pepper, then add the lamb. Mix well, cover, and leave to marinate in the
    refrigerator 24 hours.
2   Remove the lamb from the refrigerator and leave to stand 1 hour to come
    to room temperature. Melt the ghee in a heavy flameproof casserole over low
    heat. Add the fennel seeds and onions and stir-fry 3 to 4 minutes until fragrant.
    Increase the heat to high and add the lamb mixture. Stir-fry 3 to 4 minutes longer
    until the lamb is brown.
3   Stir in the tomatoes, bay leaf, and stock and bring to a boil. Cover the pan tightly
    and simmer, stirring occasionally, over a very low heat 2 hours, or until the lamb
    is meltingly tender. Remove from the heat, mix well, and sprinkle with the
    cilantro. Serve hot with bread and chutney.

075 Kashmiri Saffron, Almond & Lamb Curry

PREPARATION TIME 25 minutes, plus making the garam masala and rice
COOKING TIME 1 hour 50 minutes **SERVES** 4 to 6

1 tbsp. saffron threads
4 tbsp. sunflower oil
3 onions, sliced
2 garlic cloves, finely chopped
1 tsp. finely grated gingerroot
3 dried red chilies
8 green cardamom pods
1 tsp. fennel seeds
½ tsp. turmeric
2 tsp. ground cumin
1 tsp. ground coriander

1 tsp. Garam Masala
  (see page 11)
2lb. 4oz. boned leg of lamb,
  cut into bite-size pieces
7oz. heavy cream
⅔ cup toasted blanched almonds
½ cup plain yogurt, whisked
salt and freshly ground black pepper
1 recipe quantity North Indian
  Green Bean & Carrot Pulao
  (see page 184), to serve

1   Crumble the saffron into a small bowl, cover with 1¼ cups warm water, and
     leave to infuse 10 minutes.
2   Meanwhile, heat the oil in a large, heavy-bottomed saucepan over low heat.
     Add the onions, garlic, ginger, and chilies and fry, stirring occasionally, 8 to 10
     minutes until the onions are soft. Add the cardamom, fennel seeds, turmeric,
     cumin, coriander, and garam masala and fry 2 to 3 minutes longer until fragrant.
     Increase the heat to high, add the lamb and stir-fry 6 to 8 minutes until the
     meat is brown.
3   Stir in the saffron and soaking liquid and the cream. Season with salt and pepper,
     then lower the heat to low and simmer, covered, 1 hour. Sprinkle in the almonds
     and cook 30 minutes longer, or until the lamb is meltingly tender. Remove the
     pan from the heat, stir in the yogurt, and serve hot with rice.

076 Middle Eastern Spiced Lamb Meatballs

PREPARATION TIME 20 minutes, plus 30 minutes chilling and making the bread
COOKING TIME 15 minutes **SERVES** 4–6

2 tbsp. sunflower oil
1 onion, finely chopped
2 garlic cloves, very finely chopped
2 tsp. salt
1 tsp. cinnamon
½ tsp. dried mint, crumbled
¼ tsp. ground allspice
1lb. 12oz. ground lamb

1¼ cups fresh breadcrumbs
1 large egg, lightly beaten
2 tbsp. currants
1¼ cups black sesame seeds
1¼ cups sesame seeds
1 recipe quantity Turkish Pide Bread
  (see page 190), to serve
thick plain yogurt, whisked, to serve

1   Heat the oil in a small nonstick skillet over medium-low heat. Add the onion and
     garlic and fry, stirring frequently, 5 minutes, or until soft. Set aside to cool slightly.
2   Transfer the onion mixture to a bowl and stir in the salt, cinnamon, mint, and
     allspice. Add the lamb, breadcrumbs, egg, and currants and mix well. Roll the
     mixture into 30 bite-size meatballs.
3   Spread the sesame seeds over two separate plates. Roll half of the meatballs in
     the black sesame seeds until coated and arrange them on a baking sheet. Roll
     the remaining meatballs in the white sesame seeds and put them on the baking
     sheet (use two baking sheets, if necessary). Cover loosely with plastic wrap and
     chill 30 minutes to firm up.
4   Preheat the oven to 400°F and take the baking sheets out of the refrigerator.
     Bake the meatballs 8 to 10 minutes until golden and just cooked through.
     Serve the meatballs hot with the bread and the yogurt for dipping.

077 Sindhi Lamb Curry

PREPARATION TIME 15 minutes, plus making the curry powder, garam masala, and rice
COOKING TIME 1 hour 30 minutes   SERVES 4

1lb. 12oz. lamb neck tenderloin,
  cut into bite-size chunks
1 tbsp. ground cardamom
2 tbsp. Curry Powder (see page 11)
4 large tomatoes, coarsely chopped
2 red onions, finely chopped

2 tsp. Garam Masala (see page 11)
2 tbsp. tomato paste
salt and freshly ground black pepper
1 recipe quantity Saffron Rice
  (see page 180), to serve

1 Put the lamb in a bowl, sprinkle the cardamom and curry powder over and toss
to mix well. Transfer to a heavy-bottomed saucepan and add the tomatoes,
onions, garam masala, and tomato paste.
2 Add 3 cups water, season well with salt and pepper, and bring to a boil over
high heat. Cover tightly, lower the heat to low, and simmer, stirring occasionally,
1½ hours, or until the meat is tender. Remove from the heat and leave to stand
5 minutes before serving. Serve hot with rice.

078 Sri Lanka Mutton Curry

PREPARATION TIME 10 minutes, plus 30 minutes marinating and making the curry powder
and bread   COOKING TIME 1 hour 45 minutes   SERVES 4

1lb. 12oz. boneless mutton or lamb,
  cut into bite-size pieces
3 tbsp. white wine vinegar
2 onions, coarsely chopped
5 garlic cloves, chopped
2 tbsp. peeled and finely grated
  gingerroot

⅓ cup sunflower oil
4 tbsp. Sri Lankan Curry Powder
  (see page 12)
10 to 12 curry leaves
2 cups coconut milk
1 recipe quantity Spice-Filled Naan
  (see page 195), to serve

1 Put the mutton in a bowl, drizzle the vinegar over, and leave to marinate
30 minutes. Meanwhile. put the onions, garlic, and ginger in a small food
processor and blend until the mixture forms a smooth paste. Heat the oil in
a heavy-bottomed saucepan over medium-high heat, add the onion paste and
stir-fry 2 to 3 minutes until light brown. Add the curry powder and curry leaves
and stir-fry 3 minutes until coated.
2 Drain the mutton, reserving the vinegar, and add the meat to the pan. Stir-fry
5 minutes, or until brown, then add the coconut milk and reserved vinegar. Bring
to a boil, lower the heat to low, and simmer, covered, 1½ hours, or until the
mutton is tender. Serve hot with bread.

079 Burmese Lamb Curry

PREPARATION TIME 10 minutes, plus making the curry paste and rice
COOKING TIME 50 minutes   SERVES 4

4 tbsp. peanut oil
1lb. 12oz. boneless lamb, diced
15oz. canned crushed tomatoes
2 tbsp. Burmese Curry Paste
  (see page 13)

2 tsp. turmeric
10oz. baby new potatoes
chopped cilantro leaves, to serve
1 recipe quantity Burmese Golden
  Rice (see page 185), to serve

1 Heat 1 tablespoon of the oil in a heavy-bottomed saucepan over medium-high
heat. Add the lamb and fry, stirring occasionally, 8 to 10 minutes until brown,
then mix in the tomatoes, curry paste, and turmeric. Stir in the potatoes and add
enough water to just cover the meat. Bring to a boil, then lower the heat to low.
2 Simmer 35 to 40 minutes until the lamb and potatoes are tender, adding more
water if the curry begins to dry out. Sprinkle with cilantro and serve with rice.

080 Raan of Lamb

PREPARATION TIME 20 minutes, plus 24 hours marinating, 1 hour standing, and making the curry powder and bread   COOKING TIME 2 hours 15 minutes   SERVES 4

1 leg of lamb, about 3lb. 5oz.
2 tbsp. mild Curry Powder
   (see page 11)
2 garlic cloves, very finely chopped
3 tsp. ground coriander
2 tsp. ground cumin

1 tsp. ground cloves
2 tsp. cinnamon
⅔ cup plain yogurt
1 recipe quantity Roomali Roti
   (see page 194), to serve

1   Put the lamb in a large stainless steel or other nonreactive dish and, using a sharp knife, make deep gashes all over the flesh to let the marinade penetrate deeply.
2   Put all of the remaining ingredients in a bowl and mix well. Pour the marinade over the lamb and rub it all over the meat. Cover and leave to marinate in the refrigerator 24 hours.
3   Remove the lamb from the refrigerator 1 hour before cooking and leave it to come to room temperature. Preheat the oven to 350°F.
4   Put the lamb on a nonstick roasting tray and spoon any remaining marinade over. Cover loosely with foil and bake 1½ hours until brown.
5   Remove the foil and baste the lamb by spooning the pan juices over it. Return the pan to the oven and bake, uncovered, 40 to 45 minutes longer, or until cooked to your liking. Remove from the oven, cover again with foil, and leave to rest 10 to 15 minutes, then carve into thin slices and serve with bread.

081 Minted Lamb

PREPARATION TIME 25 minutes, plus 24 hours marinating, 1 hour standing, and making the curry paste, bread, and chutney   COOKING TIME 25 minutes   SERVES 4

4 racks of lamb, each with 4 or 5 ribs,
   French-trimmed, about 1lb. 12oz.
   total weight
2 cups finely chopped mint leaves
1 cup finely chopped cilantro leaves
2 tsp. finely grated garlic
2 tsp. peeled and finely grated
   gingerroot
2 red chilies, finely chopped
4 tbsp. sunflower oil

3 tbsp. Tandoori Curry Paste
   (see page 14)
juice of 1 lime
4 tbsp. coconut cream
1 tsp. honey
1 recipe quantity Roomali Roti
   (see page 194), to serve
1 recipe quantity Indian Red Cabbage
   Chutney (see page 202), to serve

1   Put the racks of lamb on a work surface and, using a small sharp knife, prick the flesh side all over, then transfer to a shallow nonreactive dish.
2   Put all of the remaining ingredients in a blender or small food processor and blend 2 to 3 minutes until the mixture forms a fairly smooth paste. Rub this paste all over the lamb, then cover and leave to marinate in the refrigerator 24 hours.
3   Remove the lamb from the refrigerator 1 hour before cooking and leave it to come to room temperature. Preheat the oven to 350°F and line a baking tray with parchment paper.
4   Put the lamb, flesh-side up, in the baking tray and bake 20 to 25 minutes until cooked to your liking. Remove from the oven and cover with foil. Leave the lamb to rest 5 to 6 minutes before serving, then serve with bread and chutney.

82 Moroccan Spiced Lamb Shanks

PREPARATION TIME 20 minutes, plus making the couscous　**COOKING TIME** 2 hours 50 minutes
SERVES 4

2 tbsp. olive oil
4 lamb shanks, each about 10oz.,
　trimmed of excess fat
¾ tsp. cinnamon
¾ tsp. ground ginger
½ tsp. ground cumin
½ tsp. ground allspice
¼ tsp. freshly grated nutmeg

1 large onion, chopped
15oz. canned crushed tomatoes
1 tsp. salt
1 cup plus 2 tbsp. chicken stock
　or water
cilantro leaves, to serve
couscous, to serve
harissa, to serve

1　Preheat the oven to 300°F. Heat the oil in a large flameproof casserole over
　medium-high heat. Add the lamb and fry 6 to 8 minutes until brown. Transfer
　the shanks to a plate, using a slotted spoon, and set aside.
2　Lower the heat to medium, add the spices to the casserole and fry 1 to 2 minutes,
　or until fragrant. Add the onion and fry 4 to 5 minutes longer, then return the
　lamb to the casserole.
3　Add the tomatoes, salt, and enough of the stock or water to almost cover the
　shanks. Bring to a boil, then remove from the heat, cover tightly, and carefully
　transfer to the oven. Bake 2 to 2½ hours until the meat is falling off the bone.
　Alternatively, cook this entirely on the stovetop; simmer, covered, over very low
　heat 2 to 2½ hours, using a heat diffuser if needed to prevent the shanks from
　catching on the bottom of the casserole.
4　Carefully lift the shanks out of the casserole (the meat will be loose on the bone)
　and put them in a bowl, then cover. Continue simmering the cooking liquid over
　low heat 5 to 10 minutes until it becomes slightly thickened, then use an
　immersion blender to blend it into a sauce. Transfer the sauce to a bowl, rinse
　out the casserole, and strain the sauce back into it. Return the lamb shanks and
　reheat slowly if needed. Sprinkle with cilantro leaves and serve hot with couscous
　and a small bowl of harissa.

083 Eggplants Stuffed with Curried Lamb

PREPARATION TIME 20 minutes, plus making the curry paste   **COOKING TIME** 40 minutes
SERVES 4

2 large eggplants, cut in half
  lengthwise
4 tbsp. sunflower oil
1 onion, thinly sliced
1 tsp. peeled and finely grated
  gingerroot
1 tsp. cayenne pepper
1 tbsp. Tandoori Curry Paste
  (see page 14)
2 garlic cloves, finely chopped

¼ tsp. ground turmeric
1 tsp. ground coriander
2 tsp. dried mint
1 tomato, finely chopped
1lb. 5oz. ground lamb
1 red bell pepper, seeded and
  finely diced
2 tbsp. chopped cilantro leaves
2 tbsp. chopped mint leaves
salt

1 Preheat the oven to 350°F. Using a sharp knife and a spoon, scoop out most
   of the eggplant flesh and reserve for use in another recipe. Put the eggplants,
   cut-side up, on a baking sheet and set aside.
2 Heat the oil in a large skillet over low heat. Add the onions and stir-fry
   4 to 5 minutes until soft, then add the ginger, cayenne, curry paste, garlic,
   turmeric, coriander, dried mint, and tomato. Stir-fry 4 to 5 minutes longer until
   well coated, then season with salt. Add the ground lamb and continue stir-frying
   5 to 6 minutes over high heat until brown. Stir in the red pepper and chopped
   cilantro and mint, then remove from the heat.
3 Carefully spoon the lamb mixture into the prepared eggplant shells. Bake
   20 to 25 minutes until hot. Serve hot.

084 Jamaican Coconut Lamb Curry

PREPARATION TIME 20 minutes, plus making the curry powder and bread
COOKING TIME 2 hours 15 minutes   SERVES 4

2 tbsp. sunflower oil
1 onion, halved and thinly sliced
2 tsp. peeled and finely grated
  gingerroot
2 tsp. finely grated garlic
3 tbsp. mild Curry Powder
  (see page 11)
1 tsp. cinnamon
1lb. 12oz. boneless lamb tenderloin

1¾ cups coconut milk
scant 1 cup lamb stock
⅔ cup freshly grated or
  shredded coconut
salt and freshly ground black pepper
chopped cilantro leaves, to serve
1 recipe quantity Trinidadian Roti
  Paratha (see page 189), to serve

1   Heat the oil in a large, heavy-bottomed saucepan over low heat. Add the onion
    and stir-fry 4 to 5 minutes until soft. Stir in the ginger, garlic, curry powder, and
    cinnamon and stir-fry 2 to 3 minutes longer until fragrant.
2   Add the lamb and stir-fry 4 to 5 minutes until the meat is light brown, then
    stir in the coconut milk and stock. Bring to a boil and season well with salt and
    pepper, then cover the pan tightly and lower the heat to low. Simmer very slowly
    (using a heat diffuser if necessary, to prevent the meat from sticking to the pan)
    1½ to 2 hours, stirring occasionally, until the lamb is tender. Meanwhile, if using
    shredded coconut, soak it in warm water 20 minutes, then drain.
3   Remove the lamb from the heat and sprinkle the grated coconut over. Sprinkle
    with cilantro and serve hot with bread.

085 Persian Lamb & Lentil Curry

PREPARATION TIME 30 minutes, plus making the curry powder, rice, and chutney
COOKING TIME 2 hours 15 minutes   SERVES 4

1lb. 12oz. boned lamb shoulder
  or leg, cut into large chunks
6 tbsp. red lentils, rinsed and drained
6 tbsp. yellow split peas, rinsed
  and drained
10oz. butternut squash, peeled,
  seeded, and coarsely chopped
8oz. potatoes, peeled and chopped
  into chunks
1 tsp. turmeric
4 tbsp. sunflower oil
2 large onions, coarsely chopped
2 tsp. cumin seeds

1 tbsp. ground coriander
1 tsp. peeled and finely grated
  gingerroot
1 tbsp. finely grated garlic
1 tbsp. Curry Powder (see page 11)
2 tsp. tamarind paste
2 tsp. honey
salt and freshly ground black pepper
1 recipe quantity Saffron Rice
  (see page 180), to serve
1 recipe quantity Sweet Mango
  Chutney (see page 213), to serve

1   Put the lamb, lentils, split peas, squash, potatoes, and turmeric in a large,
    heavy-bottomed saucepan. Season well with salt and pepper, then add enough
    water to just cover. Bring to a boil over high heat, then lower the heat to low
    and simmer 1 to 1½ hours until the meat is tender.
2   Remove the meat from the mixture with a slotted spoon, transfer to a plate,
    and set aside. Using a hand-held electric mixer or immersion blender, puree the
    vegetable mixture until fairly smooth. Return the meat to the pan and set aside.
3   Heat 3 tablespoons of the oil in a large skillet over low heat. Add the onions and
    stir-fry 15 to 20 minutes until golden brown. Set half of the onions aside and add
    the rest to the meat mixture.
4   Heat the remaining oil in the same skillet over low heat. Add the cumin seeds,
    coriander, ginger, garlic, and curry powder and stir-fry 2 to 3 minutes until
    fragrant. Stir this mixture into the meat curry along with the tamarind paste and
    honey until well mixed. Simmer 10 to 15 minutes until hot. Sprinkle with the
    reserved onions and serve hot with rice and chutney.

086 Caribbean Lamb Curry

PREPARATION TIME 15 minutes, plus making the rice and chutney
COOKING TIME 1 hour 45 minutes   SERVES 4

2 tbsp. sunflower oil
1lb. 12oz. boned leg of lamb,
    cut into bite-size cubes
2 onions, finely chopped
2 tsp. peeled and finely grated
    gingerroot
1 Scotch bonnet or habanero chili,
    thinly sliced
1 red bell pepper, seeded and
    chopped
2 tsp. ground allspice
3 tsp. ground cumin

1 cinnamon stick
pinch of grated nutmeg
15oz. canned crushed tomatoes
finely grated zest and juice of 2 limes
4 tbsp. packed light brown sugar
1¼ cups fresh or frozen peas
salt and freshly ground black pepper
1 recipe quantity Jamaican Plantain
    Rice (see page 179), to serve
1 recipe quantity Jamaican Peach
    Chutney (see page 211),
    to serve

1   Heat half of the oil in a large, heavy-bottomed saucepan over medium-high heat. Add the lamb, in batches, and cook, turning occasionally, 3 to 4 minutes until light brown. Transfer to a plate, using a slotted spoon, and set aside.
2   Heat the remaining oil in the same pan over medium-high heat and add the onions, ginger, chili, red pepper, allspice, cumin, cinnamon, and nutmeg. Stir-fry 3 to 4 minutes until soft and fragrant, then return the lamb to the pan and add the tomatoes, lime zest and juice, and sugar. Season with salt and pepper.
3   Bring to a boil, then lower the heat to low. Cover the pan tightly and simmer 1½ hours, or until the lamb is tender. Five minutes before the end of cooking, stir in the peas. Ladle into bowls and serve with rice and chutney.

087 Tandoori Lamb Chops

PREPARATION TIME 10 minutes, plus at least 4 hours marinating and making the curry paste, bread, and raita   COOKING TIME 15 minutes   SERVES 4

12 lamb chops, about 5oz. each
½ cup plain yogurt
4 tbsp. tomato paste
4 tbsp. Tandoori Curry Paste
    (see page 14)
1 tsp. peeled and finely grated
    gingerroot
1 tsp. cayenne pepper

2 tsp. salt
3 tbsp. lemon juice
sliced tomato, cucumber, and red
    onion, to serve
1 recipe quantity Saag Roti
    (see page 192), to serve
1 recipe quantity Corn Raita
    (see page 212), to serve

1   Arrange the chops in a single layer in a shallow, stainless steel or other nonreactive dish. Put the yogurt, tomato paste, curry paste, ginger, cayenne, salt, and lemon juice in a small bowl. Mix well, then rub the mixture into the lamb. Cover and leave to marinate in the refrigerator 4 to 5 hours, or overnight if time permits.
2   Preheat the oven to 425°F and line a baking sheet with parchment paper. Spread the lamb chops in a single layer on the baking sheet and bake 12 to 15 minutes, or until the lamb is cooked to your liking. Serve hot with sliced tomato, cucumber, and red onion and with bread and raita.

088 Lamb Rogan Josh

PREPARATION TIME 20 minutes, plus making the curry paste, rice, and raita
COOKING TIME 3 hours **SERVES** 4

2 tbsp. sunflower oil
1lb. 12oz. boneless lamb shoulder,
 cut into large bite-size pieces
2 large onions, halved and
 thickly sliced
3 garlic cloves, very finely chopped
2 tsp. peeled and finely grated
 gingerroot
2 cassia bark or
 cinnamon sticks
2 tsp. cayenne pepper
2 tsp. paprika
6 green cardamom pods
4 tbsp. Tandoori Curry Paste
 (see page 14)

15oz. canned crushed tomatoes
6 tbsp. tomato paste
1 tsp. sugar
2½ cups lamb stock
4 to 6 potatoes, peeled and halved
salt and freshly ground black pepper
chopped cilantro leaves,
 to serve
plain yogurt, whisked,
 to drizzle
1 recipe quantity Mushroom Pulao
 (see page 183), to serve
1 recipe quantity Raita
 (see page 204), to serve

1 Heat half of the oil in a large, heavy-bottomed flameproof casserole over
 medium-high heat. Working in batches, add the lamb and stir-fry 3 to 4 minutes
 until brown. Transfer to a plate, using a slotted spoon, and set aside.
2 Add the remaining oil to the casserole and lower the heat to medium. When
 the oil is hot, add the onions and fry, stirring frequently, 10 to 12 minutes until
 soft and light brown.
3 Add the garlic, ginger, cassia, cayenne, paprika, and cardamom and stir-fry
 1 to 2 minutes, then add the curry paste and lamb. Stir-fry 2 to 3 minutes
 until well coated Stir in the tomatoes, tomato paste, sugar, stock, and potatoes.
 Season well with salt and pepper and bring the mixture to a boil.
4 Lower the heat to very low and cover tightly. Simmer very slowly 2 to 2½ hours
 (using a heat diffuser, if possible) until the lamb is meltingly tender. Sprinkle
 with cilantro, drizzle with yogurt, and serve hot with rice and raita.

089 Lamb Korma

PREPARATION TIME 15 minutes, plus making the curry paste, bread, and chutney
COOKING TIME 1 hour 10 minutes **SERVES** 4

2 tbsp. sunflower oil
1lb. 12oz. lamb neck tenderloin,
 thinly sliced
2 tbsp ghee or butter
1 onion, finely chopped
2 garlic cloves, finely chopped
2 tsp. peeled and finely grated
 gingerroot
½ cup very finely ground almonds
1 tbsp. white poppy seeds

5 tbsp. Korma Curry Paste
 (see page 15)
1¾ cups lamb stock
1 cup plus 2 tbsp. light cream
salt and freshly ground black pepper
1 recipe quantity Naan
 (see page 190), warm, to serve
1 recipe quantity Mint & Cilantro
 Chutney (see page 201), to serve

1 Heat the oil in a large, nonstick skillet over medium-high heat. Working in
 batches, add the lamb and stir-fry 2 to 3 minutes until brown. Transfer to a
 plate, using a slotted spoon, and set aside.
2 Add the ghee to the pan and lower the heat to medium. When the ghee is
 hot, add the onion, garlic, and ginger and stir-fry 3 to 4 minutes until the
 onion is soft. Stir in the ground almonds, poppy seeds, and curry paste and
 stir-fry 1 to 2 minutes until fragrant.
3 Add the lamb, stock, and cream to the pan and bring to a boil, then reduce
 the heat to low and season well with salt and pepper. Simmer, uncovered,
 55 minutes to 1 hour until the lamb is very tender, stirring occasionally. Serve
 hot with bread and chutney.

090 Turkish Apricot & Lamb Curry

PREPARATION TIME 20 minutes, plus making the bread   **COOKING TIME** 1 hour 45 minutes
SERVES 4

4 tbsp. sunflower oil
1lb. 12oz. boned shoulder of lamb,
   cut into bite-size pieces
1 onion, finely chopped
3 garlic cloves, finely grated
2 tsp. turmeric
1 tsp. ground ginger
1 tsp. cinnamon
1 tsp. paprika
large pinch of freshly grated nutmeg
1⅔ cups golden raisins

1 cup dried apricots
15oz. canned crushed tomatoes
1¼ cups vegetable or lamb stock
salt and freshly ground black pepper
thick plain yogurt, whisked,
   to drizzle (optional)
chopped mint leaves, to serve
   (optional)
1 recipe quantity Besan Roti
   (see page 193), to serve

1   Heat half of the oil in a large, heavy-bottomed saucepan. Add the lamb,
    working in batches, and stir-fry 3 to 4 minutes until brown. Transfer to a plate,
    using a slotted spoon, and set aside.
2   Heat the remaining oil in the pan and add the onion, garlic, turmeric, ginger,
    cinnamon, paprika, nutmeg, golden raisins, and dried apricots. Stir-fry
    1 to 2 minutes until fragrant, then add the lamb. Stir-fry 2 to 3 minutes.
3   Stir in the tomatoes and stock and season well with salt and pepper. Bring to a
    boil, then lower the heat to low, cover tightly, and simmer slowly (using a heat
    diffuser if possible) 1½ hours, or until thick. Drizzle with yogurt and sprinkle
    with mint, if desired, and serve hot with bread.

091 Tandoori Pork Chops

PREPARATION TIME 10 minutes, plus at least 24 hours marinating and making the curry paste, biryani, and pickle COOKING TIME 30 minutes SERVES 4

3 garlic cloves, finely grated
1 tsp. peeled and finely grated
   gingerroot
juice of 2 large lemons
1 tbsp. ground cumin
3 tbsp. Tandoori Curry Paste
   (see page 14)
1 cup plus 2 tbsp. plain yogurt
8 thick pork chops, about
   7oz. each

salt and freshly ground black pepper
chopped mint leaves, to serve
1 recipe quantity Spicy Spinach
   Biryani with Cauliflower
   (see page 185), to serve
1 recipe quantity
   Spiced Carrot Pickle
   (see page 212), to serve

1   Put the garlic, ginger, lemon juice, cumin, curry paste, and yogurt in a bowl and mix well, then season well with salt and pepper.
2   Arrange the pork chops in a single layer in a shallow stainless steel or other nonreactive bowl and pour the yogurt mixture over. Toss to coat well, then cover and leave to marinate in the refrigerator 24 to 48 hours.
3   Preheat the oven to 400°F and line a baking tray with parchment paper. Put the chops on the baking tray and bake 25 to 30 minutes until cooked to your liking. Sprinkle with mint and serve hot with rice and pickle.

092 Burmese Dry Pork Curry

PREPARATION TIME 15 minutes, plus making the rice and pickle COOKING TIME 25 minutes SERVES 4

1 large onion, coarsely chopped
2 garlic cloves, crushed
1 tsp. peeled and finely grated
   gingerroot
1 tsp. turmeric
1 tsp. cayenne pepper
1 tbsp. sesame oil
2 tbsp. sunflower oil
1lb. 12oz. pork tenderloin,
   thinly sliced

2 tbsp. finely chopped lemongrass
2 tbsp. tamarind paste
1 tbsp. fish sauce
chopped cilantro leaves, to serve
1 recipe quantity Burmese Golden
   Rice (see page 185), to serve
1 recipe quantity Burmese Cucumber
   Pickle (see page 203), to serve

1   Put the onion, garlic, ginger, turmeric, and cayenne in a food processor and blend 1 minute, or until the mixture forms a paste.
2   Heat the oils in a nonstick skillet over medium-high heat. Carefully add the spice paste (it will splutter) and stir-fry 2 to 3 minutes until fragrant. Add the pork, mix well, and stir-fry 10 to 12 minutes longer until light brown.
3   Stir in the lemongrass, tamarind paste, and fish sauce and stir-fry 5 to 8 minutes until the pork is cooked through. Sprinkle with cilantro and serve hot with rice and pickle.

093 Spicy Pork & Potato Curry

PREPARATION TIME 20 minutes, plus making the rice   COOKING TIME 1 hour 50 minutes
SERVES 4

3 tbsp. sunflower oil
1 onion, finely chopped
2 bay leaves
2 red chilies, seeded and finely
  chopped
2 garlic cloves, finely chopped
1lb. 12oz. pork tenderloin, cut into
  bite-size chunks
2 tsp. ground coriander
1 tsp. ground cumin
½ tsp. turmeric
½ tsp. cayenne pepper

½ tsp. cinnamon
1⅓ cups finely chopped tomatoes
3 cups chicken stock
4 large potatoes, peeled and cut
  into bite-size chunks
½ cup finely chopped cilantro
  leaves
salt and freshly ground black
  pepper
1 recipe quantity Lemon Rice
  (see page 182), to serve

1   Heat the oil in a large saucepan over low heat. Add the onion, bay leaves, chilies,
    and garlic and stir-fry 4 to 5 minutes until the onion is soft.
2   Increase the heat to high and add the pork. Stir-fry 6 to 8 minutes until the meat
    is light brown. Add the coriander, cumin, turmeric, cayenne, and cinnamon and
    season well with salt and pepper. Stir-fry 3 to 4 minutes longer.
3   Add the tomatoes and stock and bring to a boil. Cover, lower the heat to low,
    and simmer slowly 1 hour, stirring occasionally. Add the potatoes and cook
    25 to 30 minutes longer until the meat and potatoes are tender. Remove from
    the heat, stir in the chopped cilantro, and serve warm with rice.

094 Rice Noodles with Sticky Lemon Pork

PREPARATION TIME 5 minutes, plus 1 hour marinating   COOKING TIME 10 minutes   SERVES 4

4 pork chops, about 7oz. each
½ cup sweet chili sauce, plus extra
  to serve
juice of 2 lemons
9oz. dried rice noodles

1 small handful flat-leaf parsley
  leaves, chopped
1 small handful cilantro, chopped
½ cucumber, peeled into ribbons with
  a potato peeler
salt and freshly ground black pepper

1   Put the pork chops, sweet chili sauce, and half of the lemon juice in a stainless
    steel or other nonreactive bowl and mix well. Season with salt and pepper, then
    cover and leave to marinate in the refrigerator 1 hour.
2   Preheat the broiler to medium. Put the noodles in a heatproof bowl and cover
    with boiling water. Leave to stand 10 minutes, or until soft, then drain well and
    return to the bowl.
3   Meanwhile, arrange the pork chops on the broiler rack and broil 4 to 5 minutes
    on each side until cooked through.
4   Stir the parsley, cilantro, cucumber, and remaining lemon juice into the noodles,
    toss well, and season with salt and pepper. Serve immediately, topped with the
    pork chops.

095 Pork Rendang

PREPARATION TIME 15 minutes, plus making the crêpes   **COOKING TIME** 2 hours 50 minutes
SERVES 4

2 tbsp. sunflower oil
1lb. 12oz. pork tenderloin,
  cut into large pieces
2 onions, finely chopped
1 tbsp. ground coriander
1 tsp. turmeric
6 garlic cloves, crushed
6 tbsp. very finely chopped
  lemongrass

2 or 3 bird's-eye chilies, chopped
4 tbsp. finely chopped cilantro
  (including roots and stems)
1¾ cups coconut milk
salt and freshly ground black pepper
1 recipe quantity Malaysian Roti Jala
  (see page 194), to serve

1   Preheat the oven to 300°F. Heat the oil in a deep flameproof casserole over
    medium-high heat. Add the pork and cook, stirring occasionally, 5 to 6 minutes
    until brown all over.
2   Meanwhile, put the onions, coriander, turmeric, garlic, lemongrass, chilies,
    cilantro, and coconut milk in a food processor and blend until smooth. Season
    well with salt and pepper, then pour this mixture over the pork.
3   Cover tightly and bake, turning the pork occasionally, 2½ hours, or until it is
    meltingly tender and most of the liquid has evaporated. Remove from the oven
    and leave to rest 10 to 12 minutes before serving. Cut into thick slices and
    serve with crêpes.

096 Tamarind Pork

PREPARATION TIME 20 minutes, plus 30 minutes marinating and making the rice
COOKING TIME 20 minutes   **SERVES** 4

2 tsp. fish sauce
2 tsp. light soy sauce
1lb. 12oz. pork tenderloin,
  thinly sliced
2 tbsp. tamarind paste
2 tbsp. sunflower oil
2 garlic cloves, finely chopped
1 tbsp. sugar
1 onion, halved and thinly sliced

2 tbsp. rice wine vinegar
1 small handful cilantro leaves,
  coarsely torn or chopped
1 small handful mint leaves,
  coarsely torn or chopped
⅔ cup skinless roasted peanuts,
  coarsely chopped
salt and freshly ground black pepper
jasmine rice, to serve

1   Put the fish sauce and soy sauce in a bowl. Mix well, then season with black
    pepper. Add the pork and stir to coat well. Cover and leave to marinate in the
    refrigerator 30 minutes. Put the tamarind paste and 7 tablespoons water in a
    small bowl and leave to stand 5 minutes, or until the paste dissolves.
2   Heat half of the oil in a heavy-bottomed saucepan over medium-high heat. Add
    the garlic and stir-fry 1 to 2 minutes until light golden. Add the tamarind liquid
    and half of the sugar and cook, stirring occasionally, 6 to 8 minutes until the
    liquid reduces and thickens into a syrup.
3   Put the onion, rice wine vinegar, and remaining sugar in a bowl and season lightly
    with salt. Mix well and set aside.
4   Meanwhile, heat the remaining oil in a large pan over medium-high heat. Add
    the pork, working in small batches, and fry, turning occasionally, 3 to 4 minutes
    until golden brown and cooked to your liking. Set aside.
5   Arrange the cilantro and mint leaves on a large serving dish. Spoon the marinated
    onions and any liquid that remains in the bowl over the top. Pile the pork on top
    of the onions and drizzle the caramelized tamarind syrup over. Sprinkle with the
    peanuts and serve hot.

097 Filipino Ground Pork Curry

PREPARATION TIME 10 minutes, plus making the curry powder and noodles
COOKING TIME 40 minutes   **SERVES** 4

4 tbsp. sunflower oil
1lb. 12oz. ground pork
3 garlic cloves,
  very finely chopped
2 tsp. peeled and finely grated
  gingerroot
1 tbsp. mild Curry Powder
  (see page 11)

1 tsp. turmeric
2 green chilies, chopped
2 bay leaves
1¾ cups coconut milk
1¼ cups fresh or frozen peas
juice of 1 lime
salt and freshly ground black pepper
egg noodles or rice, to serve

1 Heat the oil in a large, nonstick wok or skillet over high heat. Add the pork and stir-fry 3 to 4 minutes until brown. Transfer to a plate and set aside.
2 Add the garlic, ginger, curry powder, turmeric, and chilies to the wok and stir-fry 1 to 2 minutes until fragrant. Stir in the bay leaves and coconut milk and season with salt and pepper.
3 Bring the mixture to a boil, then lower the heat to low and simmer, uncovered, 30 minutes, stirring occasionally. Five minutes before the end of the cooking time, stir in the peas.
4 Remove from the heat and stir in the lime juice, then serve hot with noodles.

098 Nonya Pork Curry

PREPARATION TIME 25 minutes, plus at least 3 hours chilling and making the noodles
COOKING TIME 30 minutes   **SERVES** 4

1 egg
2 tsp. cornstarch
2 garlic cloves, crushed
2 tbsp. finely chopped cilantro leaves
2 red chilies, finely chopped
1lb. 12oz. ground pork
salt and freshly ground black pepper
egg noodles, to serve

NONYA CURRY SAUCE
1 tbsp. finely grated garlic
⅔ cup finely chopped shallots
1 tsp. peeled and finely grated
  galangal
6 long red chilies, halved lengthwise
  and seeded
⅓ cup sunflower oil
15oz. canned crushed tomatoes
1 tbsp. kecap asin, or 1 tbsp. dark soy
  sauce mixed with 1 tsp. fish sauce
1¾ cups coconut milk

1 Put the egg, cornstarch, garlic, cilantro, chilies, and pork in a large bowl. Season well with salt and pepper and mix well, then roll tablespoons of the mixture into balls and arrange them on a baking sheet. Cover and chill 3 to 4 hours, or overnight if time permits.
2 To make the curry sauce, put the garlic, shallots, galangal, chilies, and half of the oil in a blender or small food processor. Blend 2 to 3 minutes until the mixture forms a paste.
3 Heat the remaining oil in a large, nonstick wok or skillet over medium-high heat. Add the curry paste and stir-fry 1 to 2 minutes, then add the tomatoes, kecap asin, and coconut milk and bring to a boil. Lower the heat to low and simmer 10 minutes until thick. Carefully add the meatballs to the sauce and simmer, uncovered, 12 to 15 minutes, stirring occasionally, until cooked through. Serve hot with noodles.

Fragrant Pork Belly Curry

PREPARATION TIME 20 minutes, plus making the curry powder, rice, and bok choy
COOKING TIME 2 hours 45 minutes   **SERVES** 4

2 tbsp. sunflower oil
1lb. 12oz. belly pork, cut into bite-
   size pieces
10 curry leaves
1 tbsp. cumin seeds
1 tbsp. crushed coriander seeds
1 onion, finely chopped
2 tsp. finely grated garlic
2 tsp. peeled and finely grated
   gingerroot

2 tbsp. Curry Powder (see page 11)
2 tbsp. white wine vinegar
2 cinnamon sticks
2 star anise
6 green cardamom pods, crushed
1¾ cups coconut milk
salt and freshly ground black pepper
jasmine rice, to serve
steamed bok choy, to serve

1   Preheat the oven to 300°F. Heat half of the oil in a flameproof casserole over
    medium-high heat, then add the pork. Stir-fry 4 to 5 minutes until brown.
    Transfer the pork to a plate, using a slotted spoon, and set aside.
2   Heat the remaining oil in the same casserole and add the curry leaves, cumin and
    coriander seeds, onion, garlic, and ginger. Stir-fry 3 to 4 minutes, then return the
    pork to the pan and add the curry powder. Stir-fry 2 to 3 minutes until fragrant.
3   Stir in the vinegar, cinnamon, star anise, cardamom, coconut milk, and scant
    1 cup water. Season with salt and pepper and bring to a boil. Cover tightly and
    carefully transfer the casserole to the oven. Bake 2½ hours, or until the pork is
    meltingly tender. Serve hot with rice and bok choy.

100 Japanese Pork Curry

PREPARATION TIME 15 minutes, plus making the curry sauce and rice
COOKING TIME 1 hour 5 minutes   **SERVES** 4

2 tbsp. sunflower oil
14oz. boneless pork, such
   as tenderloin, cut into small
   bite-size pieces
1 onion, thickly sliced
10oz. potatoes, peeled and cut
   into small bite-size pieces

2 carrots, cut into small bite-size
   pieces
1 cup Japanese Curry Sauce
   (see page 12)
Japanese rice, to serve

1   Heat the oil in a deep saucepan over medium-high heat. Add the pork and
    stir-fry 6 to 8 minutes until light brown. Add the onion, potatoes, and carrots
    and stir-fry 2 to 3 minutes longer until the onions are soft.
2   Add 2 cups plus 2 tablespoons water and bring to a boil. Lower the heat to low,
    cover tightly, and simmer 30 to 40 minutes until the vegetables are tender.
3   Add the curry sauce and simmer gently, stirring frequently, 15 minutes, or until
    thick. Serve hot over rice.

101 Goan Pork Vindaloo

PREPARATION TIME 15 minutes, plus at least 6 hours marinating and making the rice and raita
COOKING TIME 1 hour 40 minutes   **SERVES** 4

1lb. 12oz. boneless pork tenderloin,
   cut into bite-size pieces
4 tbsp. vindaloo paste
2 tbsp. sunflower oil
1 onion, finely chopped
1 tbsp. cayenne pepper
1 tsp. turmeric
2 tsp. ground cumin
1lb. potatoes, peeled and quartered
⅓ cup tomato paste

1 tbsp. sugar
15oz. canned crushed tomatoes
1¾ cups chicken stock
salt and freshly ground black pepper
chopped cilantro leaves, to serve
1 recipe quantity Curry Leaf
   & Coconut Rice (see page 186),
   to serve
1 recipe quantity Raita
   (see page 204), to serve

1   Put the pork in a stainless steel or other nonreactive dish. Rub the vindaloo paste
    all over the pork, cover with plastic wrap, and leave to marinate in the refrigerator
    at least to 8 hours and up to 24 hours.
2   Heat the oil in a large, heavy-bottomed saucepan over medium-high heat. When
    it is hot, add the onion and stir-fry 3 to 4 minutes until beginning to brown, then
    add the cayenne, turmeric, cumin, and pork. Stir-fry 3 to 4 minutes longer until
    the meat is light brown.
3   Stir in the potatoes, tomato paste, sugar, tomatoes, and stock. Season well with
    salt and pepper and bring to a boil. Cover tightly, lower the heat to low, and
    simmer, stirring occasionally, 1½ hours, or until the pork is tender. Sprinkle with
    chopped cilantro and serve hot with rice and raita.

02 Curried Burmese Red Pork

PREPARATION TIME 10 minutes, plus 1 hour marinating and making the curry powder and rice
COOKING TIME 1 hour 5 minutes **SERVES** 4

⅓ cup light soy sauce
⅓ cup tomato paste
1 tbsp. Curry Powder
   (see page 11)
1lb. 12oz. boneless pork loin, diced
2 tbsp. peanut oil
1 tbsp. light brown sugar

2 garlic cloves, thinly sliced
1 tbsp. peeled and finely grated
   gingerroot
1 recipe quantity Burmese-Style
   Coconut Spiced Rice (see page 184),
   to serve

1   In a stainless steel or other nonreactive dish or bowl, mix together the soy sauce, tomato paste, and curry powder. Add the pork and toss to coat evenly. Cover and leave to marinate in the refrigerator 1 hour.
2   Heat the oil in a heavy-bottomed saucepan over low heat. Add the sugar and stir 3 to 4 minutes until it dissolves and starts to caramelize. Add the garlic and ginger and stir-fry 2 minutes. Stir in the marinated pork and marinade, then cook, covered, over low heat 15 minutes, stirring occasionally.
3   Add just enough water to cover the pork, then continue cooking, covered, 45 minutes longer, or until the pork is tender and almost all the liquid evaporates. Serve hot with rice.

03 Curry Leaf Kheema

PREPARATION TIME 15 minutes, plus making the masala paste, bread, and chutney
COOKING TIME 25 minutes **SERVES** 4

1lb. 12oz. lean ground pork
3 garlic cloves, minced
1 tsp. peeled and finely grated
   gingerroot
2 tbsp. Green Masala Paste
   (see page 14)
¼ tsp. ground turmeric
4 tbsp. sunflower oil
1 large onion, peeled and finely
   chopped

10 to 12 curry leaves
2 green chilies, seeded and chopped
3 or 4 tomatoes, quartered
scant 1 cup coconut milk
4 tbsp. chopped cilantro leaves
salt
1 recipe quantity Spice-Filled Naan
   (see page 195), warmed, to serve
1 recipe quantity Mint Chutney
   (see page 204), to serve

1   Put the pork, garlic, ginger, masala paste, and turmeric in a bowl and season with salt. Mix thoroughly using your hands, then set aside.
2   Heat the oil in a large skillet over low heat. Add the onion, curry leaves, and chilies and stir-fry 2 to 3 minutes until fragrant. Increase the heat to high, add the pork mixture, and stir-fry 7 to 10 minutes until brown.
3   Add the tomatoes, coconut milk, and cilantro and continue stir-frying 10 to 12 minutes until the pork is tender. Serve hot with naan and chutney.

104 Cambodian Pork & Lemongrass Curry

PREPARATION TIME 20 minutes, plus making the noodles   **COOKING TIME** 55 minutes
SERVES 4

2 tbsp. sunflower oil
6 shallots, finely chopped
1 red chili, thinly sliced
2 tsp. peeled and finely grated
    galangal
2 tbsp. finely chopped lemongrass
2 tsp. finely grated garlic
2 tsp. crushed fenugreek seeds
1 tbsp. ground cumin
1 tsp. ground turmeric
1 tbsp. tamarind paste

finely grated zest and juice of 1 lime
1¾ cups coconut milk
8 small new potatoes, peeled
2 red bell peppers, seeded and
    cut into bite-size pieces
1lb. 12oz. pork tenderloin, cut
    into bite-size pieces
salt and freshly ground black pepper
rice noodles, to serve
sliced scallions, to serve

1   Heat the oil in a large, nonstick wok or skillet over medium-high heat. Add the
    shallots, chili, galangal, lemongrass, garlic, fenugreek seeds, cumin, and turmeric.
    Stir-fry 2 to 3 minutes until fragrant. Stir in the tamarind paste, lime zest and
    juice, coconut milk, potatoes, and red peppers. Bring to a boil, then lower the
    heat to medium and simmer, covered, 25 minutes, stirring occasionally.
2   Add the pork and season with salt and peppers. Simmer slowly, uncovered,
    25 minutes longer, stirring occasionally, or until tender. Ladle into bowls,
    sprinkle with black pepper, and serve with rice noodles and scallions.

105 Malay Devil Curry

PREPARATION TIME 10 minutes, plus making the rice   **COOKING TIME** 20 minutes   **SERVES** 4

4 tbsp. sunflower oil
1lb. 12oz. pork tenderloin, thinly
  sliced
2 tbsp. chili paste
4 garlic cloves, minced

½ tsp. mustard
1 tbsp. tamarind paste
1 tbsp. palm sugar
salt
rice, to serve

1   Heat half of the oil in a large skillet over medium-high heat. Add the pork and
    stir-fry 5 to 6 minutes until light brown. Transfer to a plate, using a slotted spoon,
    and set aside.
2   Heat the remaining oil in the pan and add the chili paste, garlic, and mustard.
    Stir-fry 4 to 5 minutes, then add 6 tablespoons to ½ cup water. Return the pork
    to the pan and stir-fry 3 to 4 minutes longer until well coated.
3   Mix the tamarind paste with ½ cup water and add it to the pan. Season well with
    salt, then stir in the palm sugar. Simmer 4 to 5 minutes until the pork is cooked
    through. Serve hot with rice.

106 Braised Pork Belly

PREPARATION TIME 15 minutes, plus making the rice and greens
COOKING TIME 2 hours 30 minutes   **SERVES** 4

1lb. 12oz. belly pork, trimmed and
  cut into 12 pieces (ask the butcher
  on the meat counter to do this
  for you)
1¾ cups good-quality beef stock
⅓ cup light soy sauce
finely grated zest and juice of
  1 large orange
1 tbsp. peeled and finely shredded
  gingerroot
2 garlic cloves, sliced

1 tbsp. cayenne pepper
1 tbsp. dark muscovado sugar
3 cinnamon sticks
3 cloves
10 whole black peppercorns
2 or 3 star anise
salt
1 recipe quantity Classic Egg-Fried
  Rice (see page 178), to serve
steamed greens, to serve

1   Put the pork in a wok with a lid and cover with water, then bring to a boil over
    high heat. Cover, lower the heat, and simmer slowly 30 minutes. Drain the pork,
    then return it to the wok, add all of the remaining ingredients and season with
    salt. Add just enough water to cover the pork.
2   Bring to a boil over high heat, then cover tightly, lower the heat to low, and cook,
    stirring occasionally, 1½ hours, or until the pork is tender.
3   Remove the lid and simmer 30 minutes longer, stirring occasionally, until the meat
    is very tender. Serve the meat and the juices with rice.

107 Black Pork Curry

PREPARATION TIME 15 minutes, plus making the curry powder and rice
COOKING TIME 1 hour 50 minutes   SERVES 4

2 onions, chopped
1¼in. piece gingerroot, peeled
  and chopped
4 garlic cloves, chopped
2 tbsp. sunflower oil
2 tbsp. Sri Lankan Curry Powder
  (see page 12)
6 curry leaves
1 cinnamon stick
8 cardamom pods

1lb. 12oz. boneless pork leg,
  cut into large cubes
1 tbsp. wine vinegar
1 tbsp. tamarind paste
scant 1 cup coconut milk
1 red chili, seeded and thinly sliced
salt
1 recipe quantity Lemon Rice
  (see page 182), to serve

1   Put the onions, ginger, and garlic in a food processor and blend 1 minute, or until finely chopped.
2   Heat the oil in a large pan or wok over low heat. Add the onion mixture and fry 2 to 3 minutes, stirring continuously so it doesn't burn. Add the curry powder, curry leaves, cinnamon stick, and cardamom and fry, stirring, 1 minute until fragrant. Add the pork and stir until well coated.
3   Stir in the vinegar, tamarind paste, and scant 1 cup water and season with salt. Lower the heat to low and simmer, covered, 1½ hours, stirring occasionally, or until the pork is tender.
4   Stir in the coconut milk and gently simmer 15 minutes longer. Stir in the chili just before serving, then serve hot with rice.

108 Bangkok Sour Pork Curry

PREPARATION TIME 20 minutes, plus making the curry paste and noodles
COOKING TIME 2 hours 10 minutes   SERVES 4

1 tbsp. sunflower oil
1 onion, finely chopped
1 tsp. peeled and finely grated
  galangal
3 tbsp. Thai Red Curry Paste
  (see page 15)
1lb. 12oz. thick pork steaks,
  cut into bite-size pieces
3½ cups chicken stock

½ cup finely chopped cilantro
  (including roots and stems)
2 lemongrass stalks, crushed
4 tsp. tamarind paste
1 tbsp. grated palm sugar
6 kaffir lime leaves
1 small handful Thai basil leaves
thick egg noodles, to serve

1   Preheat the oven to 300°F. Heat the oil in a large flameproof casserole over low heat. Add the onion and fry 3 to 4 minutes until soft. Add the galangal, curry paste, and pork and stir-fry 4 to 5 minutes until light brown.
2   Add the stock, cilantro, lemongrass, tamarind paste, palm sugar, and lime leaves and bring to a boil, then cover and carefully transfer to the oven. Bake 2 hours, or until the pork is tender.
3   Transfer the curry to a serving bowl and scatter over the basil leaves just before serving. Serve hot with thick egg noodles.

109 Burmese Pork Curry

PREPARATION TIME 15 minutes, plus making the curry paste and bread
COOKING TIME 2 hours   **SERVES** 4

4 tbsp. peanut oil
1lb. 12oz. lean pork,
   cut into 1in. pieces
2 tbsp. Burmese Curry Paste
   (see page 13)
2 onions, sliced
1¼ cups chicken stock

2 lemongrass stalks,
   lightly crushed
salt and freshly ground black pepper
cilantro leaves, to garnish
1 recipe quantity Burmese Paratha
   (see page 191), to serve

1   Heat the oil in a wide, heavy-bottomed saucepan with a tight-fitting lid over
low heat. Add the pork and fry 6 to 8 minutes until well brown. Increase the
heat to high, add the curry paste and stir-fry 2 minutes until fragrant. Add the
onions and stir-fry 4 to 5 minutes longer until soft.
2   Add the stock and season with salt and pepper, then add the lemongrass.
Cover, lower the heat to low and cook 1½ hours, or until the pork is tender.
3   Uncover and cook 15 minutes longer, if desired, until the liquid reduces.
Remove from the heat, sprinkle with cilantro leaves, and serve hot with bread.

110 Jamaican Curried Mutton

PREPARATION TIME 10 minutes, plus 1 hour marinating and making the curry powder and rice
COOKING TIME 2 hours 10 minutes   **SERVES** 4

1lb. 12oz. mutton or goat,
   cut into bite-size cubes
1 tsp. salt
1 tsp. freshly ground black pepper
1 tbsp. Curry Powder (see page 11)
1 tbsp. sunflower oil
1 onion, sliced

3½ cups beef stock
2 Scotch bonnet or habanero chilies,
   seeded and chopped
2 potatoes, peeled and diced
1 recipe quantity Jamaican Plantain
   Rice (see page 179), to serve

1   Put the mutton in a bowl. In a small bowl, mix together the salt, pepper, and
curry powder and rub the mixture into the meat. Cover and refrigerate 1 hour
to marinate.
2   Heat the oil in a heavy saucepan over medium-low heat. Add the mutton and
onion and cook, stirring, 10 to 12 minutes until the meat is brown. Add the
stock and chilies, lower the heat to low, and simmer, covered, 1½ hours until
the meat is tender.
3   Add the potatoes and continue cooking 20 to 30 minutes longer until they are
soft and the gravy is thick. Serve hot with rice.

CHAPTER 3

POULTRY & EGGS

Two of the most popular ingredients in our modern kitchens, poultry and eggs are great in curries. They offer versatility and marry well with lots of different flavors and textures. From classic favorites, such as Butter Chicken and Thai Green Chicken Curry, to enticing dishes that might be less familiar, such as Egg & Coconut Curry and Duck Jungle Curry with Bamboo Shoots, the delectable selection here will broaden your idea of what a curry has to offer.

Many of the recipes in this chapter are perfect for special occasions or gathering your friends and family around the table. For a delicious main course, for example, try Burmese Chicken Noodle Curry. In this recipe, tender pieces of chicken are slowly cooked in a succulent broth of curried coconut milk, then spooned over noodles with various toppings scattered on top. Or, expand your repertoire by trying something new, like Sri Lankan Egg Curry or Lebanese Chicken & Apple Curry.

Whichever you choose, these recipes will wow your senses—and become favorites you'll want to make again and again.

CHICKEN & SPINACH CURRY (SEE PAGE 83)

111 Filipino Chicken Adobo

PREPARATION TIME 10 minutes, plus making the rice COOKING TIME 1 hour SERVES 4

½ cup apple cider vinegar
6 tbsp. to ½ cup light soy sauce
2 cups plus 2 tbsp. chicken stock
2 bay leaves
1 tsp. freshly ground black pepper

2 tbsp. sunflower oil
1lb. 12oz. chicken thighs
15 to 20 garlic cloves, chopped
rice, to serve

1 Put the vinegar, soy sauce, stock, bay leaves, and pepper in a saucepan. Bring to a boil over high heat, then cover, lower the heat to low, and simmer 15 to 20 minutes until slightly thickened.
2 Meanwhile, heat the oil in a large, heavy-bottomed flameproof casserole over medium-high heat. Add the chicken and cook 5 minutes, turning occasionally, or until brown all over. Add the garlic and stir-fry 3 to 4 minutes, taking care not to let the garlic burn. Add the sauce and bring to a boil.
3 Cover tightly, lower the heat to low, and simmer 35 to 40 minutes until the chicken is cooked through. Serve with rice.

112 Laotian Chicken Curry

PREPARATION TIME 15 minutes, plus making the rice COOKING TIME 30 minutes SERVES 4

1lb. 12oz. skinless chicken
   thigh fillets
5 cloves
1 small bunch cilantro leaves
   with roots
2 tbsp. sunflower oil

5 shallots, sliced
3 garlic cloves, sliced
3 scallions
1 tbsp. fish sauce
½ tsp. freshly ground black pepper
rice, to serve

1 Bring 4⅓ cups water to a boil in a saucepan over low heat. Add the chicken, cloves, and cilantro and lower the heat to low. Simmer 20 to 25 minutes until the chicken is cooked through. Transfer the chicken to a plate, using a slotted spoon, and set aside until cool enough to handle, then shred the meat and set aside. Strain the cooking liquid into a clean saucepan, discarding the cloves and cilantro, and set aside.
2 Meanwhile, preheat the broiler to high. Heat the oil in a small skillet over low heat. Add the shallots and garlic and fry, stirring occasionally, 10 minutes, or until crisp and golden brown. Drain on paper towels.
3 While the shallots are cooking, put the scallions on the broiler pan and broil, turning occasionally, 3 to 4 minutes until slightly charred, then slice finely.
4 Bring the cooking liquid to a boil over high heat. Add the scallions, chicken, fish sauce, and pepper, then remove from the heat. Divide the curry into four bowls, top with the fried garlic and shallots, and serve hot with rice.

113 Penang Red Curry

PREPARATION TIME 10 minutes, plus making the curry paste and rice COOKING TIME 1 hour
SERVES 4

1lb. 12oz. chicken thighs
   and drumsticks
3 tomatoes, cut into wedges
2 red bell peppers, seeded
   and thinly sliced

2 cups Penang Red Curry Paste
   (see page 13)
Thai basil leaves, to garnish
1 recipe quantity Thai Fried Rice
   (see page 189)

1 Preheat the oven to 375°F. Arrange the chicken pieces in a single layer in a casserole and add the tomatoes and peppers. Pour the curry paste over, cover, and bake 1 hour, or until the chicken is tender and cooked through.
2 Remove from the oven and mix well. Sprinkled with basil leaves and serve hot with rice.

14 Malaysian Chicken Curry

PREPARATION TIME 35 minutes, plus making the masala paste and crêpes
COOKING TIME 1 hour   **SERVES** 4

2 garlic cloves, finely chopped
¾in. piece gingerroot, peeled and
  coarsely chopped
20 shallots, coarsely chopped
1lb. 12oz. chicken thighs
3 tbsp. sunflower oil
2 cinnamon sticks
2 cloves

2 star anise
2 tbsp. Red Masala Paste
  (see page 14)
1¼ cups coconut milk
2 large potatoes, peeled and cut into
  thick wedges
1 recipe quantity Malaysian Roti Jala
  (see page 194)

1   Put the garlic, ginger, and half of the shallots in a food processor and blend
   2 to 3 minutes until fairly smooth. Put the chicken in a wide bowl and spread
   the shallot paste all over it, then set aside to marinate 15 to 20 minutes.
2   Heat the oil in a large wok or skillet over medium-high heat. Add the remaining
   shallots and the cinnamon, cloves, and star anise and stir-fry 2–3 minutes until
   fragrant. Add the curry paste and stir-fry 2 to 3 minutes, then add the chicken
   and stir-fry 4 to 5 minutes longer until brown.
3   Add the coconut milk and just enough water to cover the chicken. Add the
   potatoes and bring the mixture to a boil, then cover, lower the heat to low,
   and simmer 40 to 45 minutes until the chicken is cooked through. Serve
   hot with crêpes.

15 Moroccan Spiced Chicken

PREPARATION TIME 15 minutes, plus making the couscous   **COOKING TIME** 1 hour   **SERVES** 4

4 tbsp. olive oil
2 onions, grated or very
  finely chopped
4 garlic cloves, finely chopped
1 large pinch of saffron threads
2 tsp. ground ginger
2 tsp. ground cumin
2 cinnamon sticks

2 tsp. smoked paprika
1lb. 12oz. chicken thighs
juice of 1 lemon
2 tbsp. chopped cilantro leaves
2 tbsp. chopped parsley
2 preserved lemons, coarsely chopped
salt and freshly ground black pepper
couscous, to serve

1   In a wide flameproof casserole or heavy-bottomed pan that can hold all of the
   chicken pieces in one layer, heat the oil over low heat. Add the onions and fry,
   stirring occasionally, 5 minutes, or until soft. Stir in the garlic, saffron, ginger,
   cumin, cinnamon, and smoked paprika and cook 1 minute longer, or until
   fragrant. Add the chicken, season with salt and pepper, and add 2 cups plus
   2 tablespoons water.
2   Bring to a boil over high heat, then lower the heat to low, cover, and simmer,
   turning the chicken a few times, 40 to 45 minutes until thick, adding a little
   more water if the mixture becomes too dry during cooking. Add the lemon juice,
   cilantro, parsley, and preserved lemons and simmer, uncovered, 5 to 10 minutes
   until the sauce thickens. Serve hot with couscous.

116 Nonya Chicken Curry

PREPARATION TIME 15 minutes, plus making the curry powder   COOKING TIME 50 minutes
SERVES 4

2 onions, finely chopped
6 garlic cloves, coarsely chopped
1 tbsp. peeled and finely grated
  gingerroot
⅓ cup sunflower oil
6 tbsp. Nonya Curry Powder
  (see page 11)
3¾ cups coconut milk
1lb. 12oz. boneless, skinless chicken
  thighs, cut into bite-size pieces

2 lemongrass stalks, crushed
8 to 10 kaffir lime leaves
1 tbsp. tamarind paste
1lb. potatoes, peeled and cut
  into bite-size pieces
1 small handful cilantro leaves,
  chopped
salt and freshly ground black pepper

1   Put the onions, garlic, ginger, and 4 tablespoons water in a food processor
    and blend 2 to 3 minutes until it forms a coarse paste.
2   Heat the oil in a wok or skillet over low heat. Add the onion paste and cook,
    stirring occasionally, 3 to 4 minutes until light brown. Sprinkle the curry
    powder over and cook, stirring, 3 to 4 minutes longer until fragrant.
3   Stir in the coconut milk and bring to a simmer. Add the chicken, lemongrass,
    lime leaves, tamarind paste, and potatoes and season well with salt and
    pepper. Bring to a boil, cover, and lower the heat to low. Simmer, stirring
    occasionally, 35 to 40 minutes until the chicken and potatoes are tender.
    Remove from the heat, stir in the cilantro and serve hot.

17 Chicken & Spinach Curry

PREPARATION TIME 15 minutes, plus at least 8 hours marinating and making the curry powder, bread, and chutney   **COOKING TIME** 1 hour 5 minutes   **SERVES** 4

5 tbsp. plain yogurt, plus extra
   to serve
2 tbsp. finely grated garlic
2 tbsp. peeled and finely grated
   gingerroot
1 tbsp. ground coriander
1 tbsp. Curry Powder (see page 11)
1lb. 12oz. boneless, skinless chicken
   thighs, cut into bite-size pieces
10oz. frozen spinach, thawed
2 tbsp. sunflower oil

1 onion, finely chopped
2 tsp. cumin seeds
1 tbsp. lemon juice
salt and freshly ground black pepper
1 red chili, sliced, to serve
cilantro leaves, to serve
1 recipe quantity Naan
   (see page 190), to serve
1 recipe quantity Sweet Mango
   Chutney (see page 213), to serve

1   Mix together the yogurt, garlic, ginger, coriander, and curry powder and season well with salt and pepper. Put the chicken in a large stainless steel or other nonreactive bowl, pour the yogurt mixture over, and toss well. Cover and leave to marinate in the refrigerator 8 to 10 hours.

2   Put the spinach in a saucepan and cook over low heat 6 to 8 minutes. Season with salt and pepper, then drain well. Transfer to a food processor and blend 2 to 3 minutes until smooth.

3   Heat the oil in a large, nonstick skillet with a lid over low heat. Add the onion and fry, stirring occasionally, 10 to 12 minutes until soft. Add the cumin seeds and cook, stirring, 1 minute, or until fragrant. Increase the heat to high and add the chicken mixture. Stir-fry 6 to 8 minutes until light brown. Add the spinach and 7 ounces water and bring to a boil.

4   Lower the heat to low, cover tightly, and simmer 25 to 30 minutes until the chicken is cooked through. Then cook, uncovered, over high heat 3 to 4 minutes, stirring frequently. Remove from the heat, stir in the lemon juice, and sprinkle with the chili and cilantro leaves. Serve hot with bread and chutney.

18 Mandalay Chicken & Shrimp Curry

PREPARATION TIME 15 minutes, plus making the curry powder and rice   **COOKING TIME** 1 hour
SERVES 4

1lb. 12oz. boneless chicken thighs,
   cut into bite-size pieces
2 large onions, coarsely chopped
5 garlic cloves, coarsely chopped
1 tsp. peeled and finely grated
   gingerroot
2 tbsp. sunflower oil
½ tsp. shrimp paste
1¼ cups coconut milk

2 tbsp. Curry Powder (see page 11)
7oz. raw jumbo shrimp, shelled
   and deveined
salt and freshly ground black pepper
chopped cilantro, to serve
sliced red chilies, to serve
1 recipe quantity Zucchini & Tamarind
   Rice (see page 186), to serve
lime wedges, to serve

1   Season the chicken pieces with salt and pepper, then set aside. Put the onions, garlic, and ginger in a food processor and blend 2 to 3 minutes until smooth, adding a little water if needed.

2   Heat the oil in a large skillet or saucepan over high heat. Add the onion mixture and shrimp paste and cook, stirring, 5 minutes, or until fragrant.

3   Lower the heat to medium and add the chicken. Cook 5 minutes, turning occasionally, until light brown. Add the coconut milk and curry powder and bring to a boil. Lower the heat to low, cover, and simmer, stirring occasionally, 40 minutes, or until thick.

4   Uncover the pan, stir in the shrimp and cook 6 to 8 minutes until the shrimp are pink and cooked through and the chicken is tender. Transfer the curry to a serving dish, and sprinkle with chopped cilantro and sliced red chilies. Serve hot with rice and lime wedges for squeezing over.

119 Malaysian Mango & Chicken Curry

PREPARATION TIME 15 minutes, plus making the curry powder, crêpes, and pickle
COOKING TIME 15 minutes   **SERVES** 4

1¼ cups chicken stock
2 tbsp. light soy sauce
2 tbsp. apple cider vinegar
2 tbsp. Curry Powder (see page 11)
2 tbsp. cornstarch
3 tbsp. sunflower oil
1lb. 12oz. boneless, skinless chicken breast halves, diced
2 red bell peppers, seeded and cut into bite-size pieces
1 tbsp. peeled and finely grated gingerroot
4 scallions, thinly sliced
2 mangoes, peeled, pitted, and cut into bite-size pieces
1 recipe quantity Malaysian Roti Jala (see page 194), to serve
1 recipe quantity Pickled Green Chilies (see page 208), to serve

1   In a bowl, whisk together the stock, soy sauce, vinegar, curry powder, and cornstarch and set aside.
2   Heat half of the oil in a wok or large skillet over high heat. Add the chicken and stir-fry 6 to 8 minutes until just cooked through. Transfer to a plate and cover to keep warm.
3   Add the remaining oil to the wok. When it is hot, add the peppers and stir-fry 2 minutes, or until soft, then add the ginger and stir-fry 30 to 40 seconds longer, or until fragrant. Add the stock mixture and return the chicken to the wok. Cook, stirring, 4 to 5 minutes over high heat until the sauce thickens and the chicken is hot.
4   Stir in the scallions and mangoes, then toss to coat all the ingredients and serve hot with crêpes and pickle.

120 Thai Baked Yellow Chicken Curry

PREPARATION TIME 15 minutes, plus making the rice   **COOKING TIME** 45 minutes   **SERVES** 4

2 red chilies, coarsely chopped
2 shallots, coarsely chopped
3 garlic cloves, chopped
2 tbsp. finely chopped lemongrass
1 tbsp. peeled and finely chopped galangal or gingerroot
2 tsp. turmeric
1 tsp. cayenne pepper
1 tsp. ground coriander
1 tsp. ground cumin
¼ tsp. cinnamon
3 tbsp. fish sauce
1 tbsp. palm sugar
4 kaffir lime leaves, finely shredded
1¾ cups coconut milk
juice of ½ lime
8 to 12 large chicken drumsticks
7oz. baby new potatoes, peeled
10 to 12 Thai basil leaves
jasmine rice, to serve

1   Preheat the oven to 375°F. Put the chilies, shallots, garlic, lemongrass, galangal, turmeric, cayenne pepper, coriander, cumin, cinnamon, fish sauce, palm sugar, lime leaves, coconut milk, and lime juice in a food processor and blend 2 to 3 minutes until fairly smooth.
2   Arrange the chicken in a single layer in an ovenproof casserole. Scatter the potatoes over, add the spice paste, and toss to coat evenly. Cover and bake 40 to 45 minutes until the chicken is cooked through. Sprinkled with basil leaves and serve hot with rice.

21 Lebanese Chicken & Apple Curry

PREPARATION TIME 10 minutes, plus making the curry powder and bread
COOKING TIME 1 hour 15 minutes   **SERVES** 4

4 eggs, at room temperature
3 tbsp. sunflower oil
1 onion, chopped
2 garlic cloves, minced
2 tbsp. Curry Powder (see page 11)
1lb. 12oz. boneless, skinless chicken
   breasts, cut into bite-size cubes

2 apples, cored and thinly sliced
1 tbsp. tomato paste
1 cup coconut milk
3¼ cups chicken stock
2 tbsp. cornstarch
sliced mint leaves, to serve
toasted pita bread, to serve

1 Bring a saucepan of water to a boil. Add the eggs and boil 6 minutes. Drain
   and leave to stand until cool enough to handle, then peel and set aside.
2 Heat the oil in a deep saucepan over low heat. Add the onion and cook, stirring
   occasionally, 5 minutes until soft. Add the garlic and curry powder and cook,
   stirring, 1 to 2 minutes, or until fragrant.
3 Add the chicken and fry 5 minutes until lightly golden, then stir in the apples,
   tomato paste, coconut milk, and stock and bring to a boil. Lower the heat
   to low, cover, and simmer 45 minutes, or until thick.
4 In a small bowl, mix together the cornstarch and 2 tablespoons cold water, then
   add it to the pan. Continue cooking 5 minutes longer, until the sauce thickens.
   If the sauce is still too runny, uncover the pan and simmer a little longer until
   it reduces. Add the whole eggs and cook 2 to 3 minutes until warmed through.
   Sprinkle with mint and serve hot with bread.

122 Thai Green Chicken Curry

PREPARATION TIME 15 minutes, plus making the curry paste and rice
COOKING TIME 35 minutes **SERVES** 4

1 tbsp. sunflower oil
3 tbsp. Thai Green Curry Paste
 (see page 15)
2 green chilies, finely chopped
1lb. 12oz. boneless, skinless chicken
 thighs, cut into bite-size pieces
1¾ cups coconut milk
scant 1 cup chicken stock
6 kaffir lime leaves
2 tbsp. fish sauce
1 tbsp. grated palm sugar

7oz. pea eggplants, left whole,
 or 1 large eggplant, cut into
 bize-sized pieces
3oz. green beans, trimmed
1¾oz. canned bamboo shoots,
 rinsed and drained
1 large handful Thai sweet
 basil leaves
1 large handful cilantro leaves
juice of 1 lime
jasmine rice, to serve

1 Heat the oil in a large, nonstick wok or saucepan over medium-high heat. Add the curry paste and chilies and stir-fry 2 to 3 minutes until fragrant, then add the chicken. Stir-fry 5 to 6 minutes until the chicken is light brown. Stir in the coconut milk, stock, lime leaves, fish sauce, palm sugar, and pea eggplants.
2 Simmer, uncovered, 10 to 15 minutes, stirring occasionally. Add the green beans and bamboo shoots and continue simmering 6 to 8 minutes until tender. Remove from the heat and stir in the basil, cilantro, and lime juice. Divide into bowls and serve hot with rice.

123 Thai Chicken Meatball Curry

PREPARATION TIME 20 minutes, plus making the curry paste, noodles, and bok choy
COOKING TIME 30 minutes **SERVES** 4

1lb. 12oz. ground chicken
1¼ cups fresh breadcrumbs
1⅔ cups chopped cilantro leaves
4 tbsp. finely chopped lemongrass
3 red chilies, seeded and finely
 chopped
2 tbsp. sunflower oil

2 to 3 tbsp. Thai Red Curry Paste
 (see page 15)
1¾ cups coconut milk
1 tbsp. tomato paste
salt and freshly ground black pepper
egg noodles, to serve
steamed bok choy, to serve

1 Preheat the oven to 350°F. In a bowl, mix together the chicken and breadcrumbs until well combined, then season generously with salt and pepper. Divide the mixture into 25 to 30 small balls and put them on a plate.
2 Mix together half of the cilantro with the lemongrass and chilies and spread the mixture on a plate. Carefully roll the chicken balls in the mixture to coat.
3 Working in two batches, if necessary, heat the oil in a wok or saucepan over medium heat. Add the meatballs and fry 10 minutes, turning once, until light brown. Transfer the meatballs to a baking dish and bake 10 minutes, or until the juices run clear when a meatball is pierced with a fork.
4 Meanwhile, wipe out the wok, reheat it over high heat, and add the curry paste. Stir-fry 30 seconds, then stir in the coconut milk and simmer 1 to 2 minutes until slightly reduced. Add the tomato paste and mix well. Stir the meatballs into the curry sauce. Sprinkle with the remaining cilantro and serve hot with noodles and bok choy.

124 Chicken Yakitori

PREPARATION TIME 15 minutes, plus 30 minutes soaking and making the rice
COOKING TIME 12 minutes   SERVES 4 to 6

6 tbsp. thick dark soy sauce
3 tbsp. mirin
1 tbsp. rice wine
4 tbsp. honey
1lb. 12oz. boneless, skinless chicken
   breasts, cut into 1in. pieces
2 red bell peppers, seeded and cut
   into 1in. pieces

6 to 8 scallions, cut into
   1¼in. pieces
10 shiitake mushrooms,
   stems discarded, halved
1 recipe quantity Japanese
   Mushroom Rice (see page 170),
   to serve

1   Mix together the soy sauce, mirin, rice wine, and honey and set aside. If using
wooden skewers, soak 12 of them in cold water at least 30 minutes.
2   Thread the chicken onto the skewers, alternating with the peppers, scallions,
and mushrooms. Heat a cast-iron griddle over medium-high heat. Brush the
chicken with the soy sauce glaze and cook 10 to 12 minutes, turning frequently
and brushing the tops each time with a little of the glaze, until the chicken is
cooked through and has a dark rich glaze. Serve hot with rice.

125 Lemongrass Chicken

PREPARATION TIME 15 minutes, plus making the curry powder and rice
COOKING TIME 2 hours 20 minutes   SERVES 4

1 tbsp. sunflower oil
12 large chicken drumsticks
1 onion, finely chopped
4 garlic cloves, minced
6 tbsp. very finely chopped
   lemongrass

1 red chili, finely chopped
2 tbsp. Curry Powder (see page 11)
1 tbsp. grated palm sugar
1¾ cups chicken stock
salt and freshly ground black pepper
jasmine rice, to serve

1   Preheat the oven to 275°F. Heat the oil in a large flameproof casserole over
medium-high heat. Add the chicken and cook, turning occasionally, 5 to 6
minutes until brown. Transfer to a plate, using a slotted spoon, and set aside.
2   Add the onion to the casserole and cook, stirring occasionally, over low heat
10 minutes, or until soft. Stir in the garlic, lemongrass, chili, and curry powder
and cook, stirring, 1 to 2 minutes until well mixed.
3   Return the chicken to the casserole and add the sugar and stock. Bring to a boil,
season with salt and pepper, and cover tightly. Bake 1½ to 2 hours until tender.
Serve hot with rice.

126 African Chicken Curry

PREPARATION TIME 20 minutes, plus at least 6 hours marinating and making the curry powder
and rice   COOKING TIME 1½ hours   SERVES 4

1 chicken, about 1lb. 12oz.
6 garlic cloves, finely chopped
4 tbsp. sunflower oil, plus extra
   for greasing
4 tsp. peeled and grated gingerroot
2 tbsp. Curry Powder (see page 11)

1 tsp. cinnamon
juice of 2 large lemons
½ cup plain yogurt
1 tbsp. honey
salt and freshly ground black pepper
rice, to serve

1   Put the chicken in a large bowl. In another bowl, mix together all of the
remaining ingredients, season with salt and pepper, and rub it over the chicken.
Leave to marinate, covered, in the refrigerator 6 to 8 hours.
2   Preheat the oven to 300°F and lightly oil a baking dish. Put the chicken and
marinade in the dish. Roast 1½ hours, or until cooked through, covering with
foil for the last 30 to 40 minutes of roasting. Serve hot with rice.

127　Korean Chicken Wings

PREPARATION TIME 5 minutes, plus at least 6 hours marinating and making the salad
COOKING TIME 40 minutes　**SERVES** 4

12 large chicken wings
⅔ cup soy sauce
6 tbsp. sugar
2 tbsp. finely chopped chives
1 tbsp. sesame seeds

4 garlic cloves, minced
2 tsp. cayenne pepper
all-purpose flour, to dust
1 lemon, quartered, to serve
mixed salad leaves, to serve

1　Put the chicken wings in a wide, stainless steel or other nonreactive bowl. Mix
together the soy sauce, sugar, chives, sesame seeds, garlic, and cayenne. Pour
this mixture over the chicken and toss well. Cover and leave to marinate in the
refrigerator 6 to 8 hours, or overnight if time permits.

2　Preheat the oven to 375°F. Lift the chicken out of the marinade and dust lightly
with flour, then transfer to a nonstick baking tray and bake 35 to 40 minutes
until the chicken is cooked through and golden. Serve hot with salad leaves
and lemon wedges for squeezing over.

28 Chicken Massaman Curry

PREPARATION TIME 10 minutes, plus making the curry paste and rice
COOKING TIME 40 minutes   SERVES 4

2 tbsp. sunflower oil
1 large onion, sliced
⅓–½ cup Massaman Curry Paste
   (see page 13)
2 cups plus 2 tbsp. coconut milk
1lb. 12oz. boneless, skinless chicken
   breasts, cut into bite-size cubes

2 tbsp. fish sauce
2 tbsp. lime juice
1 tsp. sugar
3oz. Thai eggplants
2 tbsp. chopped Thai basil
jasmine rice, to serve

1   Heat the oil in a skillet over low heat. Add the onion and cook, stirring
    occasionally, 6 to 8 minutes until soft. In a small bowl, mix together the curry
    paste and a little of the coconut milk, add it to the pan, and fry 1 minute. Add
    the chicken and cook 3 minutes, mixing well Stir in the fish sauce, lime juice,
    sugar, and remaining coconut milk. Lower the heat to low and cook, stirring
    occasionally, 20 minutes, or until thick.
2   Slice the eggplants in half lengthwise. Increase the heat to high and add them
    to the chicken. Cook 5 minutes, or until tender, then remove from the heat, stir
    in the basil, and serve hot with rice.

29 Chicken Xacutti

PREPARATION TIME 20 minutes, plus at least 6 hours marinating and making the garam masala
and rice   COOKING TIME 50 minutes   SERVES 4

2lb. 4oz. chicken thighs and
   drumsticks
2 tbsp. shredded coconut
1 tbsp. sunflower oil
2 large onions, finely chopped
1 tbsp. tomato paste
4 red chilies, left whole
1 tsp. ground cloves
2 tbsp. Garam Masala (see page 11)
1 cinnamon stick
chopped cilantro leaves, to serve
rice, to serve
lime wedges, to serve

XACUTTI MARINADE
1 tbsp. garlic puree or grated garlic
1 tbsp. ginger puree or grated
   gingerroot
2 tbsp. finely chopped cilantro leaves
1 tbsp. tamarind paste
1 tsp. turmeric
1 tsp. cayenne pepper

1   Put all of the ingredients for the marinade in a large bowl and mix well. Add the
    chicken and toss to coat well. Cover and leave to marinate in the refrigerator
    6 to 8 hours, or overnight if time permits.
2   Put the coconut in a small, dry skillet over medium-low heat and dry-roast, stirring
    continuously, 2 to 3 minutes until lightly golden. Watch carefully to make sure
    it does not scorch. Remove from the heat and set aside.
3   Heat the oil in a heavy saucepan over low heat. Add the onions and cook, stirring
    occasionally, 8 to 10 minutes until soft and light brown. Stir in the coconut,
    tomato paste, chilies, cloves, garam masala, and cinnamon stick.
4   Add the chicken and marinade and stir-fry over high heat 5 minutes, or until well
    coated. Add 2 cups plus 2 tablespoons water and bring to a boil, then lower the
    heat to low and simmer, covered, 25 to 30 minutes until the chicken is tender and
    cooked through and the sauce is thick. Sprinkle with chopped cilantro and serve
    hot with rice and lime wedges for squeezing over.

130 Kerala Chicken & Coconut Curry

PREPARATION TIME 15 minutes, plus making the garam masala and rice
COOKING TIME 1 hour   SERVES 4

2 tbsp. sunflower oil
2 onions, finely chopped
1 to 2 red chilies, seeded if liked
4 garlic cloves, finely grated
   or crushed
2 tsp. peeled and finely grated
   gingerroot
2 cassia bark or cinnamon sticks
1 tsp. crushed cardamom seeds
1 tbsp. ground coriander
2 tsp. ground cumin
½ tsp. turmeric
1 tsp. Garam Masala (see page 11)

1lb. 12oz. boneless, skinless chicken
   thighs, cut into bite-size pieces
15oz. canned crushed tomatoes
2 tsp. palm sugar or light
   brown sugar
1¾ cups coconut milk
salt
chopped cilantro leaves,
   to serve
1 recipe quantity Curry Leaf
   & Coconut Rice (see page 186),
   to serve
1 lime, cut into wedges, to serve

1   Heat the oil in a large wok or saucepan over low heat. Add the onions and cook, stirring occasionally, 10 to 12 minutes until golden. Add the chilies, garlic, ginger, cassia bark, cardamom, coriander, cumin, turmeric, and garam masala and cook, stirring occasionally, 1 minute, or until fragrant

2   Add the chicken and stir-fry over high heat 2 to 3 minutes, then stir in the tomatoes and sugar and stir-fry 2 to 3 minutes longer. Add the coconut milk and season with salt. Bring to a boil, then lower the heat to low, cover, and simmer, stirring occasionally, 35 to 40 minutes until the chicken is tender and the sauce thickens slightly. Sprinkle the cilantro over and serve hot with rice and lime wedges for squeezing over.

131 Tandoori Chicken Kebabs

PREPARATION TIME 15 minutes, plus at least 3 hours marinating and making the tandoori paste, bread, and accompaniments   COOKING TIME 10 minutes   SERVES 4

2lb. 4oz. boneless, skinless chicken
   breasts, cut into bite-size pieces
scant 1 cup plain yogurt
3 tbsp. Tandoori Curry Paste
   (see page 14) or tandoori powder
1 tbsp. finely grated garlic
1 tbsp. peeled and finely grated
   gingerroot

juice of 2 limes
salt and freshly ground black pepper
1 recipe quantity Naan
   (see page 190), to serve
1 recipe quantity Raita
   (see page 204), to serve
1 recipe quantity Mint & Cilantro
   Chutney (see page 201), to serve

1   Put the chicken in a large stainless steel or other nonreactive bowl. In a small bowl, mix together the yogurt, tandoori paste, garlic, ginger, and lime juice and season well with salt and pepper. Pour this mixture over the chicken and toss to coat evenly, then cover and leave to marinate in the refrigerator 3 to 4 hours, or overnight if time permits.

2   Preheat the broiler to medium-high. If using wooden skewers, soak 8 of them in cold water for at least 30 minutes to prevent scorching. Thread the chicken pieces onto the skewers and broil 4 to 5 minutes on each side until cooked through and the edges are lightly charred in places. Serve hot with bread, raita, and chutney.

132 Jamaican Curried Chicken

PREPARATION TIME 15 minutes, plus making the curry powder, rice, and chutney
COOKING TIME 1 hour 10 minutes **SERVES** 4 to 6

3 tbsp. sunflower oil
1lb. 12oz. boneless
  chicken thighs
1 large onion, finely chopped
3 garlic cloves, finely chopped
2 thyme sprigs
2 tbsp. Curry Powder (see page 11)
1 tbsp. peeled and finely grated
  gingerroot
1¾ cups coconut milk
scant 1 cup chicken stock

1 Scotch bonnet or habanero chili,
  left whole
juice of 1 lime
4 large potatoes, peeled and
  coarsely chopped
salt and freshly ground black pepper
1 recipe quantity Vegetable Jollof
  Rice (see page 188)
1 recipe quantity Jamaican Peach
  Chutney (see page 211)

1 Heat the oil in a large saucepan over medium-high heat. Add the chicken, onion, and garlic and fry, turning the chicken occasionally, 5 minutes, or until it is light brown. Add the thyme, curry powder, and ginger and stir-fry 1 minute. Stir in the coconut milk, stock, chili, lime juice, and potatoes.
2 Bring to a boil, then cover, lower the heat to low, and simmer 1 hour, or until the chicken is tender. Season well with salt and pepper and remove and discard the chili. Serve hot with rice and chutney.

133 Indonesian Chicken Opor

PREPARATION TIME 15 minutes, plus making the rice **COOKING TIME** 35 minutes **SERVES** 4

2 red chilies
5 candlenuts or macadamia nuts
1 small onion, coarsely chopped
3 garlic cloves, chopped
1 tbsp. ground coriander
1 tsp. fennel seeds
2 tsp. peeled and finely chopped
  galangal or gingerroot
1 tsp. shrimp paste
1lb. 12oz. boneless chicken thighs

2 cups plus 2 tbsp. coconut milk
1 tbsp. tamarind paste
2 tbsp. finely chopped lemongrass
2 kaffir lime leaves
1 tsp. salt
1 tsp. palm sugar
2 tbsp. shredded coconut
1 recipe quantity Indonesian-Style
  Quick Fried Rice (see page 175),
  to serve

1 Put the chilies, candlenuts, onion, garlic, coriander, fennel seeds, galangal, and shrimp paste in a blender or small food processor and blend 2 to 3 minutes until fairly smooth, adding a little water if needed.
2 Put the chicken and coconut milk in a heavy-bottomed saucepan and bring to a boil over high heat. Add the spice paste, tamarind paste, lemongrass, lime leaves, salt, and sugar and lower the heat to low. Simmer slowly, stirring occasionally, 25 to 30 minutes until the chicken is cooked through.
3 Meanwhile, put the coconut in a small, dry skillet over a medium-low heat and dry-roast, stirring continuously, 2 to 3 minutes until light golden. Watch carefully to make sure it does not scorch.
4 Sprinkle the coconut over the chicken curry and serve hot with rice.

134 Ground Chicken Korma with Peas

PREPARATION TIME 10 minutes, plus making the curry powder, chutney, and rice
COOKING TIME 35 minutes   SERVES 4

2 tbsp. olive oil
1 onion, chopped
2 garlic cloves, crushed
8oz. potatoes, peeled and cut
    into ¾in. cubes
1lb. 12oz. ground chicken
1¼ cups frozen peas
1 tbsp. mild Curry Powder
    (see page 11)

scant 1 cup vegetable stock
2 tbsp. Sweet Mango Chutney
    (see page 213)
salt and freshly ground black pepper
chopped cilantro leaves, to serve
plain yogurt, to serve
1 recipe quantity Saffron Rice
    (see page 180), to serve

1   Heat the oil in a saucepan over low heat. Add the onion and garlic and fry, stirring
    occasionally, 5 minutes until soft and starting to color. Add the potatoes and
    chicken and cook, stirring, 5 minutes, or until the chicken is brown. Add the peas,
    curry powder, stock, and chutney.
2   Season with salt and pepper. Bring to a boil, cover tightly, and lower the heat
    to low, then simmer 20 minutes until thick. Remove from the heat, sprinkle with
    cilantro, and serve with yogurt and rice.

135 Butter Chicken

PREPARATION TIME 25 minutes, plus 24 hours marinating and making the curry powder
and bread   COOKING TIME 1 hour 10 minutes   SERVES 4

1 cup unsalted raw cashew nuts
1 tbsp. fennel seeds
4 tbsp. Curry Powder (see page 11)
4 garlic cloves, crushed
2 tsp. peeled and finely grated
    gingerroot
2 tbsp. white wine vinegar
½ cup tomato paste
⅔ cup plain yogurt
1lb. 12oz. boneless, skinless chicken
    thighs, cut into large bite-size
    pieces

3 tbsp. butter
1 large onion, finely chopped
1 cassia bark or cinnamon stick
4 green cardamom pods
1 tsp. cayenne pepper
15oz. canned crushed tomatoes
⅔ cup chicken stock
scant 1 cup light cream
salt and freshly ground black pepper
1 recipe quantity Wholewheat
    Paratha (see page 193), to serve

1   Put the cashew nuts, fennel seeds, and curry powder in a small nonstick skillet
    and dry-roast over medium-low heat, stirring continuously, 1 to 2 minutes
    until fragrant.
2   Put the cashew mixture, garlic, ginger, vinegar, tomato paste, and half of the
    yogurt in a blender or food processor and blend 2 to 3 minutes until smooth.
    Transfer to a large nonreactive bowl and add the remaining yogurt and the
    chicken. Toss well, then cover and leave to marinate in the refrigerator 24 hours.
3   Melt the butter in a large, nonstick wok or saucepan over low heat. Add the
    onion, cassia bark, and cardamom and stir-fry 6 to 8 minutes until the onion
    is soft and translucent. Add the chicken mixture and cook, stirring, 10 minutes.
    Season well with salt and pepper.
4   Stir in the cayenne, tomatoes, and stock and bring to a boil. Lower the heat
    to low, and simmer, uncovered, 40 to 45 minutes, stirring occasionally, until thick.
    Stir in the cream and cook 4 to 5 minutes loner. Serve hot with warm bread.

136 Chettinad Chicken

PREPARATION TIME 10 minutes, plus making the curry powder and rice **COOKING TIME** 1 hour
SERVES 4

4 tbsp. ghee or butter
2 bay leaves
8 green cardamom pods
1 cinnamon stick
1 tsp. fennel seeds
2 tsp. cumin seeds
20 whole black peppercorns
6 to 8 dried red chilies
3 cloves
15 to 20 curry leaves

2 onions, finely chopped
4 tbsp. Madras Curry Powder
  (see page 12)
1 tomato, chopped
1lb. 12oz. chicken thighs
1 recipe quantity Lemon Rice
  (see page 182), to serve
plain yogurt, lightly whisked,
  to serve

1   Heat the ghee in a large saucepan over medium-high heat. When it is hot, add the bay leaves, cardamom, cinnamon, fennel and cumin seeds, peppercorns, chilies, and cloves and stir-fry 1 to 2 minutes until fragrant. Add the curry leaves and onions and stir-fry 8 to 10 minutes longer until the onions are soft and just lightly colored. Add the curry powder and continue stir-frying 4 to 6 minutes, adding a little water to prevent the mixture sticking.
2   Stir in the tomato, including any juices, and stir-fry 3 to 4 minutes longer until the tomato breaks down. Add the chicken thighs and stir until well coated, then add just enough water to cover. Bring to a boil, lower the heat to low, and simmer, covered, 30 to 35 minutes until the chicken is cooked through. Serve hot with rice and yogurt.

137 Bombay Chicken Curry

PREPARATION TIME 10 minutes, plus making the curry powder, rice, and chutney
COOKING TIME 45 minutes   **SERVES** 4

2 tbsp. sunflower oil
2 onions, chopped
2 garlic cloves, minced
1 tsp. ground ginger
1 tsp. turmeric
2 tsp. Curry Powder (see page 11)
1lb. 12oz. skinless chicken thighs
15oz. canned crushed tomatoes

1¾ cups coconut milk
1¼ cups fresh or frozen peas
chopped cilantro leaves, to serve
1 recipe quantity Lemon Rice
  (see page 182)
1 recipe quantity Sweet Mango
  Chutney (see page 213)
poppadoms, to serve

1   Heat half of the oil in a large skillet or saucepan over low heat. Add the onions and fry, stirring occasionally, 6 to 8 minutes until soft and golden. Add the garlic, ginger, turmeric, and curry powder and cook 1 minute, stirring often, until fragrant. Transfer to a plate and set aside.
2   Heat the remaining oil in the same pan over medium-high heat. Add the chicken and cook, turning occasionally, 5 to 6 minutes until brown all over. Add the onion mixture and cook, stirring with a wooden spoon, 1 minute, or until the chicken is coated in the mixture.
3   Stir in the tomatoes and coconut milk and lower the heat to low. Simmer 25 to 30 minutes until the chicken is cooked through, adding the peas about 5 minutes before the end of the cooking time. Sprinkle with cilantro and serve hot with rice, chutney, and poppadoms.

138 Curried Red Lentils & Chicken

PREPARATION TIME 15 minutes, plus making the curry powder and rice
COOKING TIME 45 minutes   **SERVES** 4

2 tbsp. sunflower oil
2 onions, thinly sliced
2 garlic cloves, minced
2 tbsp. Curry Powder (see page 11)
1 tsp. cumin seeds
1lb. 2oz. boneless, skinless chicken
　breasts, thinly sliced
2 cups chicken stock

heaped ¾ cup split red lentils,
　rinsed and drained
6 tbsp. coconut cream
⅓ cup raw cashew nuts
1 tomato, finely diced
1 green chili, thinly sliced
sliced cucumber, to serve
basmati rice, to serve

1　Heat half of the oil in a large pan over low heat. Add the onions and fry, stirring
　occasionally, 8 to 10 minutes until soft and translucent. Stir in the garlic, curry
　powder, and cumin seeds and cook 1 to 2 minutes longer until fragrant.
2　Add the chicken and remaining oil and cook, stirring, 2 to 3 minutes until the
　chicken is coated in the spice mixture. Stir in the stock and lentils and bring to
　a boil. Cover, lower the heat to low, and simmer, stirring occasionally, 25 minutes,
　or until the lentils are tender and the chicken is cooked through. Stir in the
　coconut cream and simmer, covered, 5 minutes longer, or until well mixed.
3　Meanwhile, put the cashew nuts in a small skillet and dry-roast over medium
　heat, stirring frequently, 2 to 3 minutes until golden brown.
4　Divide the curry into four bowls, top with the cashews, and sprinkle the tomato
　and chili over. Serve hot with rice and cucumber.

139 Crispy Spiced Chicken on Herbed Rice Noodles

PREPARATION TIME 20 minutes   **COOKING TIME** 15 minutes   **SERVES 4**

10oz. flat dried rice noodles
1 tsp. sesame oil
4 scallions, thinly sliced
1 red chili, seeded and thinly sliced
4 tbsp. chopped cilantro
4 tbsp. chopped mint leaves
3 tbsp. chopped skinless roasted
  peanuts
1 cup rice flour

1 tbsp. Chinese five-spice powder
1 tsp. cayenne pepper
1lb. 12oz. boneless, skinless chicken
  breasts, cut into thick strips
2 egg whites, lightly beaten
salt
4 tbsp. sunflower oil, plus extra
  as needed

1   Put the noodles in a large heatproof bowl, cover with boiling water, and leave
    to soak 4 to 5 minutes until soft. Drain and transfer to a serving dish. Toss in the
    sesame oil, scallions, chili, cilantro, mint, and peanuts and set aside.
2   Put the rice flour, five-spice powder, and cayenne in a large bowl, season with
    salt, and mix well. Dip the chicken strips in the egg whites, then toss them in the
    seasoned flour to coat well, shaking off any excess.
3   Heat the oil in a wok over medium-high heat. Working in batches, fry the chicken
    3 to 4 minutes until crisp and golden. Drain on paper towels.
4   Divide the noodles onto four plates, top with the chicken, and serve immediately.

140 Creamy Chicken Curry

PREPARATION TIME 15 minutes, plus making the bread and pickle   **COOKING TIME** 35 minutes
SERVES 4

4 tbsp. ghee or butter
2 bay leaves
1 cinnamon stick
1 tsp. ground cardamom
4 cloves
2 tsp. cumin seeds
1 large onion, peeled and finely
  chopped
2 tbsp. finely grated garlic
2 tbsp. peeled and finely grated
  gingerroot
1 tbsp. ground coriander

1 tbsp. ground cumin
7oz. canned crushed tomatoes
1lb. 12oz. boneless, skinless chicken
  thighs, cut into bite-size pieces
1 tsp. cayenne pepper
½ cup light cream
salt
1 recipe quantity Puri (see page 191),
  to serve
1 recipe quantity Singapore Mango
  Pickle (see page 210), to serve

1   Heat the ghee in a large skillet over high heat. When it is very hot, add
    the bay leaves, cinnamon, cardamom, cloves, and cumin seeds and stir-fry
    30 seconds, or until fragrant. Add the onion and stir-fry 4 to 5 minutes until
    the onion is soft, then add the garlic, ginger, coriander, and cumin and stir-fry
    1 minute. Add the tomatoes and continue stir-frying 1 minute longer.
2   Add the chicken, cayenne, and 1 cup plus 2 tablespoons water and season well
    with salt. Bring to a boil, then cover the pan, lower the heat to medium-low, and
    simmer 15 minutes, turning the chicken pieces occasionally.
3   Stir in the cream and cook, uncovered, over high heat 7 to 8 minutes longer,
    stirring occasionally, until the sauce thickens. Serve hot with bread and pickle.

141 Vietnamese Chicken & Ginger Curry

PREPARATION TIME 15 minutes, plus making the nuoc mau and rice
COOKING TIME 25 minutes **SERVES** 4

1lb. 12oz. boneless, skinless chicken
  thighs, cut into 1in.-chunks
2in. piece gingerroot, peeled
  and finely grated
3 tbsp. Nuoc Mau (Vietnamese
  Caramel Sauce; see page 207)

2 tbsp. fish sauce, plus extra
  as needed
¼ tsp. salt
2 scallions, green tops only,
  finely chopped, to serve
rice, to serve

1 Put the chicken, ginger, nuoc mau, fish sauce, salt, and 2 tablespoons water
   in a saucepan and mix well. Cover and bring to a boil over medium heat. Stir
   again, then replace the lid and simmer, stirring frequently, 10 to 15 minutes
   until the chicken is cooked through and tender.
2 Remove the lid and continue cooking 5 minutes, or until the sauce reduces
   and the color deepens to a rich reddish brown. Remove from the heat, cover,
   and leave to stand 5 minutes. Adjust the flavor with extra fish sauce if needed.
   Sprinkle with the scallions and serve hot with rice.

142 Visayan Chicken Curry

PREPARATION TIME 10 minutes, plus 30 minutes marinating and making the curry powder,
rice, and sauce **COOKING TIME** 50 minutes **SERVES** 4

1lb. 12oz. chicken drumsticks
  and thighs
2 tbsp. Curry Powder
  (see page 11)
3 tbsp. sunflower oil
4 garlic cloves, finely chopped
1 onion, sliced

4 small tomatoes, chopped
2 chicken stock cubes
3¼ cups coconut milk
3 potatoes, peeled and quartered
rice, to serve
1 recipe quantity Vietnamese Shallot
  Sauce (see page 207), to serve

1 Put the chicken in a stainless steel or other nonreactive bowl and sprinkle the
   curry powder over. Toss well, then leave to marinate, covered, in the refrigerator
   30 minutes.
2 Heat the oil in a large saucepan over low heat. Add the garlic, onion, and
   tomatoes and fry, stirring, 3 to 4 minutes. Crumble in the stock cubes, add
   the chicken, and stir-fry 4 to 5 minutes until thick. Add the coconut milk and
   the potatoes and cook over low heat 30 to 40 minutes until the chicken is
   tender and cooked through. Serve hot with rice and shallot sauce.

143 Fried Chicken with Mushrooms, Burmese Style

PREPARATION TIME 10 minutes, plus making the curry powder, bread, and chutney
COOKING TIME 20 minutes **SERVES** 4

3 tbsp. sunflower oil
1 onion, thinly sliced
3 garlic cloves, finely chopped
7 cups sliced button mushrooms
1lb. 12oz. boneless, skinless chicken
  breasts, thinly sliced

1 tbsp. light soy sauce
1 tsp. Curry Powder (see page 11)
1 recipe quantity Burmese Paratha
  (see page 191), to serve
1 recipe quantity Burmese Tomato
  Chutney (see page 201), to serve

1 Heat the oil in a large wok or skillet over low heat. Add the onion and fry, stirring
   occasionally, 5 to 6 minutes until light brown. Add the garlic, mushrooms, and
   chicken and stir-fry over high heat 6 to 8 minutes.
2 Stir in the soy sauce and curry powder and continue stir-frying 2 to 3 minutes
   until the chicken is cooked through. Serve hot with bread and chutney.

44 Balti Chicken

PREPARATION TIME 15 minutes, plus making the curry powder, rice, and chutney
COOKING TIME 20 minutes **SERVES** 4

3 tbsp. sunflower oil
2 onions, thinly sliced
2 red chilies, seeded and
  thinly sliced
6 to 8 curry leaves
3 garlic cloves, minced
1 tsp. peeled and finely grated
  gingerroot
1 tbsp. ground coriander
2 tbsp. Madras Curry Powder
  (see page 12)
1lb. 12oz. ground chicken

1¼ cups fresh or frozen peas
juice of 1 lemon
1 small handful mint leaves,
  chopped
1 small handful cilantro leaves,
  chopped
salt
1 recipe quantity Saffron Rice
  (see page 180), to serve
1 recipe quantity Spiced Tomato
  Chutney (see page 210), to serve

1 Heat the oil a large wok or skillet over low heat. Add the onions, chilies, and
   curry leaves and cook, stirring, 4 to 5 minutes until the onions are soft. Add
   4 tablespoons water and continue cooking, stirring occasionally, 2 to 3 minutes
   longer until the liquid almost all evaporate.
2 Add the garlic, ginger, coriander, curry powder, and chicken and stir-fry over
   high heat 6 to 8 minutes until the chicken is well coated. Add the peas and
   5 tablespoons water and continue stir-frying over high heat 3 to 4 minutes
   until the chicken is brown and cooked through. Remove from the heat and
   stir in the lemon juice, mint, and cilantro leaves. Season with salt and serve
   hot with rice and chutney.

45 Curried Chicken Livers

PREPARATION TIME 15 minutes, plus making the curry powder, rice, and pickle
COOKING TIME 4 minutes **SERVES** 4

1 large handful cilantro leaves
1 large handful mint leaves
2 hearts of lettuces, leaves separated
  and shredded
4 plum tomatoes, coarsely chopped
1 tbsp. Curry Powder (see page 11)
1 tsp. ground cumin
1 tsp. ground coriander
1 tsp. crushed fennel seeds
½ tsp. cayenne pepper
1 tsp. peeled and finely grated
  gingerroot

1 tsp. finely chopped garlic
2 tbsp. white vinegar
1lb. 12oz. chicken livers, trimmed
4 tbsp. sunflower oil
a pinch of paprika
salt and freshly ground black pepper
1 lemon, cut into wedges, to serve
1 recipe quantity Turmeric Rice with
  Chickpeas (see page 180), to serve
1 recipe quantity Spiced Carrot Pickle
  (see page 212), to serve

1 Put the cilantro and mint leaves, lettuce, and tomatoes in a bowl, toss lightly,
   and set aside.
2 In a large bowl, mix together the curry powder, cumin, coriander, fennel seeds,
   cayenne, ginger, garlic, and vinegar to make a smooth paste, then season well
   with salt and pepper. Add the chicken livers and spread the mixture over them
   to coat completely.
3 Heat the oil in a large skillet over high heat. Add the chicken livers, and stir-fry
   3 to 4 minutes until light brown and still slightly pink on the inside.
4 Divide the lettuce mixture onto four plates, top with the chicken livers, and
   sprinkle the paprika over. Serve warm with lemon wedges for squeezing over
   and with rice and pickle.

146 Indonesian-Style Spicy Broiled Chicken

PREPARATION TIME 15 minutes, plus making the rice and salad **COOKING TIME** 20 minutes
SERVES 4

3 red chilies, coarsely chopped
4 garlic cloves, coarsely chopped
1 large onion, coarsely chopped
2 tbsp. finely chopped lemongrass
1 tbsp. peeled and finely chopped
  gingerroot
4 chicken breast halves, about
  7oz. each

scant 1 cup coconut milk
4 kaffir lime leaves
sunflower oil, for greasing
salt
1 recipe quantity Indonesian-Style
  Quick Fried Rice (see page 175),
  to serve
green salad, to serve

1   Put the chilies, garlic, onion, lemongrass, ginger, and scant 1 cup water in a food processor and blend 2 to 3 minutes until fairly smooth.
2   Put the chicken, coconut milk, and lime leaves in a large skillet and season well with salt. Bring to a boil over high heat, then lower the heat to low and simmer 4 to 5 minutes, then stir in the chili mixture and cook 10 minutes longer, or until the sauce reduces by half. Transfer the chicken to a plate and discard the sauce.
3   Preheat the broiler to medium-high and arrange the chicken in a single layer on a lightly greased broiler rack. Broil 3 to 4 minutes on each side until slightly charred, then serve hot with rice and salad.

147 Malaysian Red Sambal Chicken

PREPARATION TIME 20 minutes, plus 30 minutes soaking and making the crêpes and pickle
COOKING TIME 25 minutes **SERVES** 4

1lb. 12oz. boneless, skinless chicken
  breast halves, cut into large pieces
2 tbsp. sunflower oil
1 recipe quantity Malaysian Roti Jala
  (see page 194), to serve
1 recipe quantity Pickled Papaya
  (see page 208), to serve

RED SAMBAL
8 to 10 dried red chilies
3 large onions, finely chopped
6 garlic cloves, chopped
1½oz. shrimp paste
scant 1 cup sunflower oil
1 tbsp. sugar
2 tbsp. tomato paste
1 tsp. salt
juice of 2 limes

1   To make the sambal, put the chilies in a heatproof bowl, cover with hot water, and leave to soak 30 minutes. Drain and transfer to a food processor. Add the onions, garlic, and shrimp paste and blend 2 to 3 minutes until smooth.
2   Heat the oil in a wok or saucepan over low heat. Add the paste and cook, stirring, 5 minutes, or until fragrant. Stir in the sugar, tomato paste, salt, and lime juice, then remove from the heat and leave to cool.
3   Bring a large saucepan of water to a boil. Add the chicken, lower the heat to low, and cook 12 to 15 minutes until cooked through. Drain and leave to cool.
4   Just before serving, heat the oil in a skillet over medium-high heat. Add the chicken and stir-fry 3 to 4 minutes until light brown. Divide the chicken onto four plates and top each portion with 1 to 2 tablespoons of the sambal. Serve hot with crêpes and pickle.

148 Chicken Kofta Curry

PREPARATION TIME 20 minutes, plus at least 1 hour chilling and making the curry powder, rice, and chutney **COOKING TIME** 55 minutes **SERVES** 4

2 tsp. peeled and finely grated
  gingerroot
4 tsp. finely grated garlic
1 tsp. ground cinnamon
½ cup finely chopped cilantro leaves,
  plus extra to serve
1lb. 12oz. ground chicken
3 tbsp. sunflower oil
1 onion, finely chopped
2 tbsp. Curry Powder (see page 11)

15oz. canned crushed tomatoes
scant 1 cup chicken stock
1 cup plus 2 tbsp. light cream
salt and freshly ground black pepper
1 recipe quantity Turmeric Rice with
  Chickpeas (see page 180),
  to serve
1 recipe quantity Spiced Tomato
  Chutney (see page 210), to serve

1 Put the ginger, garlic, cinnamon, cilantro, and chicken in a bowl and season well with salt and pepper. Using your hands, mix well, then roll tablespoons of the mixture into bite-size balls and put them on a baking sheet. Cover and leave in the refrigerator 1 to 2 hours.

2 Heat 2 tablespoons of the oil in a large, nonstick skillet over medium-high heat. Add the chicken balls, working in batches, and fry 5 minutes, turning occasionally, or until light brown. Transfer the chicken balls to a plate, using a slotted spoon, cover, and set aside to keep warm.

3 Add the remaining oil to the pan and lower the heat to medium. Add the onion and cook, stirring, 4 to 5 minutes until soft, then stir in the curry powder and cook, stirring, 1 to 2 minutes until fragrant.

4 Add the tomatoes, stock, and cream and bring to a boil, then lower the heat to low and simmer, uncovered, 10 to 15 minutes until well mixed. Add the chicken balls to the pan and stir gently to coat. Simmer 10 to 15 minutes until cooked through. Sprinkle with cilantro just before serving with rice and chutney.

149 Curried Jerk Chicken, Grenada Style

PREPARATION TIME 15 minutes, plus at least 6 hours marinating and making the curry powder, rice, and chutney **COOKING TIME** 35 minutes **SERVES** 4 to 6

3lb. 3oz. chicken thighs and
  drumsticks
1 recipe quantity Vegetable Jollof
  Rice (see page 188), to serve
1 recipe quantity Tobago Tamarind
  Chutney (see page 210), to serve

CURRIED JERK MARINADE
1 tbsp. Curry Powder (see page 11)
2 Scotch bonnet or habanero chilies,
  coarsely chopped

10 scallions, roughly sliced
2 onions, coarsely chopped
3 garlic cloves,
  coarsely chopped
1 tbsp. peeled and finely grated
  gingerroot
2 tbsp. thyme leaves
4 tbsp. sunflower oil
2 tsp. sugar
2 tsp. salt
scant 1 cup coconut cream

1 Put all the ingredients for the jerk marinade in a food processor and blend 1 to 2 minutes until smooth. Transfer to a glass or ceramic dish, add the chicken pieces, and mix well to coat in the marinade. Cover and leave to marinate 6 to 8 hours, or overnight in the refrigerator.

2 Preheat the oven to 400°F. Heat a griddle or cast-iron skillet over high heat. When it is very hot, add the chicken pieces and cook, turning frequently, 5 minutes until brown on all sides. Transfer to a roasting pan and roast 30 minutes, or until cooked through. Serve hot with rice and chutney.

150 Green Chicken Kebabs

PREPARATION TIME 20 minutes, plus at least 4 hours marinating and making the kachumber
COOKING TIME 10 minutes   **SERVES** 4

scant 1 cup low-fat plain yogurt
2 garlic cloves, crushed
2 tsp. peeled and finely grated
  gingerroot
2 tsp. ground cumin
1 tsp. ground coriander
1 green chili, finely chopped
1 large handful cilantro leaves,
  chopped
1 small handful mint leaves, chopped

juice of 2 limes
1lb. 12oz. boneless, skinless chicken
  breasts, cut into bite-size pieces
2 tbsp. chopped skinless roasted
  peanuts
salt
1 recipe quantity Kachumber
  (see page 200)
lime wedges, to serve

1   Put the yogurt, garlic, ginger, cumin, coriander, chili, cilantro and mint leaves, and lime juice in a blender and blend 2 to 3 minutes until fairly smooth. Season lightly with salt.
2   Put the chicken in a large bowl, pour the yogurt mixture over, and toss to coat evenly. Cover with plastic wrap and leave to marinate in the refrigerator 4 to 6 hours, or overnight, if time permits.
3   If using wooden skewers, soak them in cold water at least 30 minutes before cooking. Preheat the broiler to medium-high. Thread the chicken pieces onto the skewers and broil, turning frequently, 8 to 10 minutes until cooked through and light brown. Sprinkle with the peanuts and serve hot with kachumber and lime wedges for squeezing over.

151 Green Masala Chicken

PREPARATION TIME 10 minutes, plus making the masala paste and rice
COOKING TIME 40 minutes **SERVES** 4

2 tbsp. sunflower oil
1 onion, finely chopped
1lb. 12oz. boneless, skinless chicken
   thighs, cut into 1in. pieces
1 tsp. turmeric
4 tbsp. Green Masala Paste
   (see page 14)

2½ cups plus 2 tbsp. coconut milk
1 small handful cilantro leaves,
   chopped
salt
1 recipe quantity Saffron Rice
   (see page 180), to serve

1   Heat the oil in a large, deep saucepan over medium-high heat. Add the onion and fry, stirring frequently, 5 minutes until soft. Add the chicken and turmeric and fry, stirring occasionally, 7 minutes until the chicken is lightly golden in places. Stir in the masala paste and fry 1 minute longer, or until fragrant.

2   Add the coconut milk, season with salt, and bring to a boil. Lower the heat to low and simmer 20 to 25 minutes until the sauce is slightly reduced and the chicken is tender and cooked through. Remove from the heat and stir in the cilantro. Serve hot with rice.

152 Burmese-Style Chicken Curry

PREPARATION TIME 15 minutes, plus making the curry paste, curry powder, and rice
COOKING TIME 1 hour **SERVES** 4

⅓ cup sunflower oil
8 shallots, thinly sliced
1lb. 12oz. boneless, skinless chicken
   thighs, cut into large pieces
1 tbsp. Thai Red Curry Paste
   (see page 15)
1 tbsp. Nonya Curry Powder
   (see page 11)

½ cup coconut milk
4 tbsp. tomato paste
2 tbsp. fish sauce
1 tbsp. palm sugar
3 large tomatoes, cut into wedges
1 small bunch cilantro leaves,
   coarsely chopped
jasmine rice, to serve

1   Heat the oil in a medium skillet over low heat. Add the shallots and cook, stirring occasionally, 6 to 8 minutes until soft and lightly golden. Transfer to a plate, using a slotted spoon, reserving the oil in the pan, then set aside.

2   Put the chicken in the pan and stir in the curry paste and curry powder until evenly coated. Add enough water to just cover and bring to a boil over high heat. Lower the heat to low, cover tightly, and simmer 20 to 25 minutes until the chicken is cooked through.

3   Stir in the coconut milk, tomato paste, fish sauce, palm sugar, and tomatoes. Cook, stirring occasionally, over low heat 15 to 20 minutes until smooth and creamy. Remove from the heat, stir in the cilantro, and serve hot with rice.

153 Balinese Chicken

PREPARATION TIME 35 minutes, plus making the rice   COOKING TIME 15 minutes   SERVES 4

2 green mangoes, peeled, pitted, and
   cut into matchsticks
2 red chilies, coarsely chopped
1 tsp. whole black peppercorns
4 candlenuts or macadamia nuts
1 cup plus 2 tbsp. coconut milk
1 tsp. palm sugar

1 tbsp. lime juice
1lb. 12oz. boneless, skinless chicken
   breasts, thinly sliced
1 tbsp. chopped mint leaves
salt
1 recipe quantity Pilau Rice
   (see page 180), to serve

1   Put the mangoes in a colander and sprinkle lightly with salt, then leave to stand
   20 minutes. Squeeze out the moisture and set aside.
2   Put the chilies, peppercorns, and candlenuts in blender or spice mill and grind
   until the mixture forms a coarse paste. Put the paste in a saucepan and add the
   coconut milk, palm sugar, lime juice, and 2 cups plus 2 tablespoons water. Season
   with salt and bring to a boil over high heat. Lower the heat to medium low and
   add the chicken. Simmer 10 minutes, or until cooked through. Add the mango
   and cook 2 to 3 minutes, then sprinkle with the mint and serve hot with rice.

154 Burmese Chicken & Bamboo Shoot Curry

PREPARATION TIME 10 minutes, plus making the curry paste and rice
COOKING TIME 35 minutes   SERVES 4

2 tbsp. Burmese Curry Paste
   (see page 13)
1lb. 12oz. boneless, skinless chicken
   breasts, diced
15oz. canned bamboo shoots, rinsed
   and drained

1 tbsp. peanut oil
1 tsp. turmeric
1 tsp. shrimp paste
salt and freshly ground black pepper
lime wedges, to serve
rice, to serve

1   Put the curry paste, chicken, bamboo shoots, oil, turmeric, and shrimp paste
   in a heavy-bottomed saucepan. Add enough water to cover the chicken, mix well,
   and bring to a boil over high heat, then cover the pan and lower the heat to low.
2   Simmer 20 to 30 minutes until the chicken is tender and cooked through. Check
   the seasoning, adding salt and pepper as needed, and serve hot with rice and
   lime wedges for squeezing over.

155 Bhoona Chicken

PREPARATION TIME 15 minutes, plus 2 hours marinating and making the garam masala and bread
COOKING TIME 8 minutes   SERVES 4

1lb. 12oz. boneless, skinless chicken
   breasts, cut into strips
2 tbsp. sunflower oil
1 tsp. Garam Masala (see page 11)
1 recipe quantity Wholewheat
   Paratha (see page 193), to serve

MARINADE
½ cup plain yogurt
juice of 2 limes

2 garlic cloves, finely chopped
1 tsp. turmeric
1 tbsp. cayenne pepper
1 tsp. crushed cardamom seeds
1 tbsp. salt
1 tbsp. ground coriander
1 tbsp. ground cumin
1 tsp. Garam Masala
   (see page 11)
1 handful cilantro leaves, chopped

1   Mix together all of the ingredients for the marinade in a large bowl. Toss in the
   chicken and leave to marinate, covered, in the refrigerator 2 hours.
2   Heat the oil in a nonstick skillet over medium-high heat. Add the chicken and
   stir-fry 6 to 8 minutes until cooked through. Mix in the garam masala and serve
   hot with bread.

156 Quick Jerk Chicken with Rice & Peas

PREPARATION TIME 10 minutes, plus making the rice and bread   **COOKING TIME** 5 minutes
SERVES 4

4 skinless chicken breast halves,
  about 6oz. each
4 tbsp. jerk seasoning
olive oil, for greasing
  and drizzling
1 chicken stock cube
4 tbsp. coconut cream

2½ cups cold cooked long-grain
  white rice
6 to 8 scallions, coarsely chopped
15oz. canned red kidney beans,
  rinsed and drained
salt and freshly ground black pepper
1 recipe quantity Trinidadian Roti
  Paratha (see page 189), to serve

1   Preheat the broiler to high. Put the chicken breasts between two sheets of plastic
    wrap and pound with a rolling pin until evenly flattened and about ⅝ inch thick.
    Remove the plastic wrap and put the chicken on a lightly greased broiler rack.
    Spread the jerk seasoning over to coat evenly, then drizzle with olive oil. Season
    with salt and pepper and broil 3 to 4 minutes on each side until cooked through.
2   While the chicken is cooking, put ⅔ cup boiling water in a skillet over high heat
    and crumble the stock cube and coconut cream into it. Add the rice, scallions,
    and kidney beans and bring to a boil. Lower the heat to medium and cook,
    stirring, 2 to 3 minutes until completely warmed through and hot. Serve with
    the chicken and bread.

157 Silken Chicken

PREPARATION TIME 20 minutes, plus at least 6 hours marinating and making the garam masala
and bread   **COOKING TIME** 20 minutes   **SERVES** 4

4 boneless, skinless chicken breast
  halves
2 tbsp. lemon juice
scant 1 cup heavy cream
1 garlic clove, finely chopped
1 tsp. peeled and finely grated
  gingerroot

1½ tsp. Garam Masala (see page 11)
1½ tsp. cayenne
1½ tsp. ground cumin
2 tsp. dried mint
salt and freshly ground black pepper
1 recipe quantity Saag Roti
  (see page 192), to serve

1   Make 3 or 4 diagonal slashes across the top of each chicken breast, then
    arrange them in a single layer in a shallow bowl. Season generously with salt
    and pepper, squeeze the lemon juice over, and toss to coat well, then leave to
    stand 5 to 10 minutes.
2   Mix together the cream, garlic, ginger, and 1 teaspoon each of the garam masala,
    cayenne, and cumin. Pour it over the chicken to coat evenly, then cover and leave
    to marinate in the refrigerator 6 to 8 hours, or overnight.
3   Preheat the oven to 425°F. Transfer the chicken to a nonstick baking tray and
    sprinkle the mint and the remaining garam masala, cayenne, and cumin over.
    Season well with salt and pepper and bake 15 to 20 minutes until tender and
    cooked through. Serve hot with bread.

158 Filipino Chicken Curry

PREPARATION TIME 15 minutes, plus making the curry powder and rice
COOKING TIME 35 minutes   **SERVES** 4

2 to 3 tbsp. sunflower oil
1lb. 12oz. boneless chicken thighs,
   cut into bite-size pieces
3 garlic cloves, crushed
1 large onion, coarsely chopped
1 tbsp. fish sauce
3 tbsp. Curry Powder (see page 11)
3 potatoes, peeled and cut into
   small cubes

1 red bell pepper, seeded and cut
   into large squares
3 celery sticks, cut into 1¼in. pieces
1¾ cups coconut milk
salt and freshly ground black pepper
1 recipe quantity
   Tomato & Cilantro Rice
   (see page 186), to serve

1   Heat the oil in a large skillet over medium-high heat. Add the chicken and stir-fry
   6 to 8 minutes until golden all over. Add the garlic and onion and fry a few
   minutes until soft. Add the fish sauce and sprinkle the curry powder over, then
   season with salt and pepper and cook, stirring, 2 minutes until brown.
2   Add the potatoes and 1¾ cups water. Cover and bring to a boil, then lower
   the heat to medium, add the red pepper and celery, and simmer 6 to 8 minutes
   until tender. Stir in the coconut milk and continue simmering 10 minutes longer,
   or until thick. Serve hot with rice.

159 Dhaka Chicken Curry

PREPARATION TIME 15 minutes, plus making the curry powder and bread
COOKING TIME 40 minutes   **SERVES** 4

2 tbsp. sunflower oil
1 onion, thinly sliced
2 tsp. brown mustard seeds or
   1 tbsp. wholegrain mustard
2 tsp. finely grated garlic
1 tsp. turmeric
2 tsp. ground coriander
2 tbsp. Curry Powder (see page 11)

1lb. 12oz. boneless, skinless chicken
   thighs
½ cup plain yogurt, lightly whisked
salt and freshly ground black pepper
cilantro leaves, to serve
1 recipe quantity Wholewheat
   Paratha (see page 193), to serve

1   Heat the oil in a large, nonstick wok or skillet over low heat. Add the onion and
   fry, stirring occasionally, 5 to 6 minutes until soft.
2   Meanwhile, using a mortar and pestle, pound the mustard seeds and garlic into
   a coarse paste, then add the mixture to the pan. Fry, stirring, 1 minute, or until
   well mixed, then add the turmeric, coriander, and curry powder and fry, stirring,
   2 to 3 minutes until fragrant. Add the chicken and stir-fry over high heat
   5 minutes until light brown, then add 1 cup plus 2 tablespoons water. Season
   well with salt and pepper and bring to a boil.
3   Cover tightly, lower the heat to low, and simmer, stirring occasionally,
   20 to 25 minutes until the chicken is cooked through. Remove from the heat
   and stir in the yogurt. Sprinkle with cilantro leaves and serve hot with bread.

Burmese Chicken Noodle Curry

PREPARATION TIME 20 minutes, plus making the curry paste   **COOKING TIME** 55 minutes   **SERVES** 4

1lb. 12oz. boneless chicken thighs,
   cut into bite-size pieces
2 large onions, coarsely chopped
5 garlic cloves, coarsely chopped
1 tsp. peeled and finely grated
   gingerroot
3 tbsp. sunflower oil
½ tsp. Burmese shrimp paste
1¾ cups coconut milk

2 tbsp. Burmese Curry Paste
   (see page 13)
7oz. dried rice vermicelli
4 tbsp. chopped cilantro leaves
1 red onion, finely chopped
2 garlic cloves, slivered
2 red chilies, thinly sliced
salt and freshly ground black pepper
1 lime, sliced, to serve

1   Season the chicken with salt and pepper, then set aside. Put the onions, garlic, and ginger in a food processor and process 2 to 3 minutes until smooth, adding a little water if needed. Heat 2 tablespoons of the oil in a large pan over high heat. Add the onion mixture and shrimp paste and cook, stirring, 5 minutes until fragrant. Add the chicken and cook over low heat 4 to 5 minutes, turning occasionally, until light brown. Add the coconut milk and curry paste.

2   Bring to a boil, then lower the heat to low and simmer, covered, 30 minutes, stirring occasionally. Uncover the pan and cook 15 minutes loner, or until the chicken is tender. Meanwhile, heat the remaining oil in a small skillet over medium-high heat. Add the garlic and fry 1 to 2 minutes until crisp, then drain on paper towels. Toward the end of the chicken's cooking time, put the noodles in a bowl, cover with boiling water, and leave to soak for 10 minutes. Meanwhile, put the cilantro, red onion, garlic slivers, and chilies in a small bowl and mix well.

3   Drain and divide the noodles into four bowls. Ladle the curry over, and sprinkle with the cilantro mixture. Serve immediately with lime for squeezing over.

161 Duck Curry with Pea Eggplants

PREPARATION TIME 15 minutes, plus making the curry paste and rice
COOKING TIME 35 minutes   **SERVES** 4

1 tbsp. sunflower oil
3 tbsp. Thai Red Curry Paste
   (see page 15)
2 green chilies, finely chopped
1lb. 12oz. boneless duck breasts,
   cut into bite-size pieces
1¾ cups coconut milk
1 cup chicken stock
6 kaffir lime leaves
2 tbsp. fish sauce

1 tbsp. grated palm sugar
7oz. pea eggplants
3oz. green beans, trimmed
2oz. canned bamboo shoots,
   rinsed and drained
1 large handful Thai sweet
   basil leaves
1 large handful cilantro leaves
juice of 1 lime
jasmine rice, to serve

1   Heat the oil in a large, nonstick wok or saucepan over medium-high heat. Add the curry paste and chilies and stir-fry 2 to 3 minutes until fragrant. Add the duck and stir-fry 5 to 6 minutes until light brown.
2   Stir in the coconut milk, stock, lime leaves, fish sauce, sugar, and pea eggplants and simmer, uncovered, 10 to 15 minutes, stirring occasionally. Add the green beans and bamboo shoots and continue simmering 6 to 8 minutes until thickened. Remove from the heat and stir in the basil, cilantro, and lime juice. Divide into bowls and serve with rice.

62 Aromatic Duck & Bamboo Shoot Curry

PREPARATION TIME 15 minutes, plus making the curry paste and rice
COOKING TIME 1 hour   **SERVES** 4

1¾ cups coconut milk
7oz. coconut cream
4 duck legs, skinned
2 tbsp. sunflower oil
4 tbsp. Thai Red Curry Paste
 (see page 15)
1 tbsp. palm or light brown sugar
3 tbsp. fish sauce

15oz. canned bamboo shoots,
 drained
7oz. green beans, halved
4 kaffir lime leaves
6 tbsp. finely chopped cilantro
 leaves
1 recipe quantity Thai Fried Rice
 (see page 189), to serve

1 Put the coconut milk and half of the coconut cream in a heavy-bottomed saucepan and bring to a boil over high heat. Add the duck and simmer, covered, over low heat 45 minutes, or until tender.
2 Meanwhile, put the remaining coconut cream in a skillet over low heat. Add the oil and curry paste and cook, stirring frequently, 3 to 4 minutes until the oil starts to separate. Add the sugar and cook 1–2 minutes longer.
3 Transfer the duck to a plate, using a slotted spoon, and cover to keep warm.
4 Add the cooking liquid and fish sauce to the curry paste mixture and simmer 2 minutes.
5 Shred or cut the duck meat from the bone and add it to the sauce along with the bamboo shoots, green beans, and lime leaves.
6 Cook 8 to 10 minutes until the vegetables are tender. Sprinkle with the cilantro and serve hot with rice.

63 Duck Jungle Curry with Bamboo Shoots

PREPARATION TIME 20 minutes, plus making the rice   **COOKING TIME** 30 minutes   **SERVES** 4

2 tbsp. sunflower oil
1lb. 12oz. duck breasts, sliced into
 thin strips
1¾ cups chicken stock
1 tbsp. fish sauce
2oz. canned bamboo shoots, rinsed
 and drained
7oz. pea eggplants
1 small handful Thai sweet
 basil leaves
jasmine rice, to serve

JUNGLE CURRY PASTE
1 tbsp. ground white peppercorns
4 green chilies, finely chopped
2 tsp. peeled and finely grated
 galangal
2 tbsp. very finely chopped
 lemongrass
3 kaffir lime leaves, very finely
 shredded
1 tsp. shrimp paste
6 garlic cloves, crushed
5 Thai or small shallots,
 finely chopped
3 tbsp. finely chopped cilantro root
4 tbsp. sunflower oil

1 Put all of the ingredients for the curry paste in a small food processor and blend 2 to 3 minutes until smooth, adding a little water if necessary.
2 Heat the oil in a large, nonstick wok or skillet over high heat. Add the curry paste and stir-fry 1 to 2 minutes until fragrant, then add the duck. Stir-fry 4 to 5 minutes until brown. Add the stock and fish sauce and bring to a boil. Remove the duck from the pan, using a slotted spoon, put it on a plate and cover to keep warm.
3 Add the bamboo shoots and pea eggplants to the wok, lower the heat to medium, and cook 12 to 15 minutes until tender. Return the duck to the pan and simmer slowly over low heat 3 to 4 minutes. Stir in half of the basil leaves and remove from the heat. Divide the curry into four bowls, sprinkle with the remaining basil leaves, and serve hot with rice.

164 Egg & Coconut Curry

PREPARATION TIME 15 minutes, plus making the curry powder and rice
COOKING TIME 45 minutes   SERVES 4

2 potatoes, peeled
8 eggs, at room temperature
2 tbsp. sunflower oil
1 onion, halved and thinly sliced
10 curry leaves
2 tbsp. Curry Powder (see page 11)

1 tsp. sugar
7oz. canned crushed tomatoes
1¾ cups coconut milk
salt
basmati rice, to serve

1   Bring a saucepan of lightly salted water to a boil. Add the potatoes and boil
    10 to 12 minutes until tender, then drain. Meanwhile, bring another pan of
    water to a boil, add the eggs, and boil 6 minutes. Drain and leave to stand until
    cool enough to handle, then peel and set aside. Chop the potatoes.
2   Heat the oil in a large, nonstick skillet over medium-high heat. Add the onion
    and curry leaves and cook, stirring, 5 minutes until soft. Stir in the curry powder,
    then the sugar and tomatoes. Bring to a boil, lower the heat to medium-low,
    and cook, stirring frequently, 10 minutes. Stir in the coconut milk and add the
    eggs and potatoes. Cook 15 minutes longer, or until thick. Season with salt and
    serve hot with rice.

165 Sri Lankan Egg Curry

PREPARATION TIME 20 minutes, plus making the curry powder and rice
COOKING TIME 25 minutes   SERVES 4

8 eggs, at room temperature
4 tbsp. sunflower oil
1 onion, finely chopped
10 curry leaves
3 garlic cloves, finely chopped
2 tsp. peeled and grated gingerroot
2 green chilies, finely chopped

3 tbsp. Sri Lankan Curry Powder
   (see page 12)
10oz. canned crushed tomatoes
6 tbsp. chopped cilantro leaves
salt
basmati rice, to serve

1   Bring a saucepan of water to a boil. Add the eggs and boil 6 minutes. Drain
    and leave to stand until cool enough to handle, then peel and set aside. Heat
    the oil in a skillet over low heat. Prick the eggs all over with a fork and fry them
    3 to 4 minutes until brown. Drain on paper towels and set aside.
2   Reheat the oil over low heat. Add the onion, curry leaves, garlic, ginger, chilies,
    and curry powder. Stir-fry 8 minutes, or until the onion is soft. Stir in the
    tomatoes, season with salt, and add the eggs. Bring to a boil, then lower the
    heat to low. Cook 5 minutes longer, add the cilantro, and serve hot with rice.

166 Masala Omelet

PREPARATION TIME 10 minutes, plus making the curry powder and bread
COOKING TIME 15 minutes   SERVES 4

1 tsp. sunflower oil
4 small red onions, finely chopped
2 red chilies, thinly sliced
2 garlic cloves, finely chopped
2 tbsp. Curry Powder (see page 11)

8 eggs, lightly beaten
4 tbsp. chopped cilantro leaves
1 recipe quantity Wholewheat
   Paratha (see page 193), to serve

1   Preheat the broiler to high. Heat the oil in a medium flameproof, nonstick skillet
    over low heat. Add the onions, chilies, and garlic and cook, stirring, 5 minutes,
    or until soft. Add the curry powder and fry, stirring occasionally, 1 minute. Add
    the eggs and cilantro, swirling the pan to coat the base evenly.
2   Cook 2 to 3 minutes until nearly set, then broil 2 to 3 minutes until light brown
    and set. Serve immediately with warm bread.

Spiced Scrambled Eggs

PREPARATION TIME 10 minutes, plus making the bread   COOKING TIME 15 minutes   SERVES 4

15g/½oz butter
1 onion, diced
2 large garlic cloves, finely chopped
1 red chilli, seeded and
    finely chopped
1 tsp. peeled and grated gingerroot

1 large tomato, seeded and
    finely chopped
4 tbsp. finely chopped cilantro leaves
8 large eggs
salt
1 quantity Wholewheat Paratha
    (see page 193), to serve

1   Melt the butter in a large skillet over low heat. Add the onion and fry, stirring
    occasionally, for 5 minutes or until soft but not colored. Add the garlic and chili
    and fry, stirring, for a further 1 minute. Add the ginger and cook, stirring, for
    a further 30 seconds, then add half of the tomato and a large pinch of the
    coriander. Fry for further 1 minute.
2   In a bowl, whisk the eggs until light and fluffy and season well with salt. Remove
    the pan from the heat and add the egg mixture. Return the pan to a medium-low
    heat and cook, stirring continuously with a wooden spoon, for 4–5 minutes until
    the mixture sets lightly – it should have a creamy texture. Quickly stir in the
    remaining tomato and coriander and serve immediately with warm bread.

CHAPTER 4

FISH & SHELLFISH

Growing up in the coastal city of Mumbai, in India, with wonderful

thriving fish markets selling all types of fresh fish and shellfish daily,

it is no wonder fish curries are particularly close to my heart. I can

remember going to the fish markets with my father on early Sunday

mornings and coming home with burlap sacks full of live crabs and

lobsters. As a result, many of the recipes here have become cherished

memories from my childhood. The fragrant and spicy Cochin Crab

Curry and delicate Fish Mollee are two of my all-time favorites.

There is also have a range of delicious recipes from elsewhere

around the world. Chermoula Spiced Fish from Morocco, Island

Monkfish Curry from the Seychelles, and Crayfish & Coconut Curry

from the Caribbean are just some of the wonderful curries here

that will prove irresistible.

One advantage of cooking fish and shellfish is that they require

very minimal cooking—so you can get an amazing meal ready in no

time at all. That's just one reason I'm so sure many of the recipes in

this chapter are guaranteed to become your favourite "fast food."

BANANA LEAF FISH (*SEE PAGE 117*)

168 Red Masala Broiled Mackerel

PREPARATION TIME 10 minutes, plus making the masala paste and rice
COOKING TIME 10 minutes SERVES 4

4 mackerel, about 10oz. each,
  dressed
½ cup Red Masala Paste
  (see page 14)
2 tsp. salt

1 recipe quantity Curry Leaf
  & Coconut Rice (See page 186),
  to serve
2 limes, cut into wedges, to serve

1 Preheat the broiler to medium-high. Wash the mackerel and pat dry with paper
towels. Using a sharp knife, slash the thickest part of the flesh on each side of
the fish 3 or 4 times.

2 Mix together the masala paste and salt and spread this mixture on both sides of
the fish. Put the fish on the broiler rack and broil 5 minutes on each side or until
cooked and crisp. Serve hot with rice and lime wedges for squeezing over.

169 Sri Lankan Salmon Curry

PREPARATION TIME 10 minutes, plus making the curry powder and rice COOKING TIME 1 hour
SERVES 4

2 tbsp. sunflower oil
1 large onion, chopped
4 garlic cloves,
  finely chopped
10 curry leaves
1 tsp. turmeric
2 tbsp. Sri Lankan Curry Powder
  (see page 12)

2 tomatoes, coarsely chopped
1 tbsp. tamarind paste
1¾ cups coconut milk
4 thick salmon steaks
salt
1 recipe quantity Lemon Rice
  (see page 182), to serve

1 Heat the oil in a large skillet over low heat. Add the onion, garlic, and curry leaves
and cook, stirring occasionally, over medium-low heat 8 to 10 minutes until the
onion is soft and light golden. Add the turmeric and curry powder and continue
stirring 1 to 2 minutes until fragrant. Stir in the tomatoes (including any juices),
tamarind paste, and coconut milk. Season with salt and simmer, stirring
occasionally, 15 minutes, or until slightly thickened.

2 Add the salmon steaks to the pan and spoon some of the sauce over them.
Simmer 5 minutes, then cover the pan, lower the heat to low, and cook
20 to 25 minutes until the fish is cooked through. Serve hot with rice.

170 Sri Lankan Fried Fish

PREPARATION TIME 20 minutes, plus making the curry powder, bread, and pickle
COOKING TIME 8 minutes SERVES 4

4 thick salmon steaks
1 tbsp. tamarind paste
1 tsp. turmeric
2 tbsp. Sri Lankan Curry Powder
  (see page 12)
7 tbsp. canola oil

salt and freshly ground black pepper
1 recipe quantity Naan
  (see page 190), to serve
1 recipe quantity Sri Lankan Lemon &
  Date Pickle (see page 213), to serve

1 Arrange the fish steaks in a single layer in a baking dish. Mix together the
tamarind paste, turmeric, curry powder, and 4 tablespoons warm water and
season with salt and pepper. Pour the marinade over the fish and toss to coat
well. Leave to marinate at room temperature 10 minutes.

2 Heat the oil in a wide skillet over medium-high heat. Add the salmon steaks and
fry 3 to 4 minutes on each side until crisp and cooked through. Serve hot with
bread and pickle.

171 Spiced Halibut Curry

PREPARATION TIME 15 minutes, plus 30 minutes marinating and making the curry powder and rice **COOKING TIME** 50 minutes **SERVES** 4

4 tbsp. lemon juice
4 tbsp. rice wine vinegar
2 tbsp. cumin seeds
2 tbsp. Curry Powder
  (see page 11)
1 tsp. salt
1lb. 12oz. thick halibut fillets, skinned
  and cut into large bite-size cubes
4 tbsp. sunflower oil

1 onion, finely chopped
3 garlic cloves, finely chopped
2 tsp. peeled and finely grated
  gingerroot
1lb. 12oz. canned crushed tomatoes
1 tsp. sugar
1 recipe quantity Mushroom Pulao
  (see page 183), to serve

1 Mix together the lemon juice, vinegar, cumin seeds, curry powder, and salt in
  a shallow stainless steel or other nonreactive bowl. Add the fish and turn to coat
  evenly. Cover and leave to marinate in the refrigerator 30 minutes.
2 Meanwhile, heat a wok with a lid over high heat, then add the oil. When it is hot,
  add the onion, garlic, and ginger. Lower the heat to low and cook, stirring
  occasionally, 10 minutes.
3 Stir in the tomatoes and sugar and bring to a boil over high heat. Lower the heat
  to low and cook, covered, 15 to 20 minutes, stirring occasionally, until thick.
  Gently stir in the fish and the marinade and simmer, covered, 15 to 20 minutes
  until the fish is cooked through and flakes easily. Serve with rice.

172 South Vietnamese Fish Curry

PREPARATION TIME 15 minutes, plus making the curry powder and rice
COOKING TIME 35 minutes **SERVES** 4

1 tbsp. sunflower oil
4 shallots, finely chopped
4 garlic cloves, crushed
2 tbsp. finely chopped lemongrass
1 tbsp. peeled and finely
  grated ginger
1 tbsp. Curry Powder (see page 11)
1 tsp. cinnamon
6 star anise
1¾ cups coconut cream

6 kaffir lime leaves
10oz. shelled and deveined raw
  jumbo shrimp
14oz. firm white fish fillets, such
  as cod or halibut, skinned and cut
  into bite-size pieces
20 Thai basil leaves
4 tbsp. finely chopped cilantro leaves
6 scallions, finely chopped
rice, to serve

1 To make the curry paste, heat the oil in a wok or deep heavy saucepan over
  medium-high heat. Add the shallots, garlic, lemongrass, and ginger and stir-fry
  3 to 4 minutes. Add the curry powder, cinnamon, and star anise and cook, stirring
  occasionally, 2 minutes until aromatic.
2 Add the coconut cream, lime leaves, and 1¼ cups water and bring to a boil.
  Lower the heat to medium and simmer 15 to 20 minutes until the liquid
  reduces by half.
3 Lower the heat to medium-low and add the shrimp and fish. Simmer 5 minutes,
  or until the shrimp turn pink and they and the fish are cooked through. Remove
  from the heat and stir in the chopped Thai basil, cilantro, and scallions. Serve
  hot with rice.

173 Thai Fish Ball Curry with Carrots & Snow Peas

PREPARATION TIME 20 minutes, plus making the curry paste and rice
COOKING TIME 20 minutes **SERVES** 4

1 tbsp. sunflower oil
1 tbsp. Thai Red Curry Paste
   (see page 15)
3½ cups coconut milk
2 tsp. finely grated palm sugar
4 kaffir lime leaves, finely shredded
1 tbsp. very finely chopped
   lemongrass
2 tsp. fish sauce
1 carrot, cut into matchsticks
5oz. snow peas, halved lengthwise
1 red chili, finely chopped, to serve
cilantro leaves, to serve
jasmine rice, to serve

FISH BALLS
1lb. 12oz. firm white fish fillets,
   such as cod, halibut, or pomfret,
   cut into chunks
2 garlic cloves, crushed
2 tbsp. cornstarch
2 tbsp. dark soy sauce
2 tbsp. finely chopped cilantro root
1 tsp. peeled and grated gingerroot

1   Put all of the ingredients for the fish balls in a food processor and blend
    2 to 3 minutes until the mixture forms a paste. Roll the mixture into
    35 to 40 bite-size balls and set aside.
2   Heat the oil in a large, nonstick wok or saucepan over low heat. Add the curry
    paste and fry, stirring, 1 to 2 minutes, then add the coconut milk. Bring to a boil,
    lower the heat to low, and simmer slowly, uncovered, 6 to 8 minutes until
    slightly thickened.
3   Add the fish balls, palm sugar, lime leaves, lemongrass, fish sauce, carrot,
    and snow peas. Bring back to a boil, then lower the heat to low and simmer,
    uncovered, 6 to 8 minutes until the fish balls are cooked through.
4   Ladle the curry into bowls, sprinkle with red chili and cilantro leaves, and
    serve with rice.

174 Tamarind Fish Curry

PREPARATION TIME 15 minutes, plus 30 minutes marinating and making the rice
COOKING TIME 55 minutes **SERVES** 4

1 tbsp. tamarind paste
4 tbsp. rice wine vinegar
2 tbsp. cumin seeds
1 tsp. turmeric
1 tsp. cayenne pepper
1 tsp. salt
1lb. 12oz. thick halibut or cod fillets,
  skinned and cut into large
  bite-size cubes
4 tbsp. sunflower oil

1 onion, finely chopped
3 garlic cloves, finely grated
2 tbsp. peeled and finely grated
  gingerroot
2 tsp. black mustard seeds
1lb. 12oz. canned crushed tomatoes
1 tsp. sugar
basmati rice, to serve
poppadoms, to serve

1 In a shallow stainless steel or other nonreactive bowl, mix together the tamarind
   paste, vinegar, cumin seeds, turmeric, cayenne, and salt. Add the fish and turn
   to coat evenly. Cover and leave to marinate in the refrigerator 30 minutes.
2 Meanwhile, heat a wok over high heat and add the oil. When it is hot, add the
   onion, garlic, ginger, and mustard seeds. Lower the heat to medium-low and
   cook slowly, stirring occasionally, 10 minutes until the onions have softened.
   Add the tomatoes and sugar and stir well.
3 Bring to a boil over high heat, then lower the heat to low, cover, and cook slowly,
   stirring occasionally, 15 to 20 minutes until slightly thickened.
4 Gently mix in the fish and marinade, then simmer, covered, 15 to 20 minutes until
   the fish is cooked through and flakes easily. Serve with rice and poppadoms.

175 Tandoori Fish Kebabs

PREPARATION TIME 15 minutes, plus at least 2 hours marinating and making the curry paste
and rice **COOKING TIME** 10 minutes **SERVES** 4

1½ cups plain yogurt
2 tbsp. finely grated onion
1 tbsp. finely grated garlic
1 tbsp. peeled and finely grated
  gingerroot
juice of 2 limes, plus extra lime
  wedges, to serve
3 tbsp. Tandoori Curry Paste
  (see page 14)

4 red bell peppers, seeded and cut
  into large bite-size pieces
1lb. 12oz. thick salmon fillets, skinned
  and cut into large bite-size pieces
salt and freshly ground black pepper
chopped cilantro and mint leaves,
  to serve
1 recipe quantity Turmeric Rice with
  Chickpeas (see page 180), to serve

1 In a large bowl, mix together the yogurt, onion, garlic, ginger, lime juice, and
   curry paste. Add the peppers and salmon and season well with salt and pepper.
   Toss to coat evenly, then cover and leave to marinate in the refrigerator
   2 to 4 hours.
2 Preheat the broiler or a charcoal barbecue to high. If using wooden skewers,
   soak eight of them in water for 30 minutes to prevent scorching. Alternately
   thread the fish and peppers onto the skewers and broil 4 to 5 minutes on each
   side until the fish is just cooked through. Sprinkle with cilantro and mint and
   serve hot with rice and lime wedges for squeezing over.

176 Turkish-Style Fish with Coriander & Yogurt

PREPARATION TIME 10 minutes, plus at least 4 hours marinating and making the rice
COOKING TIME 15 minutes   SERVES 4

1 cup plus 2 tbsp. plain yogurt,
  whisked
1 tbsp. ground coriander
1½ tsp. ground cardamom
2 tsp. freshly ground black pepper
juice of 1 lemon

4 thick white fish fillets, such as
  halibut, hake, or cod, about
  7oz. each, skinned
2 tbsp. finely chopped dill
salt
rice, to serve

1   In a bowl, mix together the yogurt, coriander, cardamom, pepper, and lemon
    juice, then season with salt. Arrange the fish in a single layer in a wide glass or
    ceramic dish and pour the yogurt marinade over. Toss to coat evenly, then cover
    and leave to marinate in the refrigerator 4 to 6 hours.
2   Preheat the oven to 400°F and line a baking tray with parchment paper. Remove
    the fish from the marinade and put it on the parchment. Bake 12 to 15 minutes
    until the fish is just cooked through. Serve hot with rice.

177 White Fish Curry

PREPARATION TIME 10 minutes, plus 30 minutes soaking and making the rice and relish
COOKING TIME 25 minutes   SERVES 4

1 tsp. fenugreek seeds
1lb. 12oz. firm white fish fillets,
  such as halibut, pomfret, or hake,
  skinned and cut into large
  bite-size pieces
1 tsp. turmeric
2 tsp. salt
1 onion, thinly sliced

2 garlic cloves, finely chopped
8 curry leaves
2 cups plus 2 tbsp. coconut milk
juice of ½ lemon, to taste
freshly ground black pepper
jasmine rice, to serve
1 recipe quantity Sri Lankan Coconut
  Relish (see page 213), to serve

1   Put the fenugreek seeds in a small bowl, cover with cold water, and leave to soak
    30 minutes, then drain. Pat the fish dry with paper towels, then rub them all over
    with the turmeric and the salt and set aside.
2   Put the fenugreek seeds, onion, garlic, curry leaves, and coconut milk in
    a saucepan and season well with salt and pepper and cook, stirring occasionally,
    over low heat 12 to 15 minutes until the onions are soft.
3   Stir well, then add the fish and simmer over low heat 10 minutes until cooked
    through. Remove from the heat and drizzle with lemon juice to taste. Serve with
    rice and relish

178 Allepy Fish Curry

PREPARATION TIME 15 minutes, plus 30 minutes soaking and making the curry powder and rice
COOKING TIME 20 minutes   **SERVES** 4

4 dried chilies
1 cup freshly grated or shredded
    coconut
1 tbsp. paprika
3 tbsp. Curry Powder (see page 11)
scant 1 cup coconut milk
2 tbsp. tamarind paste
2 green chilies, halved lengthwise

1in. piece gingerroot, peeled
    and grated
1 small onion, finely chopped
4 mackerel fillets, about 7oz. each,
    dressed
salt
basmati rice, to serve

1 Put the dried chilies in a bowl, add enough hot water to just cover and leave to soak 30 minutes. If using shredded coconut, soak it in warm water 20 minutes, then drain.
2 Put the chilies and soaking liquid, paprika, curry powder, coconut, and coconut milk in a blender or food processor. Blend 1 to 2 minutes until the mixture forms a smooth paste. Transfer the paste to a heavy-bottom skillet. Stir in 7 tablespoons water and bring to a slow simmer over medium-low heat.
3 Stir in the tamarind paste, green chilies, ginger, and onion and season with salt, then simmer 2 to 3 minutes. Add the fish and stir once to coat it in the mixture.
4 Simmer, covered, over low heat 10 to 15 minutes until the fish is just cooked. Remove from the heat and serve hot with rice.

179 Banana Leaf Fish

PREPARATION TIME 30 minutes, plus making the rice   **COOKING TIME** 25 minutes   **SERVES** 4

1 cup freshly grated or shredded
    coconut
fresh banana leaves, cut into 4 x 10in.
    squares, for wrapping
2 tsp. ground cumin
2 tsp. ground coriander
1½ tsp. light brown sugar
4 green chilies, seeded and chopped
⅔ cup chopped cilantro leaves
4 tbsp. chopped mint leaves
5 garlic cloves, chopped

1 tsp. peeled and finely grated
    gingerroot
3 tbsp. sunflower oil
4 thick cod fillets, about 7oz. each,
    skinned
juice of 2 limes
salt
1 recipe quantity Curry Leaf
    & Coconut Rice (see page 186),
    to serve

1 If using shredded coconut, soak it in warm water 20 minutes, then drain.
2 Preheat the oven to 400°F. Dip the banana leaves into a pan of very hot water 10 to 15 seconds to soften, then wipe dry with paper towels.
3 Put the cumin, coriander, sugar, coconut, chilies, cilantro and mint leaves, garlic, and ginger in a blender and blend until the mixture forms a paste (or use a mortar and pestle). Heat 1 tablespoon of the oil in a skillet over low heat, add the paste, and cook, stirring, 1 to 2 minutes until fragrant. Season with salt, then remove from the heat and arrange them on a work surface.
4 Spread the paste liberally over both sides of each piece of fish. Put one piece of fish on each banana leaf, drizzle with the lime juice, and fold the edges of the leaf around the fish to form a package, securing each one with bamboo skewers or string. Put the packages on a baking sheet and bake 15 to 20 minutes until cooked through. Serve hot with rice.

180 Cambodian Spiced Fish in Coconut Cream

PREPARATION TIME 15 minutes, plus making the rice   **COOKING TIME** 15 minutes   **SERVES** 4

2 tbsp. finely chopped
  lemongrass
1 tbsp. peeled and finely chopped
  galangal or gingerroot
3 red chilies, coarsely chopped
4 garlic cloves, coarsely chopped
4 thick cod fillets, about 7oz. each,
  skinned and cut into large
  bite-size pieces

5 tbsp. sunflower oil
scant 1 cup coconut cream
1 tbsp. fish sauce
2 tbsp. chopped skinless roasted
  peanuts
1 small handful Thai basil leaves
rice, to serve

1   Put the lemongrass, galangal, chilies, garlic, and scant 1 cup water in a small food processor and blend 1 to 2 minutes until the mixture forms a smooth paste, then set aside. Meanwhile, pat the fish dry with paper towels.

2   Heat the oil in a nonstick skillet over low heat. Add the fish and fry, turning once, 4 to 5 minutes until light brown and cooked through. Transfer the fish to a plate and cover to keep warm.

3   Drain all but 2 tablespoons of the oil from the pan and lower the heat to low. Add the spice paste and cook, stirring, 5 minutes until thick. Add the coconut cream and fish sauce and cook, stirring, over high heat 5 minutes. Return the fish to the pan, add the peanuts and basil, and gently toss well. Serve hot with rice.

181 Chermoula Spiced Fish

PREPARATION TIME 30 minutes, plus making the rice   **COOKING TIME** 20 minutes   **SERVES** 4

4 thick halibut or cod fillets,
  about 7oz. each, skinned
sunflower oil, for greasing
salt
1 recipe quantity Lebanese Herbed
  Rice with Chickpeas (see page 178),
  to serve
1 lemon, cut into wedges, to serve

CHERMOULA
1 large bunch cilantro, leaves picked
  and coarsely chopped
4 garlic cloves, finely chopped
1 tsp. ground cumin
1 tsp. ground paprika
1 tsp. cayenne pepper
6 tbsp. olive oil
3 tbsp. white wine vinegar

1   Arrange the fish in a single layer in a lightly greased baking dish and season with salt, then set aside.

2   Put all of the ingredients for the chermoula in a blender or food processor and blend 1 to 2 minutes until smooth. Spoon the marinade over the fish, coating the fillets evenly, and leave to marinate 15 to 20 minutes.

3   Preheat the oven to 375°F. Bake the fish 15 to 20 minutes until cooked through. Serve hot with rice and lemon wedges for squeezing over.

182 Broiled Galangal & Turmeric Cod

PREPARATION TIME 15 minutes, plus 30 minutes marinating and making the dipping sauce
COOKING TIME 12 minutes **SERVES** 4

1oz. galangal or ginger root,
   peeled and thinly sliced
4 tsp. Greek-style yogurt
1¼ tsp. turmeric
1½ tsp. palm sugar
1½ tsp. palm or rice vinegar
1 tsp. shrimp paste
1lb. 12oz. cod or halibut fillets,
   skinned and cut into
   3in. chunks
8oz. rice vermicelli
4 tsp. sunflower oil
salt

TO SERVE
½ iceberg lettuce, leaves separated
1 small handful Thai sweet
   basil leaves
⅓ cup whole skinless roasted peanuts
1 cup Nuoc Cham Dipping Sauce
   (see page 204)

1 Using a mortar and pestle, ground the galangal until mushy. Using your fingers, squeeze the pulverized galangal into a medium bowl to extract as much juice as you can from the pulp. You should end up with about 2 teaspoons.

2 Add the yogurt, turmeric, sugar, vinegar, and shrimp paste and season with salt. Add the cod and toss to evenly coat the fish. Set aside to marinate 30 minutes. Meanwhile, bring a large saucepan of water to a boil and boil the rice vermicelli 4 minutes or until cooked, then drain, rinse well, and transfer to a small bowl, then add the oil and toss well.

3 Preheat the broiler to high. Remove the cod pieces from the marinade and put them on the broiler pan. Broil 4 minutes on each side, or until just cooked through. Transfer the fish to a warm plate and serve hot in the small bowls, with the lettuce, basil, noodles, peanuts, and dipping sauce. Provide each guest with a small bowl and chopsticks and let them help themselves.

183 Hot & Sour Thai Fish Curry

PREPARATION TIME 15 minutes, plus making the rice **COOKING TIME** 25 minutes **SERVES** 4

2 garlic cloves
5 dried red chilies
1 tsp. salt
1 tsp. turmeric
2 tbsp. finely chopped lemongrass,
   plus 2 lemongrass stalks, lightly
   crushed with a rolling pin
2 to 3 tbsp. shrimp paste

1 tbsp. fish sauce
1 tsp. palm sugar
2 tbsp. freshly squeezed lemon juice
1 tbsp. tamarind paste
1 cup pineapple, cut into small
   bite-size pieces
4 salmon fillets, 7oz. each, skinned
jasmine rice, to serve

1 Put the garlic, chilies, salt, turmeric, chopped lemongrass, and shrimp paste in a blender or small food processor and blend 1 to 2 minutes until smooth, adding a little water if needed.

2 Transfer the paste to a large skillet and add the fish sauce, palm sugar, lemongrass stalks, and 1¾ cups water. Bring to a boil over high heat, then lower the heat to medium and simmer 8 to 10 minutes.

3 In a small bowl, mix together the lemon juice, tamarind paste, scant 1 cup water and add it, along with the pineapple, to the pan. Mix well, then add the salmon fillets and cook slowly 8 to 10 minutes until cooked through. Remove from the heat and serve hot with rice.

184 Island Monkfish Curry

PREPARATION TIME 15 minutes, plus making the curry powder and rice
COOKING TIME 25 minutes   SERVES 4

2 tbsp. sunflower oil
2 onions, finely chopped
2 tbsp. Curry Powder (see page 11)
1 tsp. turmeric
1lb. 12oz. monkfish tail fillets,
   skinned and cut into large
   bite-size pieces
2 garlic cloves, chopped

1 tsp. peeled and finely grated
   gingerroot
1 star anise
1 tbsp. thyme leaves
½ tsp. tamarind paste
2 cups fish stock
1 recipe quantity Saffron Rice
   (see page 180), to serve

1 Heat the oil in a heavy-bottomed pan over low heat. Add the onion and fry
8 to 10 minutes until light golden. Stir in the curry powder and turmeric and
fry 1 minute longer, or until fragrant, then add all of the remaining ingredients.

2 Simmer over low heat, stirring occasionally, 10 to 12 minutes until the fish
is cooked through. Serve hot with rice.

185 Kochi Fish Curry

PREPARATION TIME 20 minutes, plus making the rice   COOKING TIME 25 minutes   SERVES 4

2 tbsp. freshly grated or
   shredded coconut
1 tsp. turmeric
1 tbsp. cayenne pepper
4 tbsp. sunflower oil
1 tsp. mustard seeds
20 curry leaves
2 onions, thinly sliced
4 green chilies, seeded and sliced
1in. piece gingerroot, peeled and
   cut into matchsticks

6 garlic cloves, finely chopped
1lb. 12oz. pomfret or halibut
   fillets, skinned and cut into
   large pieces
1¾ cups coconut milk
1 tbsp. tamarind paste
salt
1 recipe quantity Mushroom Pulao
   (see page 183), to serve

1 If using shredded coconut, soak it in warm water for 20 minutes, then drain.

2 In a small bowl, mix together the turmeric, cayenne, and coconut.

3 Heat the oil in a large saucepan over low heat. Add the mustard seeds and curry
leaves and when they begin to pop after 30 to 40 seconds, add the onions,
chilies, ginger, and garlic. Fry, stirring occasionally, 5 minutes, or until the onions
are golden. Stir in the turmeric mixture and cook 1 to 2 minutes.

4 Add the fish, then stir in the coconut milk and 1¼ cups water. Stir in the tamarind
paste and cook, stirring occasionally, 15 minutes, or until the fish is cooked
through. Season with salt and serve hot with rice.

186 Madras Fish Curry

PREPARATION TIME 15 minutes, plus making the curry powder and idlis
COOKING TIME 18 minutes   SERVES 4

1 tbsp. sunflower oil
2 tbsp. Madras Curry Powder
   (see page 12)
4 large mackerel, dressed, each
   cut crosswise into 4 or 5 pieces
1 red onion, chopped

1 handful cilantro leaves, chopped
finely grated zest and juice of 2 limes
1¾ cups coconut milk
1 recipe quantity Idlis (see page 179),
   to serve

1 Heat the oil in a large skillet over low heat. Add the curry powder and stir-fry
1 to 2 minutes until fragrant. Add the fish, onion, and cilantro and stir to coat.

2 Add the lime zest and juice and coconut milk and cook 15 minutes, or until the
fish is cooked through. Serve hot with idlis.

187 Vietnamese Crab Cakes

PREPARATION TIME 10 minutes, plus 1 hour chilling   **COOKING TIME** 6 minutes   **SERVES** 4

1lb. 5oz. mixed white and brown
   crabmeat
2½ cups fresh breadcrumbs
2 Thai or small shallots, finely
   chopped
1 garlic clove, chopped
1 red chili, finely chopped
2 tbsp. chopped cilantro leaves

1 tbsp. fish sauce
1 small egg, beaten
scant 1 cup canola oil, for frying
freshly ground black pepper
sweet chili sauce, to serve
Chinese chive flowers or chopped
   chives, to serve

1   Put the crabmeat, breadcrumbs, shallots, garlic, chili, cilantro, fish sauce, and egg
in a bowl. Season with pepper and mix well, using your hands. Divide the mixture
into 12 equal portions and shape into patties. Put them on a plate, cover with
plastic wrap, and leave to chill in the refrigerator for 1 hour, or until they are firm.

2   Heat the oil in a large skillet over medium-high heat. Add the crab cakes
and cook without moving them 2 to 3 minutes until brown and crunchy
underneath. Carefully turn them over and cook on the other side 2 to 3 minutes
longer until brown and crunchy. Drain on paper towels. Work in batches, to avoid
overcrowding the pan, and add more oil to the pan before each batch, if
necessary. Serve hot with sweet chili sauce and chive flowers alongside.

188 Indonesian Fish Skewers with Rice Noodles

PREPARATION TIME 20 minutes, plus making the curry paste
COOKING TIME 10 minutes SERVES 4

4 trout fillets, about 7oz. each,
  skinned and trimmed
½ tsp. turmeric
1 tbsp. Mild Curry Paste
  (see page 11)
juice of 2 lemons
2 tbsp. canola oil, plus extra
  for greasing
7oz. thin rice noodles

1 red chili, seeded and
  thinly sliced
6 scallions, finely shredded
4 tbsp. coarsely chopped mint leaves,
  plus extra, to garnish
4 tbsp. coarsely chopped
  cilantro leaves
3 tbsp. coarsely chopped
  chili-roasted peanuts
salt and freshly ground black pepper

1 If using wooden skewers, soak four of them in cold water at least 30 minutes to prevent scorching. Meanwhile, put the fish in a large bowl. In another bowl, mix together the turmeric, curry paste, lemon juice, and 1 tablespoon of the canola oil and pour it over the fish. Season with salt and pepper and toss well, then set aside.

2 Put the rice noodles in a heatproof bowl and cover with boiling water. Leave to soak 4 minutes, then drain. Rinse under cold water, drain, and set aside.

3 Preheat the broiler to medium-high and grease the broiler rack with oil. Thread the skewers through each fillet and broil 5 to 6 minutes, turning once, until just cooked through. Meanwhile, heat the remaining oil in a large skillet over high heat. Add the chili, scallions, and noodles and stir-fry 2 to 3 minutes, then remove from the heat and stir in the mint and cilantro. Season with salt and pepper and divide onto four plates. Top each portion of noodles with 1 fish skewer and scatter the peanuts over. Serve hot sprinkled with extra mint.

189 Fish Mollee

PREPARATION TIME 15 minutes, plus making the rice COOKING TIME 35 minutes SERVES 4

1 onion, coarsely grated
4 garlic cloves, crushed
2 green chilies, seeded and
  finely chopped
1 tbsp. ground cumin
1 tsp. turmeric
1 tsp. ground coriander
⅔ cup finely chopped cilantro leaves
2 tbsp. sunflower oil

26 curry leaves
1¾ cups coconut milk
4 thick halibut fillets, about 8oz.
  each, skinned
scant 1 cup canola oil
salt and freshly ground black pepper
1 recipe quantity Lemon Rice
  (see page 182), to serve

1 Put the onion, garlic, chilies, cumin, turmeric, coriander, cilantro leaves, and scant 1 cup water in a food processor and blend 2 to 3 minutes until the mixture forms a smooth paste.

2 Heat the oil in a large, heavy-bottomed skillet over high heat. Add 6 of the curry leaves and stir-fry 20 to 30 seconds until fragrant. Add the spice paste and cook, stirring, over high heat 3 to 4 minutes until fragrant. Lower the heat to low, pour in the coconut milk, and simmer slowly, uncovered, 20 minutes, or until slightly thickened.

3 Add the fish to the pan in a single layer and bring the mixture back to a boil, then lower the heat again to low and simmer 5 to 6 minutes until the fish is just cooked through. Season with salt and pepper and remove from the heat.

4 When the fish is almost finished cooking, put the canola oil in a saucepan over medium-high heat and heat it to 350°F, or until a small piece of bread dropped into the oil browns in 15 seconds. Carefully scatter the remaining curry leaves into the oil and deep-fry 30 seconds, or until crisp. Remove from the pan, using a slotted spoon, and drain on paper towels.

5 Sprinkle the curry with the deep-fried curry leaves and serve hot with rice.

190 Indonesian Yellow Fish Curry

PREPARATION TIME 15 minutes, plus making the rice   **COOKING TIME** 30 minutes
SERVES 4

3 garlic cloves, finely grated
2 green chilies, seeded and
  finely chopped
2 tsp. peeled and finely grated
  gingerroot
2 tbsp. sunflower oil
1 onion, finely chopped
1 tbsp. turmeric
scant 1 cup coconut milk

2 potatoes, peeled and
  cut into small bite-size pieces
1lb. 12oz. thick cod fillets, skinned
  and cut into large bite-size pieces
2 tomatoes, coarsely chopped
3 tbsp. chopped cilantro leaves
salt
1 recipe quantity
  Aromatic Sticky Rice
  (see page 178), to serve

1   Put the garlic, chilies, and ginger in a small food processor (or use a mortar
    and pestle) and grind until the mixture forms a smooth paste.
2   Heat the oil in a large, nonstick wok or saucepan over low heat. Add the
    garlic paste and fry, stirring, 2 to 3 minutes until fragrant, then add the onion
    and turmeric and fry, stirring, 2 to 3 minutes longer. Stir in the coconut milk
    and scant 1 cup water, then add the potatoes. Bring to a boil over high heat,
    then lower the heat to low and simmer, stirring occasionally, 10–12 minutes.
3   Season the fish with salt and add it and the tomatoes to the pan. Bring the
    mixture back to a boil, then lower the heat to low again and simmer
    6 to 8 minutes until the fish is cooked through. Remove from the heat,
    sprinkle with the cilantro, and serve hot with rice.

191 Kerala Fish Curry

PREPARATION TIME 15 minutes, plus making the rice   **COOKING TIME** 15 minutes   **SERVES** 4

1 tsp. tamarind paste
1 tsp. cayenne pepper
2 tsp. ground cumin
1 tsp. turmeric
2 tbsp. sunflower oil
3 garlic cloves, finely chopped
1lb. 12oz. thick white fish fillets, such
  as halibut or pomfret, skinned and
  cut into large bite-size pieces

1 tsp. peeled and finely grated
  gingerroot
1 red chili, thinly sliced
½ cup coconut cream
6 tbsp. finely chopped cilantro leaves
salt
basmati rice, to serve
poppadoms, to serve

1   Put the tamarind, cayenne, cumin, and turmeric in a small bowl. Add
    4 tablespoons water and mix well, then set aside.
2   Heat the oil in a large, nonstick wok or skillet over low heat. Add the garlic
    and cook, stirring, 2 to 3 minutes until light brown. Stir in the tamarind
    mixture and ⅔ cup water and cook 2 minutes.
3   Stir in the coconut cream, then add the fish. Cook, stirring continuously,
    6 to 8 minutes until the fish is just cooked through. Remove from the heat,
    season with salt, and stir in the cilantro. Serve hot with rice and poppadoms.

192 Burmese Steamed Fish Curry

PREPARATION TIME 25 minutes, plus making the curry powder and rice
COOKING TIME 25 minutes **SERVES** 4

8 white fish fillets, such as flounder
  or sole, about 3oz. each, skinned
4 tsp. salt
2 tsp. ground black pepper
2 tsp. turmeric
2 onions, 1 chopped and 1 sliced
4 garlic cloves, coarsely chopped
1 tsp. finely grated gingerroot

1 tsp. Curry Powder
  (see page 11)
1 tbsp. coconut cream
1 tbsp. ground rice
2 tsp. sesame oil
8 large cabbage leaves,
  thick central rib removed
rice, to serve

1 Sprinkle the fish fillets with half of the salt, pepper, and turmeric, then set aside.
2 Put the chopped onion, garlic, ginger, curry powder, and coconut cream
  in a blender and blend 1 to 2 minutes until smooth. Transfer the mixture
  to a large bowl and stir in the remaining salt, pepper, and turmeric, as well
  as the ground rice and sesame oil. Add the fish and mix well.
3 Put 1 cabbage leaf on a clean work surface and top with 1 fish fillet, followed
  by some of the spice mixture and sliced onion. Fold the edges of each cabbage
  leaf over each fillet to enclose, then wrap in foil to make a package.
4 Arrange the package in a steamer and steam over simmering water
  20 to 25 minutes, topping up the water with boiling water as needed. Serve
  with rice, letting everyone unwrap their packages themselves.

193 Thai Shrimp & Pineapple Curry

PREPARATION TIME 15 minutes, plus making the rice **COOKING TIME** 10 minutes **SERVES** 4

2 tbsp. finely chopped lemongrass
2 red chilies, thinly sliced
1 tbsp. peeled and finely grated
  gingerroot
½ onion, finely chopped
4 garlic cloves, crushed
1 tsp. turmeric
1 tsp. ground coriander
3 kaffir lime leaves, finely shredded
1 tbsp. palm sugar
1 tbsp. fish sauce

juice of 1 lime
1¾ cups coconut milk
24 raw jumbo shrimp, peeled
  and deveined
7oz. pineapple flesh, cut into
  bite-size cubes
3oz. cherry tomatoes
6 tbsp. coarsely chopped cilantro
  leaves
jasmine rice, to serve

1 Put the lemongrass, chilies, ginger, onion, garlic, turmeric, coriander, lime leaves,
  palm sugar, fish sauce, lime juice, and coconut milk in a food processor. Blend
  1 to 2 minutes until the mixture forms a smooth paste.
2 Transfer the mixture to a large wok or skillet and bring to a boil over high heat.
  Lower the heat to medium and stir in the shrimp, pineapple, and tomatoes.
  Simmer slowly 6 to 8 minutes until the shrimp turn pink and are cooked through.
  Remove from the heat, stir in the cilantro leaves, and serve hot with rice.

Crayfish & Coconut Curry

PREPARATION TIME 10 minutes, plus making the curry powder   **COOKING TIME** 18 minutes
SERVES 4

2 tbsp. sunflower oil
1 onion, finely chopped
2 garlic cloves, crushed
1 Scotch bonnet or habanero chili,
   seeded and finely chopped
1 tbsp. thyme leaves
1 tbsp. mild Curry Powder
   (see page 11)

1 red bell pepper, seeded and cut
   into small bite-size pieces
6 scallions, thinly sliced
7oz. canned crushed tomatoes
1¾ cups coconut milk
1lb. 12oz. cooked fresh crayfish meat
salt and freshly ground black pepper
sliced coconut, to serve

1   Heat the oil in a large, heavy-bottomed skillet over low heat. Add the onion,
    garlic, chili, and thyme and fry, stirring occasionally, 5 minutes, or until the
    onion is soft. Stir in the curry powder and cook 1 minute, or until fragrant.
2   Add the red pepper, scallions, and tomatoes and cook, stirring, 1 minute longer,
    or until combined, then add the coconut milk and bring to a boil. Lower the heat
    to medium-low and simmer 5 minutes.
3   Add the crayfish and cook 4 to 5 minutes until heated through. Season to taste
    with salt and pepper and serve hot with coconut.

195 Vietnamese Shrimp Noodles

PREPARATION TIME 20 minutes **COOKING TIME** 2 minutes **SERVES** 4

⅓ cup sugar
7 tbsp. fish sauce
juice of 4 limes
3 red chilies, thinly sliced
4 garlic cloves, finely chopped
1 tbsp. peeled and finely grated
   gingerroot
9oz. glass noodles

1¼ cups chili-roasted peanuts,
   coarsely chopped
1lb. 5oz. shelled and deveined
   cooked jumbo shrimp, with tails
   left intact
1 small cucumber, finely chopped
1 small bunch cilantro leaves,
   coarsely chopped

1 Put the sugar, fish sauce, lime juice, chilies, garlic, and ginger in a small bowl
   and mix together until the sugar dissolves.
2 Put the noodles in a bowl, cover with boiling water, and leave to soak 5 minutes,
   or until soft. Drain well in a colander, then rinse under cold running water and
   drain again.
3 Transfer the noodles to a large serving bowl. Toss in the fish sauce mixture
   and most of the peanuts, reserving a few for later. Stir in the shrimp, cucumber,
   and cilantro and toss again, then sprinkle the remaining peanuts over and serve.

196 Tobago Jerk Mussel Curry

PREPARATION TIME 15 minutes, plus making the curry powder and rice
COOKING TIME 12 minutes   SERVES 4

1lb. 12oz. fresh mussels, well
   scrubbed and beards removed
6 scallions, coarsely chopped
2 garlic cloves, crushed
1 Scotch bonnet or habanero chili,
   chopped
1 tbsp. thyme leaves

1 tbsp. Curry Powder (see page 11)
finely grated zest and juice of 1 lime
4 tbsp. sunflower oil
7oz. canned crushed tomatoes
rice, to serve
1 lemon, cut into wedges, to serve

1 Sort through the mussels, discarding any that have cracked or broken shells.
   Tap each mussel lightly on a work surface and discard any that do not close
   (this means they are already dead and should not be eaten).
2 Put the scallions, garlic, chili, thyme, curry powder, lime zest and juice, and oil
   in a food processor. Blend 1 to 2 minutes until the mixture forms a coarse paste.
   If the mixture is too dry, add a little more oil.
3 Heat a large wok or saucepan over medium-high heat until smoking hot. Add the
   paste and stir-fry 1 to 2 minutes until fragrant. Add the mussels and tomatoes,
   then cover the wok with a lid and cook 8 to 10 minutes until the mussels have
   opened. Discard any mussels that remain closed. Serve hot with rice and lemon
   wedges for squeezing over.

197 Spiced Mussels

PREPARATION TIME 15 minutes, plus making the curry powder and salad
COOKING TIME 18 minutes   SERVES 4

1lb. 12oz. fresh mussels, well
   scrubbed and beards removed
4 tbsp. sunflower oil
2 shallots, very finely chopped
1 red chili, slit lengthwise and seeded
1¼in. piece gingerroot, peeled and
   cut into thin shreds
2 garlic cloves, cut into thin shreds
2 plum tomatoes, finely chopped

1 tbsp. Curry Powder (see page 11)
scant 1 cup coconut milk
1 large handful cilantro leaves,
   chopped
3 tbsp. grated fresh coconut
   (optional)
mixed salad leaves or steamed
   vegetables, to serve

1 Sort through the mussels, discarding any that have cracked or broken shells.
   Tap each mussel lightly on a work surface and discard any that do not close
   (this means they are already dead and should not be eaten).
2 Heat the oil in a large wok with a lid or saucepan over low heat. Add the shallots,
   chili, ginger, and garlic and cook, stirring occasionally, 3 to 4 minutes. Stir in the
   tomatoes, curry powder, and coconut milk and cook over high heat, stirring
   occasionally, 4 to 5 minutes until well mixed and slightly thickened.
3 Stir in the mussels, then cover the wok or pan tightly and continue cooking over
   high heat 6 to 8 minutes until the mussels open. Discard any that remain closed.
   Stir in the cilantro and sprinkle the grated coconut over, if using. Serve
   immediately with salad.

198 Sri Lankan Cilantro Shrimp

PREPARATION TIME 15 minutes, plus making the curry powder and rice
COOKING TIME 6 minutes **SERVES** 4

1lb. 12oz. raw shrimp, peeled and
deveined
1 tbsp. Sri Lankan Curry Powder
(see page 12)
1 tsp. shrimp paste
4 garlic cloves, crushed
2 shallots, grated

½ cup finely chopped cilantro leaves
3 egg whites, lightly beaten
4 tbsp. rice flour
5 tbsp. sunflower oil
salt and freshly ground black pepper
rice, to serve

1   Using a sharp knife, slit the shrimp lengthwise along the back, then put them
in a bowl. In a separate bowl, mix together the curry powder, shrimp paste, garlic,
shallots, cilantro, egg whites, and flour. Season well with salt and pepper, then stir
this mixture into the shrimp and mix to coat well.
2   Heat half of the oil in a large, nonstick skillet over medium-high heat. Fry
half the shrimp 2 to 3 minutes, turning once, until pink and cooked through,
then drain on paper towels. Repeat with the remaining oil and shrimp. Serve
hot with rice.

199 Sri Lankan Crab Curry

PREPARATION TIME 15 minutes, plus making the curry powder   **COOKING TIME** 35 minutes
SERVES 4

1 tbsp. sunflower oil
1 large onion, finely chopped
3 garlic cloves, finely chopped
1 tsp. peeled and finely grated
gingerroot
1 red chili, finely chopped
10 curry leaves
1 tbsp. Sri Lankan Curry Powder
(see page 12)

2 tsp. cinnamon
1 tsp. turmeric
1¾ cups coconut milk
scant 1 cup chicken or fish stock
2 small to medium cooked crabs
juice of 1 lemon
salt and freshly ground black pepper

1   Heat the oil in a large, nonstick wok or saucepan over medium-high heat. Add
the onion, garlic, ginger, and chili and stir-fry 1 to 2 minutes, then add the curry
leaves, curry powder, cinnamon, and turmeric. Stir-fry 2 to 3 longer minutes
until fragrant.
2   Add the coconut milk and stock and bring to a boil. Lower the heat to low and
simmer, stirring occasionally, 10 to 15 minutes.
3   Meanwhile, lift off the back shell of each crab and remove and discard the gills,
liver, and brain matter. Rinse the crabs well, separate the claws from the bodies
and cut each body in half. Add the crab pieces to the wok and simmer, covered,
10 to 15 minutes. Remove from the heat and stir in the lemon juice. Season well
with salt and pepper and serve hot.

200 Masala Crab Cakes

PREPARATION TIME 20 minutes, plus making the masala paste and at least 5 hours chilling
COOKING TIME 25 minutes   **SERVES** 4

14oz. fresh white crabmeat
14oz. white fish fillet, such
  as cod or halibut, skinned and
  coarsely chopped
2 tbsp. Red Masala Paste
  (see page 14)
2 garlic cloves, minced
1 red chili, seeded and finely chopped

4 tbsp. finely chopped red onion
4 tbsp. chopped cilantro leaves,
  plus extra to serve
1 egg, beaten
2½ cups fresh breadcrumbs
sunflower oil, for brushing
salt and freshly ground black pepper
1 lemon, cut into wedges, to serve

1 Put the crabmeat, fish, red masala paste, garlic, chili, onion, cilantro, egg, and
breadcrumbs in a food processor. Season well with salt and pepper and blend
2 to 3 minutes until well mixed. Transfer to a bowl and mix well, using your
hands. Cover and leave to chill 5 to 6 hours, or overnight, if possible, to let
the mixture firm up and the flavors combine.

2 Preheat the oven to 400°F. Line a baking sheet with parchment paper and brush
it lightly with oil. Divide the crab mixture into 12 equal portions and shape each
one into a round cake.

3 Arrange the crab cakes on the baking sheet, brush with a little oil, and bake
20 to 25 minutes until light brown and cooked through. Serve hot with lemon
wedges for squeezing over.

201 Scallop & Spinach Curry

PREPARATION TIME 10 minutes, plus making the curry powder, rice, and salad
COOKING TIME 13 minutes   **SERVES** 4

2 tbsp. canola oil
2 tsp. black mustard seeds
4 garlic cloves, minced
1 tsp. peeled and finely grated
  gingerroot
1 tbsp. Curry Powder (see page 11)
15oz. canned crushed tomatoes
¼ tsp. sugar

7oz. baby spinach leaves,
  coarsely chopped
1lb. 12oz. scallops with or without
  roe attached
4 tbsp. heavy cream
salt and freshly ground black pepper
basmati rice, to serve
mixed salad leaves, to serve

1 Heat the oil in a large skillet over high heat. Add the mustard seeds and, as soon
as they start to pop after a few seconds, add the garlic, ginger, curry powder,
tomatoes, sugar, and scant 1 cup water and bring to a boil. Lower the heat
to medium and cook, covered, 3 to 4 minutes, stirring frequently, then uncover
and increase the heat to high.

2 Add the spinach and cook, stirring frequently, 3 to 4 minutes until it wilts. Add
the scallops and cook 3 to 4 minutes longer until they are just cooked through.
Remove from the heat and stir in the cream. Season well with salt and pepper
and serve hot with rice and salad.

202 Spiced Scallop Curry

PREPARATION TIME 10 minutes, plus making the masala paste and rice
COOKING TIME 20 minutes **SERVES** 4

3 tbsp. sunflower oil
¼ tsp. turmeric
1 tsp. cumin seeds
2 small red chilies, seeded
  and chopped
1 onion, finely chopped
6 tomatoes, diced
3 tbsp. Red Masala Paste (see page 14)

1 tsp. ground cumin
1lb. 12oz. scallops, with or without
  roe attached
½ cup finely chopped cilantro leaves
salt and freshly ground black pepper
rice, to serve
1 lemon, cut into wedges, to serve

1   Heat the oil in a skillet over low heat. Add the turmeric, cumin seeds, and chilies and cook, stirring, 30 seconds until fragrant. Add the onion and cook, stirring occasionally, 10 minutes until soft but not colored.
2   Stir in the tomatoes and masala paste and simmer 5 minutes, or until the tomatoes have cooked down to a thick sauce. Stir in the cumin and season with salt and pepper.
3   Add the scallops and cook 2 to 3 minutes until the scallops are just cooked through. Check the seasoning and adjust as needed. Stir in the cilantro and serve hot with lemon wedges for squeezing over.

203 Shrimp in Caramel Sauce

PREPARATION TIME 15 minutes, plus making the sauce and rice **COOKING TIME** 10 minutes
SERVES 4

1lb. 12oz. raw jumbo shrimp,
  shelled and deveined
1 tsp. salt
½ tbsp. fish sauce
2 tbsp. Nuoc Mau (Vietnamese
  Caramel Sauce; see page 207)

1 onion, thinly sliced
½ tsp. freshly ground black pepper
4½ tsp. sunflower oil
1 scallion, green part only,
  thinly sliced
rice, to serve

1 Put the shrimp, salt, fish sauce, and nuoc mau in a shallow saucepan and bring
to a boil over high heat. Stir in the onion and pepper and continue cooking
over high heat 8 to 10 minutes, stirring occasionally, to coat the shrimp well
in the sauce. They will curl up and release their juices to combine with the other
ingredients and concentrate into a dark sauce. Add a little water if the sauce
becomes too dry.

2 Remove from the heat and stir in the oil to coat the shrimp. Sprinkle the scallion
on top and serve hot with rice.

204 South Indian Shrimp & Mango Curry

PREPARATION TIME 20 minutes, plus making the rice and salad **COOKING TIME** 25 minutes
SERVES 4

4 garlic cloves, finely chopped
2 tbsp. ground coriander
1 tbsp. paprika
1 tbsp. jaggery or palm sugar
2 tsp. peeled and finely grated
  gingerroot
2 tsp. ground cumin
1 tsp. cayenne pepper
½ tsp. turmeric

1 mango, peeled, pitted, and sliced
1¾ cups coconut milk
1 tbsp. tamarind paste
2 tsp. salt
2lb. 4oz. large unshelled raw shrimp,
  with heads and tails left intact
chopped cilantro leaves, to garnish
rice, to serve
cucumber and tomato salad, to serve

1 Put the garlic, coriander, paprika, jaggery, ginger, cumin, cayenne, and turmeric
in a wok or saucepan and mix well. Stir in 1¾ cups water and then bring the
mixture to a boil over high heat. Lower the heat to low and simmer, covered,
8 to 10 minutes, stirring occasionally.

2 Stir in the mango, coconut milk, tamarind paste, and salt. Bring to a simmer, then
add the shrimp. Cover, lower the heat to low, and cook 10 to 12 minutes until
the shrimp turn pink and are cooked through. Sprinkle with cilantro leaves and
serve hot with rice and salad.

205 Pepper Shrimp, Chettinad Style

PREPARATION TIME 15 minutes, plus making the rice   **COOKING TIME** 12 minutes   **SERVES** 4

2 tbsp. sunflower oil
3 dried red chilies, roughly crushed
1 tsp. crushed black peppercorns
1 tsp. crushed fennel seeds
  or star anise
10 small shallots, finely chopped
4 garlic cloves, finely chopped

2 tbsp. tomato paste
1lb. 12oz. raw jumbo shrimp,
  shelled and deveined
2 tbsp. green peppercorns
  (in brine), drained
salt
basmati rice, to serve

1   Heat the oil in a large pan over low heat. Add the chilies, black peppercorns, and
    fennel and cook, stirring, 1 to 2 minutes. Increase the heat to high and add the
    shallots, garlic, and tomato paste. Season with salt and mix well, then cook for
    2 to 3 minutes.
2   Add the shrimp and cook, stirring, 1 to 2 minutes until well coated. Stir in ⅓ cup
    plus 1 tablespoon water and cook 3 to 4 minutes longer until the shrimp are pink
    and are cooked through. Remove from the heat, stir in the green peppercorns,
    and serve hot with rice.

206 Pickled Shrimp Curry

PREPARATION TIME 20 minutes, plus making the rice   **COOKING TIME** 40 minutes   **SERVES** 4

4 tbsp. sunflower oil
8 shallots, finely chopped
6 to 8 curry leaves
1 tbsp. finely grated garlic
1 tbsp. peeled and finely grated
  gingerroot
3 red chilies, halved
  lengthwise
1 tbsp. ground coriander
2 tsp. cumin seeds

2 tsp. black mustard seeds
2 tsp. nigella seeds
2 tsp. fennel seeds
15oz. canned crushed tomatoes
1lb. 12oz. small raw shrimp,
  peeled and deveined
6 tbsp. finely chopped cilantro leaves
salt and freshly ground black pepper
basmati rice, to serve

1   Heat the oil in a large, nonstick wok or skillet over low heat. Add the shallots
    and cook, stirring occasionally, 10 minutes until light golden. Add the curry
    leaves, garlic, ginger, and chilies and stir 1 minute longer.
2   Add the coriander and the cumin, mustard, nigella, and fennel seeds. Season
    with salt and pepper and cook, stirring, 1 to 2 minutes until fragrant.
3   Stir in the tomatoes. Bring to a boil, lower the heat to low, and simmer, stirring
    occasionally, 20 to 25 minutes until thick. Add the shrimp and cook over high
    heat 3 to 4 minutes until the shrimp turn pink and are cooked through.
    Remove from the heat, stir in the cilantro leaves, and serve hot with rice.

207 Caribbean Curried Lobster

PREPARATION TIME 10 minutes, plus making the curry powder and rice
COOKING TIME 20 minutes   **SERVES** 4

2 tbsp. butter
1 onion, finely chopped
2 garlic cloves, finely chopped
2 tbsp. Curry Powder (see page 11)
2 scallions, thinly sliced

2 large tomatoes, finely chopped
1lb. 12oz. cooked fresh lobster meat,
  coarsely chopped
2 tsp. cornstarch
rice, to serve

1   Melt the butter in a large skillet over low heat. Add the onion, garlic, curry
    powder, scallions, and tomatoes and fry, stirring occasionally, 6 to 8 minutes.
    Add the lobster and stir-fry 6 to 8 minutes until pink and opaque.
2   Mix the cornstarch with scant 1 cup cold water and add it to the pan. Mix well,
    then cook 5 to 6 minutes until thick. Serve hot with rice.

208 Masala Fennel Shrimp

PREPARATION TIME 15 minutes, plus making the curry powder and rice
COOKING TIME 20 minutes **SERVES** 4

1 tbsp. sunflower oil
10 to 12 curry leaves
2 large shallots, halved and
   thinly sliced
2 tsp. finely grated garlic
1 tsp. peeled and finely grated
   gingerroot
1 tbsp. fennel seeds

1 tbsp. Curry Powder (see page 11)
5 large tomatoes, seeded
   and chopped
1lb. 12oz. raw jumbo shrimp,
   shelled and deveined, with tails
   left intact
salt
rice, to serve

1   Heat the oil in a large wok or nonstick skillet over low heat. Add the curry leaves and cook, stirring, 30 seconds, then add the shallots and continue stirring for 4 to 5 minutes longer until light brown.
2   Add the garlic, ginger, and fennel seeds, lower the heat to low, and cook slowly, stirring, 2 to 3 minutes. Stir in the curry powder, then add the tomatoes (including any juices). Increase the heat to high and stir-fry 3 to 4 minutes.
3   Add the shrimp and continue stir-frying 6 to 7 minutes until the shrimp turn pink and are just cooked through. Remove from the heat, season lightly with salt, and serve hot with rice.

209 Malaysian Scallop Curry

PREPARATION TIME 15 minutes, plus making the rice   **COOKING TIME** 25 minutes   **SERVES** 4

1 tbsp. cayenne pepper
1 tsp. ground coriander
2 tsp. ground cumin
2 garlic cloves, crushed
8 Thai or small shallots, finely
   chopped
6 tbsp. finely chopped lemongrass
1 tsp. peeled and finely grated
   galangal or gingerroot
1 tbsp. grated palm sugar
½ tsp. shrimp paste
2 tbsp. finely chopped skinless
   raw peanuts

2½ cups plus 2 tbsp. coconut milk
7oz. sugar snap peas, trimmed
1lb. 12oz. scallops, with or without
   roe attached

TO SERVE
Thai basil leaves
chopped skinless roasted peanuts
thinly sliced red chilies
jasmine rice

1   Put the cayenne, coriander, cumin, garlic, shallots, lemongrass, galangal, palm sugar, shrimp paste, and raw peanuts in a blender or food processor. Add the coconut milk and blend 2 to 3 minutes until fairly smooth.
2   Transfer the mixture to a large wok and bring it to a boil over high heat. Lower the heat to low and simmer, uncovered, 12 to 15 minutes, stirring occasionally, until thick.
3   Add the peas and scallops and bring back to a boil. Lower the heat to low and simmer 6 to 8 minutes until the scallops are cooked through. Remove from the heat, sprinkle with basil leaves, roasted peanuts, and red chilies and serve hot with rice.

210   Thai Braised Mussels

PREPARATION TIME 15 minutes, plus making the curry paste and rice
COOKING TIME 10 minutes   **SERVES** 4

3lb. 5oz. fresh mussels, well scrubbed
    and beards removed
1 tbsp. sunflower oil
6 garlic cloves, coarsely chopped
1 tbsp. peeled and finely chopped
    gingerroot
1 tsp. Thai Green Curry Paste
    (see page 15)
3 to 4 large red chilies, split in half
    lengthwise
6 scallions, finely chopped

1¾ cups coconut milk
2 lemongrass stalks, halved
    lengthwise
3 tbsp. light soy sauce
finely grated zest and juice of 2 limes
1 tsp. sugar
1 large handful cilantro leaves,
    chopped
salt and freshly ground black pepper
jasmine rice, to serve

1.   Sort through the mussels, discarding any that have cracked or broken shells. Tap each mussel lightly on a work surface and discard any that do not close (this means they are already dead and should not be eaten).
2.   Heat the wok over high heat and add the oil. When it is hot, add the garlic, ginger, curry paste, chilies, and scallions and stir-fry 30 seconds.
3.   Stir in the coconut milk, lemongrass, soy sauce, lime zest and juice, and sugar. Bring to a boil, then add the mussels. Bring back to a boil, cover with a lid, and continue boiling 5 to 6 minutes until all the mussels open. Discard any that remain closed. Remove from the heat, and stir in the cilantro. Season with salt and pepper and serve hot with rice.

211   Malabari Shrimp

PREPARATION TIME 15 minutes, plus making the curry powder, bread, and chutney
COOKING TIME 8 minutes   **SERVES** 4

1 tbsp. Curry Powder (see page 11)
1 tsp. tamarind paste
1 tsp. cayenne pepper
2 tsp. ground cumin
1 tsp. turmeric
2 tbsp. sunflower oil
3 garlic cloves, finely chopped
1lb. 12oz. large raw jumbo shrimp,
    shelled and deveined, with tails
    left intact

1 tsp. peeled and finely grated
    gingerroot
1 red chili, thinly sliced
½ cup coconut milk
6 tbsp. finely chopped cilantro leaves
salt
1 recipe quantity Naan
    (see page 190), to serve
1 recipe quantity Sweet Mango
    Chutney (see page 213), to serve

1.   Put the curry powder, tamarind paste, cayenne, cumin, and turmeric in a small bowl. Add 4 tablespoons water and mix well. Set aside.
2.   Heat the oil in a large, nonstick wok or skillet over low heat. Add the garlic and shrimp and cook, stirring, 2 to 3 minutes until well coated.
3.   Stir in the ginger, chili, and tamarind mixture, and then stir in 7 tablespoons water. Simmer 2 minutes, then add the coconut milk. Simmer slowly 2 to 3 minutes, stirring continuously, until the shrimp turn pink and are just cooked through. Remove from the heat, season with salt, and stir in the cilantro. Serve hot with bread and chutney.

212 Spiced Shrimp

PREPARATION TIME 10 minutes, plus 30 minutes marinating and making the rice
COOKING TIME 20 minutes   **SERVES** 4

1lb. 12oz. raw jumbo shrimp,
  shelled and deveined,
  with tails left intact
juice of 1 lime
1 tsp. salt
1 tbsp. sunflower oil
1 onion, finely chopped
¾in. piece gingerroot, peeled and
  finely chopped

3 garlic cloves, finely chopped
2 tsp. cayenne pepper
2 tsp. paprika
4 tsp. tomato paste
1 tsp. sugar
3 to 4 tbsp. chopped cilantro leaves,
  to serve
basmati rice, to serve

1 Put the shrimp in a bowl and sprinkle the lime juice and salt over. Leave
   to marinate in the refrigerator 30 minutes, then drain, reserving the juices.
2 Heat the oil in a large skillet over low heat. Add the onion, ginger, and garlic
   and cook, stirring occasionally, 10 to 12 minutes until very soft, then add the
   cayenne pepper and paprika and cook, stirring, 30 seconds.
3 Add the shrimp and reserved juice and stir-fry over high heat 3 to 4 minutes
   until the shrimp start to turn pink. Add the tomato paste and sugar and stir-fry
   2 minutes. Sprinkle with cilantro leaves and serve hot with rice.

213 Japanese Seafood Curry

PREPARATION TIME 15 minute, plus making the curry sauce and rice
COOKING TIME 30 minutes   **SERVES** 4

2 tbsp. sunflower oil
1 garlic clove, finely chopped
1 tsp. peeled and finely grated
  gingerroot
1 onion, finely chopped
1¼ cups Japanese Curry Sauce
  (see page 12)

1 medium squid, dressed,
  cut into thick slices
8 raw jumbo shrimp, shelled
  and deveined
8 scallops, with or without roe
  attached
Japanese rice, to serve

1 Heat the oil in a nonstick saucepan over low heat. Add the garlic, ginger,
   and onion and cook, stirring occasionally, 8 to 10 minutes until soft and
   translucent. Add the curry sauce and 1¼ cups water and bring to a boil
   over high heat.
2 Lower the heat to medium and simmer 15 minutes, or until thick. Mix in
   the squid, shrimp, and scallops and simmer 5 minutes longer, or until
   cooked through. Serve hot with rice.

214 Cochin Crab Curry

PREPARATION TIME 15 minutes, plus making the rice   **COOKING TIME** 40 minutes   **SERVES** 4

2 cooked fresh crabs
3 onions, finely chopped
6 garlic cloves, finely chopped
1 tbsp. peeled and finely grated
  gingerroot
½ tsp. fenugreek seeds
10 curry leaves

1 cinnamon stick
2 tsp. cayenne pepper
1 tsp. turmeric
1¾ cups coconut milk
salt and freshly ground black pepper
basmati rice, to serve

1 Divide each crab into 4 portions, breaking each body in half and separating the
   large claws from the body. Leave the legs attached.
2 Put all of the remaining ingredients in a large saucepan. Season with salt and
   pepper, then simmer, covered, over a medium-low heat 30 minutes.
3 Add the crabs and cook 10 minutes until heated through. Serve hot with rice.

215 Chili-Seared Squid

PREPARATION TIME 30 minutes **COOKING TIME** 10 minutes **SERVES** 4

1 garlic clove, finely chopped
1 red chili, seeded and thinly
    sliced plus extra to serve
2 tsp. salt
1 tsp. peeled and finely grated
    gingerroot
1 tsp. ground coriander
1 tsp. ground cumin
1 tsp. cayenne pepper

1 tsp. tomato paste
juice of 2 lemons
1lb. 12oz. fresh squid, cleaned
4 tbsp. canola oil
1 small red onion, very thinly sliced
1 large handful cilantro leaves,
    chopped
1 small handful mint leaves,
    chopped

1   In a small bowl, mix together the garlic, red chili, salt, ginger, coriander,
    cumin, cayenne, tomato paste, and lemon juice. Put the squid in another
    bowl and pour over the spice mixture, then toss to coat evenly. Cover and
    leave to stand at room temperature 12 to 15 minutes.

2   Cut a series of shallow, diagonal lines over the surface of the squid, using
    a sharp knife, then cut it into bite-size rings or pieces. Heat the oil in a large
    skillet over very high heat. Working in batches, lift the squid from the
    marinade and cook it 1 to 2 minutes, turning once, until it turns opaque,
    then transfer to a serving bowl and cover to keep warm while you cook
    the remaining squid.

3   Stir the onion and cilantro and mint leaves into the squid, toss to mix well,
    and serve hot with extra chili.

216 Chili, Ginger & Soy Seared Scallops

PREPARATION TIME 10 minutes, plus making the rice   **COOKING TIME** 5 minutes   **SERVES** 4

24 scallops, with or without
  roe attached
4 tbsp. canola oil
4 tbsp. light soy sauce
4 tbsp. Chinese cooking wine
  (Shaoxing wine) or dry sherry

2 red chilies, thinly sliced
3in. piece gingerroot, peeled
  and finely grated
6 scallions, thinly sliced
salt and freshly ground black pepper
rice, to serve

1 Put the scallops on a plate and season lightly with salt and pepper.
2 Heat the oil in a large, heavy-bottomed skillet over high heat. When the oil
  is very hot, add the scallops, arranging them in a circle around the pan. Cook
  1 to 2 minutes on each side, then remove from the pan and arrange on a plate.
3 Mix together the soy sauce and wine and sprinkle it over the scallops. Scatter
  a little chili, ginger, and scallion over each one and serve hot with rice.

217 Burmese Dry Shrimp Curry

PREPARATION TIME 10 minutes, plus making the curry paste and rice
COOKING TIME 8 minutes   **SERVES** 4

1 onion, coarsely chopped
4 garlic cloves, chopped
1 tsp. peeled and finely grated
  gingerroot
2 tsp. Burmese Curry Paste
  (see page 13)
1 tsp. turmeric
½ tsp. cayenne pepper

2 tbsp. sesame oil
1 tbsp. sunflower oil
1lb. 12oz. raw large shrimp, shelled
  and deveined
4 tbsp. chopped cilantro leaves
4 scallions, thinly sliced
salt
rice, to serve

1 Put the onion, garlic, ginger, curry paste, turmeric, and chili powder in a food
  processor and blend 1 to 2 minutes until fairly smooth. Season with salt.
2 Heat the oils in a large saucepan over low heat. Add the onion paste and stir-fry
  2 minutes. Add the shrimp and stir-fry 4 to 5 minutes until pink and cooked
  through. Stir in the cilantro and scallions and serve hot with rice.

218 Filipino Shrimp & Pineapple Curry

PREPARATION TIME 15 minutes, plus making the curry paste and rice
COOKING TIME 20 minutes   **SERVES** 4 to 6

4 tbsp. sunflower oil
1 eggplant, cut into bite-size cubes
1 tbsp. Thai Green Curry Paste
  (see page 15)
1¾ cups coconut milk
1½ cups pineapple cut into
  bite-size cubes

3 tbsp. pineapple juice
2 or 3 green chilies, left whole
1lb. 12oz. unshelled raw jumbo
  shrimp
1 tbsp. fish sauce
rice, to serve

1 Heat half of the oil in a large wok or skillet over low heat. Add the eggplant
  and stir-fry 5 to 6 minutes. Add the remaining oil and the curry paste and stir-fry
  3 to 4 minutes longer until fragrant.
2 Stir in the coconut milk, then lower the heat to low and cook 4 to 5 minutes.
3 Add the pineapple, pineapple juice, chilies, and shrimp and bring back to a boil.
  Stir-fry 3 to 4 minutes until the shrimp turn pink and are cooked through. Stir
  in the fish sauce and serve hot with rice.

CHAPTER 5

VEGETABLES

Vegetables, legumes, and even fruit form the basis of some of the most classic and beloved curries around the world. Dishes such as Sri Lankan Coconut Dal and Saag Paneer are, for me, among the ultimate comfort foods. Like most of the recipes in this chapter, they're also incredibly easy to make and provide a great option when you're looking to get dinner on the table quickly or want to entertain without a lot of hassle.

Some of the recipes here might surprise you, especially if ingredients such as okra, cashew nuts, papaya, tofu, and mango are not part of your everyday cooking routine. Try Papaya in Coconut Milk from the Philippines, Cashew Nut Curry from Sri Lanka, or South Indian Mango & Yogurt Curry and discover how these foods can transform a meal into something truly special.

Whether you're in the mood for a hearty Red Lentil Curry with Mustard Seeds & Tamarind or a light, delicate Nonya Laksa with Bean Sprouts, these recipes present an astoundingly diverse collection of flavors and textures that will inspire you time and time again.

AACHARI BAINGAN (*SEE PAGE 140*)

219 Burmese Dry Bitter Melon Curry

PREPARATION TIME 30 minutes, plus 30 minutes standing and making the curry powder, rice, and pickles COOKING TIME 35 minutes SERVES 4

2 bitter melons (carilla or Kerala),
   about 1lb. 5oz. total weight
1 tbsp. turmeric
3 tbsp. peanut oil
1 small onion, halved and thinly sliced
1 tbsp. Curry Powder (see page 11)
½ tsp. cayenne pepper
3 tomatoes, coarsely chopped

2 tbsp. dark soy sauce
1 to 2 tbsp. light soy sauce
salt and freshly ground black pepper
1 recipe quantity Burmese Golden
   Rice (see page 185), to serve
1 recipe quantity Burmese Cucumber
   Pickle (see page 203), to serve

1   Using a vegetable peeler, lightly scrape off the skin and blisters from the melons, just enough to remove any raised parts. Slice thinly, transfer to a colander, and sprinkle with salt. Leave to stand 30 minutes, then rinse well under cold running water to remove the bitter juices. Drain on paper towels and transfer to a bowl. Sprinkle the turmeric over and toss well.

2   Heat the oil in a large skillet over low heat. Add the onion and fry, stirring occasionally, 4 to 5 minutes until soft. Add the curry powder, cayenne, and the tomatoes and continue frying, stirring, 8 to 10 minutes until fragrant.

3   Stir in the melon and fry, stirring occasionally, 10 to 15 minutes until soft. Stir in the dark soy sauce and cook 2 to 3 minutes longer, then season with salt and pepper and stir in the light soy sauce. Serve hot with rice and pickle.

220 Aachari Baingan

PREPARATION TIME 30 minutes, plus making the rice and raita
COOKING TIME 50 minutes SERVES 4

1 tbsp. peeled and finely grated
   gingerroot
2 tbsp. finely grated garlic
15oz. canned crushed tomatoes
1 cup plus 2 tbsp. sunflower oil
1lb. 12oz. baby eggplants,
   halved lengthwise
2 tsp. fennel seeds
2 tsp. nigella seeds

1 tbsp. ground coriander
¼ tsp. turmeric
1 tsp. paprika
salt and freshly ground black pepper
1 recipe quantity Mushroom Pulao
   (see page 183), to serve
1 recipe quantity Raita
   (see page 204), to serve

1   Put the ginger, garlic, and half the tomatoes in a blender and blend 2 to 3 minutes until smooth, then set aside.

2   Heat half the oil in a large, heavy-bottomed skillet over low heat. Working in batches, add as many eggplants as you can fit in a single layer, cut-side down. Cook 3 to 4 minutes on each side until light brown, then remove from the pan, using a slotted spoon, and drain on paper towels.

3   Add the fennel and nigella seeds to the pan and cook, stirring, 1 to 2 minutes until fragrant. Add the tomato mixture and cook, stirring, 2 to 3 minutes longer. Add the coriander, turmeric, paprika, and remaining tomatoes and season well with salt and pepper. Simmer over low heat, stirring frequently, 6 to 8 minutes until smooth and thick.

4   Add the eggplants and toss gently to coat evenly, then cover and cook 10 to 12 minutes. Remove from the heat and leave to stand 10 to 15 minutes. Serve warm with rice and raita.

221 Five-Spice Eggplant

PREPARATION TIME 10 minutes, plus making the rice   **COOKING TIME** 15 minutes   **SERVES** 4

1lb. 12oz. eggplants, sliced
  into thin rounds
2 egg whites
6 tbsp. cornstarch
1 tbsp. Chinese five-spice powder
1 tbsp. cayenne pepper
1 tsp. salt, plus extra for seasoning

3 cups canola oil, for deep-frying,
  or more as needed
1 tbsp. mint leaves, to sprinkle
1 recipe quantity Classic Egg-Fried
  Rice (see page 178), to serve
hot chili sauce, to serve

1 Pat the eggplant slices dry with paper towels. Put the egg whites in a clean bowl and whisk until light and foamy. In another bowl, mix together the cornstarch, five-spice, chili powder, and salt and spread it over a large plate.

2 Fill a large wok or saucepan one-third full with oil and heat it to 350°F, or until a small piece of bread dropped into the oil browns in 15 seconds. Working in batches to avoid overcrowding the wok, dip the eggplants first in the egg white, then in the spice mixture. Deep-fry the slices 3 to 4 minutes until crisp and golden. Remove from the wok, using a slotted spoon, and drain on paper towels. Sprinkle with mint leaves and serve hot with rice and chili sauce.

222 Bombay Aloo

PREPARATION TIME 10 minutes, plus making the bread   **COOKING TIME** 17 minutes   **SERVES** 4

1lb. 2oz. potatoes, peeled and
  cut into 1in. cubes
4 tbsp. sunflower oil
1 to 2 tsp. black mustard seeds
1 tsp. cayenne pepper
  or paprika
4 tsp. cumin seeds
8 to 10 curry leaves

2 tsp. ground cumin
2 tsp. ground coriander
1 tsp. turmeric
6 tbsp. chopped cilantro leaves
squeeze of lemon juice
salt and freshly ground black pepper
1 recipe quantity Puri (see page 191),
  to serve

1 Bring a saucepan of lightly salted water to a boil. Add the potatoes and boil 8 to 10 minutes until tender, then drain.

2 Heat the oil in a large, nonstick wok or skillet over medium-high heat. Add the mustard seeds, cayenne, cumin seeds, and curry leaves and cook, stirring, 1 to 2 minutes until fragrant. Add the ground cumin, coriander, turmeric, and potatoes and season well with salt and pepper, then stir-fry over high heat 4 to 5 minutes until hot. Remove from the heat and stir in the cilantro leaves. Squeeze the lemon juice over and serve hot with bread.

223 Burmese Vegetable Stir-Fry with Peppers

PREPARATION TIME 15 minutes, plus making the rice   **COOKING TIME** 5 minutes   **SERVES** 4

3 tbsp. canola oil
1 red bell pepper, seeded and
  thinly sliced
1 green bell pepper, seeded and
  thinly sliced
7oz. sugar snap peas
2 bok choy, thickly sliced

8 scallions, thinly sliced
1 carrot, thinly sliced
1 garlic clove, thinly sliced
1 red chili, finely chopped
4 tbsp. light soy sauce
1 recipe quantity Burmese Golden
  Rice (see page 185), to serve

1 In a large wok or saucepan, heat the oil over high heat until hot but not smoking. Add the peppers, peas, bok choy, scallions, carrot, garlic, chili, and soy sauce.

2 Stir-fry 3 to 4 minutes until the vegetables are beginning to soften but are still crunchy. Serve hot with rice.

224 Spiced Moroccan Vegetable Stew

PREPARATION TIME 15 minutes, plus making the couscous   **COOKING TIME** 55 minutes
SERVES 4

2 tbsp. sunflower oil
1 large onion, finely chopped
2 garlic cloves, finely chopped
1 tsp. peeled and finely grated
   gingerroot
2 tsp. ground cumin
1 tsp. ground coriander
2 tsp. cinnamon
1 tsp. turmeric
1 tsp. dried chili flakes
15oz. canned crushed tomatoes

1 cup plus 2 tbsp. vegetable stock
15oz. canned chickpeas, rinsed
   and drained
1 red bell pepper, seeded and cut
   into bite-size pieces
1lb. 8oz. butternut squash, peeled
   and cut into bite-size cubes
⅔ cup golden raisins
salt and freshly ground black pepper
cilantro leaves, to serve
couscous, to serve

1   Heat the oil in a large, nonstick skillet over low heat. Add the onion and fry,
    stirring occasionally, 4 to 5 minutes until soft. Add the garlic, ginger, cumin,
    coriander, cinnamon, turmeric, chili flakes, tomatoes, and stock and bring
    to a boil. Lower the heat to low, cover the pan, and simmer 25 minutes.
2   Stir in the chickpeas, red pepper, butternut squash, and golden raisins. Simmer
    over low heat 20 to 25 minutes until the vegetables are cooked through and
    tender. Season with salt and pepper and serve hot with couscous.

225 Cambodian Vegetable Curry

PREPARATION TIME 15 minutes, plus making the curry powder and rice
COOKING TIME 1 hour   SERVES 4

1 tbsp. sunflower oil
6 shallots, coarsely chopped
1 garlic clove, chopped
1½in. piece gingerroot, peeled
  and thinly sliced
2 lemongrass stalks, cut into
  2in. pieces
1 tbsp. Curry Powder
  (see page 11)
1 red bell pepper, seeded and
  coarsely chopped
1 carrot, sliced diagonally

4 mushrooms, sliced
8oz. fried tofu, cut into
  bite-size pieces
4 cups vegetable stock
9oz. small potatoes, peeled
  and quartered
1¾ cups coconut milk
1¾oz. bean sprouts
salt and freshly ground black pepper
1 recipe quantity Saffron Rice
  (see page 180), to serve

1   Heat the oil in a large saucepan over low heat. Add the shallots and fry 3 to 4
    minutes until soft and translucent. Stir in the garlic, ginger, lemongrass, and curry
    powder and fry 5 minutes longer, or until fragrant. Stir in the red pepper, carrot,
    mushrooms, and tofu. Add the stock and season with salt and pepper.
2   Bring to a boil, stir in the potatoes and coconut milk, and bring back to a boil.
    Lower the heat to low and simmer 45 to 50 minutes until the potatoes are
    tender. Divide the curry into large wide bowls, discarding the lemongrass pieces.
    Sprinkle with the bean sprouts and serve hot with rice.

226 Caribbean Spiced Corn, Tomato & Avocado Salad

PREPARATION TIME 20 minutes, plus making the bread   COOKING TIME 9 minutes   SERVES 4

1 ear of corn
1 tbsp. chili oil
1 red bell pepper, seeded
1 avocado
2 Scotch bonnet or habanero chilies,
  seeded and finely chopped
6 tomatoes, coarsely chopped

1 small bunch cilantro leaves,
  coarsely chopped
juice of 2 limes
⅔ cup olive oil
salt and freshly ground black pepper
1 recipe quantity Trinidadian Roti
  Paratha (see page 189), to serve

1   Preheat the broiler to high or heat a charcoal barbecue until hot and the flames
    die away. Bring a saucepan of lightly salted water to a boil and cook the corn
    30 to 45 seconds, then drain and brush with the chili oil.
2   Broil the corn, turning regularly, 4 to 5 minutes until beginning to char at the
    edges. At the same time, broil the red pepper 6 to 8 minutes until the skin begins
    to blacken and blister. Cut the corn kernels from the cob, using a sharp knife, and
    put them in a bowl. Remove and discard the skin from the pepper, then cut it into
    small pieces and add it to the corn.
3   Halve, peel, and pit the avocado, then cut it into cubes. Add it to the corn, along
    with the chilies and tomatoes.
4   Put the cilantro leaves, lime juice, and olive oil in another bowl. Season well with
    salt and pepper, whisk well, and then pour the mixture over the corn mixture.
    Toss gently and serve immediately with bread.

227 Cashew Nut Curry

PREPARATION TIME 15 minutes, plus making the rice and pickle **COOKING TIME** 55 minutes
SERVES 4

1 pandanus leaf
2½ cups coconut milk
1 onion, chopped
1 tbsp. peeled and finely grated
  gingerroot
1 tsp. peeled and finely grated
  galangal
2 green chilies, seeded and
  finely chopped
8 curry leaves

1 cinnamon stick
1 tsp. turmeric
1⅔ cups raw cashew nuts
2 tbsp. chopped cilantro leaves
1 recipe quantity Lemon Rice
  (see page 182), to serve
1 recipe quantity Sri Lankan Coconut
  Relish (see page 213),
  to serve

1 Shred the pandanus leaf lengthwise into 3 sections and tie each one into
a large knot. Put it in a saucepan and add the coconut milk, onion, ginger,
galangal, chilies, curry leaves, cinnamon stick, and turmeric. Bring the mixture
to a boil over high heat, then lower the heat to medium-low and simmer
20 minutes.

2 Add the cashew nuts and cook 30 minutes longer, or until the nuts are tender.
Remove from the heat and discard the cinnamon stick and pandanus leaf.
Sprinkle the cilantro leaves over and serve hot with rice and pickle.

228 Cauliflower Curry

PREPARATION TIME 15 minutes plus making the curry powder, bread, and raita
COOKING TIME 20 minutes   **SERVES** 4

2 tbsp. sunflower oil
8 scallions, cut into 2in. pieces
2 tsp. grated garlic
2 tsp. ground ginger
2 tbsp. Curry Powder
  (see page 11)
10oz. cauliflower florets
1 red bell pepper, seeded and cut into
  small squares
1 green bell pepper, seeded and cut
  into small squares

15oz. canned crushed tomatoes
7oz. canned chickpeas, rinsed
  and drained
3 to 4 tbsp. plain yogurt
salt and freshly ground black pepper
1 large handful mint leaves, chopped,
  to serve
1 recipe quantity Naan
  (see page 190), to serve
1 recipe quantity Corn Raita
  (see page 212), to serve

1 Heat the oil in a large, nonstick skillet over low heat. Add the scallions and fry,
stirring occasionally, 2 to 3 minutes until beginning to color. Add the garlic,
ginger, and curry powder and cook, stirring, 20 to 30 seconds until fragrant, then
add the cauliflower and peppers and cook, stirring, 2 to 3 minutes longer until
well coated in the spices. Stir in the tomatoes and bring to a boil over high heat.

2 Cover, lower the heat to medium, and simmer, stirring occasionally, 10 minutes.
Add the chickpeas and season well with salt and pepper. Bring back to a boil,
then remove from the heat. Drizzle with the yogurt and sprinkle with the mint.
Serve hot with bread and raita.

229 Ceylonese Pea & Cashew Nut Curry

PREPARATION TIME 10 minutes, plus 3 hours soaking and making the curry powder, rice, and pickle   COOKING TIME 45 minutes   SERVES 4

2 cups cashew nuts
a pinch of salt, plus extra for cooking the cashews
1 tsp. turmeric
1 lemongrass stalk
2 tbsp. sunflower oil
2 onions, halved and sliced
2 garlic cloves, chopped
1 cinnamon stick
6 curry leaves
1 tsp. cayenne pepper
1 tsp. paprika

1 tbsp. Sri Lankan Curry Powder (see page 12)
1¼ cups coconut milk
1 cup frozen peas
½ cup chopped cilantro leaves
salt
1 recipe quantity Lemon Rice (see page 182), to serve
1 recipe quantity Sri Lankan Lemon & Date Pickle (see page 213), to serve

1 Put the cashews in a bowl, cover with cold water, and leave to soak 3 hours, then drain. Transfer the nuts to a pan and add 2½ cups lightly salted water, then add the turmeric and simmer over low heat, stirring occasionally 30 minutes, or until soft and creamy, then drain.
2 Meanwhile, trim off the top off the lemongrass stalk, leaving just the lower 3 to 3½ inches, then lightly bash with a wooden mallet or rolling pin to crush slightly (this helps to release the aromatic oils within) and set aside.
3 Heat the oil in a wok or saucepan over low heat. Add the onions and fry, stirring occasionally, 5 minutes until they start to color. Stir in the garlic, cinnamon, and curry leaves and 3 to 4 minutes until the onion is soft and translucent. Sprinkle the cayenne, paprika, and curry powder over and fry 30 to 40 seconds until fragrant. Add the coconut milk, lemongrass, and salt. Bring to a boil over high heat and add the cashews. Lower the heat to low and simmer 5 minutes, then add the peas. Cook 2 to 3 minutes until the peas are cooked through.
4 Remove from the heat, then remove and discard the lemongrass. Sprinkle with the cilantro leaves and serve hot with rice and pickle.

230 Chana Masala

PREPARATION TIME 15 minutes, plus making the garam masala, curry powder, bread, and raita
COOKING TIME 55 minutes   SERVES 4

4 tbsp. sunflower oil
4 garlic cloves, minced
2 tsp. peeled and finely grated gingerroot
1 large onion, coarsely grated
1 to 2 green chilies, thinly sliced
1 tsp. cayenne pepper
1 tbsp. ground cumin
1 tbsp. ground coriander
3 tbsp. plain yogurt, whisked, plus extra as needed

2 tsp. Garam Masala (see page 11)
2 tsp. tamarind paste
2 tsp. Curry Powder (see page 11)
1lb. 12oz. canned chickpeas, rinsed and drained
chopped cilantro leaves, to serve
1 recipe quantity Wholewheat Paratha (see page 193), to serve
1 recipe quantity Raita (see page 204), to serve
1 lemon, cut into wedges, to serve

1 Heat the oil in a large, heavy skillet over low heat. Add the garlic, ginger, onion, and chilies and fry, stirring occasionally, 6 to 8 minutes until the onion is light golden. Add the cayenne, cumin, coriander, yogurt, and garam masala and cook, stirring, 1 to 2 minutes longer until fragrant.
2 Stir in 2 cups plus 2 tablespoons water. Bring the mixture to a boil. Add the tamarind paste, curry powder, and chickpeas and bring back to a boil.
3 Lower the heat to low and simmer, stirring occasionally, 30 to 40 minutes until the sauce is thick and rich. Divide into four bowls and drizzle with extra yogurt, then sprinkle with cilantro leaves. Serve with bread and raita and with lemon wedges for squeezing over.

231 Chinese-Style Eggplant Curry

PREPARATION TIME 10 minutes, plus 30 minutes standing and making the rice
COOKING TIME 25 minutes SERVES 4

2 eggplants, cut into
   ½in.-thick batons
3 tbsp. hoisin sauce
2 tbsp. soy sauce
½ tsp. dried chili flakes
⅔ cup Chinese rice wine or sherry
2 tbsp. peanut oil

2 tbsp. minced garlic
2 tbsp. peeled and minced gingerroot
salt
sesame seeds, to sprinkle
1 recipe quantity Classic Egg-Fried
   Rice (see page 178), to serve

1 Put the eggplants in a colander, sprinkle with salt, and leave to drain 30 minutes, then rinse and drain well. Meanwhile, mix together the hoisin sauce, soy sauce, chili flakes, rice wine, and 1½ cups water in a bowl.
2 Heat the oil in a large wok or skillet over high heat. Add the eggplants, garlic, and ginger and stir-fry 3 to 4 minutes. Stir in the hoisin sauce mixture and then lower the heat to medium-low and simmer 15 minutes.
3 Gradually increase the heat to medium-high and then to high and cook 6 to 8 minutes until the sauce reduces to a thick glaze. Remove from the heat, sprinkle with sesame seeds, and serve hot with rice.

232 Creamy Butternut Squash Curry with Lime

PREPARATION TIME 15 minutes, plus making the curry paste and rice
COOKING TIME 25 minutes SERVES 4

1lb. 12oz. butternut squash,
   peeled, seeded, and cut into
   ¾in. cubes
1 tbsp. Thai Green Curry Paste
   (see page 15)

finely grated zest and juice of 1 lime
1¾ cups coconut milk
1 tbsp. light soy sauce
rice, to serve

1 Bring a saucepan of water to a boil, add the squash, and cook 6 minutes, or until slightly soft, then drain.
2 Heat a large saucepan over low heat. Add the curry paste and cook, stirring, 30 seconds. Stir in the lime zest and coconut milk and simmer 5 minutes. Add the squash, soy sauce, and lime juice and bring to a boil, then lower the heat to medium-low and simmer, stirring occasionally, 10 minutes, or until the squash is soft but not mushy. Serve hot with rice.

233 Spiced Cumin Potatoes

PREPARATION TIME 20 minutes, plus making the bread COOKING TIME 17 minutes SERVES 4

1lb. potatoes, peeled and cut
   into 1in. cubes
3 tbsp. sunflower oil
1 tsp. black mustard seeds
3 tsp. cumin seeds
8 to 10 curry leaves
2 tsp. ground cumin

2 tsp. ground coriander
1 tsp. turmeric
4 tbsp. chopped cilantro leaves
juice of ½ to 1 lime
salt and freshly ground black pepper
1 recipe quantity Puri (see page 191),
   to serve

1 Bring a saucepan of lightly salted water to a boil. Add the potatoes and boil for 8 to 10 minutes until tender, then drain.
2 Heat the oil in a large, nonstick skillet over medium-high heat. Add the mustard and cumin seeds and curry leaves and fry, stirring occasionally, 1 to 2 minutes. Add the ground cumin, coriander, turmeric, and potatoes, season with salt and pepper, and fry, stirring, 5 minutes, or until light brown. Stir in the cilantro leaves, squeeze the lime juice over, and serve hot with bread.

234 Creamy Paneer Curry

PREPARATION TIME 15 minutes, plus making the curry powder, bread, and pickle
COOKING TIME 35 minutes **SERVES** 4

2 tbsp. sunflower oil
8 shallots, finely chopped
2 tbsp. Curry Powder
 (see page 11)
4 tomatoes, coarsely chopped
2 tsp. finely grated garlic
2 red chilies, seeded and thinly sliced
2 tbsp. tomato paste
1 tsp. sugar
scant 1 cup light cream

1lb. paneer, cut into bite-size pieces
1⅓ cups frozen peas
salt and freshly ground black pepper
6 tbsp. finely chopped cilantro leaves,
 to sprinkle
1 recipe quantity Naan
 (see page 190), to serve
1 recipe quantity Spiced Carrot Pickle
 (see page 212), to serve

1 Heat the oil in a large, nonstick wok or skillet over medium-high heat. Add the
 shallots and fry, stirring occasionally, 2 to 3 minutes until softened. Sprinkle the
 curry powder over and cook, stirring, 1 minute, or until fragrant, then add the
 tomatoes, garlic, chilies, tomato paste, sugar, and ⅔ cup water. Bring to a boil,
 then lower the heat to low and simmer, uncovered, 15 to 20 minutes until thick.
2 Stir in the cream, paneer, and peas and simmer for 5 minutes. or until the
 paneer is heated through and the peas are cooked. Season with salt
 and pepper. Remove from the heat, stir in the chopped cilantro and serve
 with bread and pickle.

235 Curried Bangkok Bean Curd

PREPARATION TIME 15 minutes, plus making the curry paste and rice
COOKING TIME 20 minutes **SERVES** 4

6 Thai or small shallots, thinly sliced
1 tbsp. finely chopped garlic
2 tbsp. finely chopped lemongrass
1 red chili, seeded and sliced
2 tbsp. Thai Green Curry Paste
 (see page 15)
1 tbsp. light soy sauce
3 tsp. light brown sugar
4 tbsp. sunflower oil, plus extra
 as needed, for frying

1lb. firm tofu (bean curd),
 cut into ½in.-thick batons
1 cup plus 2 tbsp. coconut milk
juice of 1 lime
1 large handful cilantro leaves
1 large handful Thai basil leaves
⅓ cup skinless roasted peanuts
1 recipe quantity Aromatic Sticky Rice
 (see page 178), to serve

1 Put the shallots, garlic, lemongrass, and chili in a bowl and mix well. In another
 bowl, mix together the curry paste, soy sauce, and sugar until the sugar dissolves.
 Have the other ingredients at the ready beside the stove.
2 Heat about ½ inch oil in a skillet or large saucepan over medium-high heat. When
 it is hot, add half of the tofu in a single layer and fry 3 to 5 minutes, turning once,
 until crisp and light golden. Remove with a slotted spoon and drain on paper
 towels. Repeat with the remaining tofu, then set aside.
3 Lower the heat to medium-low and drain off all but 2 tablespoons of the oil. Add
 the shallot mixture and cook, stirring occasionally, 1 to 2 minutes until the garlic
 is lightly colored and the shallot is soft.
4 Stir in the curry paste mixture, then stir in the coconut milk. Bring to a simmer,
 add the tofu, and cook 5 minutes, or until heated through. Stir in the lime juice,
 cilantro, and basil. Sprinkle with the peanuts and serve hot with rice.

236 Nonya Laksa with Bean Sprouts

PREPARATION TIME 20 minutes, plus making the curry powder   **COOKING TIME** 45 minutes
SERVES 4

2 tbsp. canola oil
2 tbsp. finely chopped garlic
1 tbsp. peeled and finely chopped
  gingerroot
2 red chilies, sliced, plus extra to serve
2 onions, thinly sliced
4 tbsp. Nonya Curry Powder
  (see page 11)
½ tsp. turmeric
1¼ cups vegetable stock
9oz. dried rice noodles

3 eggs, at room temperature
1¾ cups coconut milk
2 tsp. chili bean sauce
1 tsp. palm sugar
1¾oz. bean sprouts
4 scallions, thinly sliced, to serve
½ cup finely chopped cilantro leaves,
  to serve
⅔ cup roasted skinless peanuts,
  coarsely chopped, to serve

1   Heat a wok or large skillet over high heat. Add the oil and, when it is very hot
    and slightly smoking, lower the heat to medium, and add the garlic, ginger,
    chilies, and onions. Cook, stirring occasionally, 5 minutes, or until fragrant. Stir
    in the curry powder, turmeric, and stock, then lower the heat to low and cook,
    covered, 20 minutes, or until thick.
2   Meanwhile, put the rice noodles in a bowl, cover with warm water, and leave
    to soak 20 minutes, or until soft, then drain well. Bring a saucepan of water
    to a boil. Add the eggs and boil 6 minutes. Drain and leave to stand until cool
    enough to handle, then peel and set aside.
3   Add the coconut milk and rice noodles to the curry mixture. Stir in the chili
    bean sauce and sugar, then add the bean sprouts. Cook 15 minutes longer,
    or until thick. Meanwhile, cut the eggs into quarters and transfer to a plate.
4   Ladle the laksa into four bowls and serve immediately with the scallions,
    cilantro leaves, eggs, peanuts, and extra red chili sprinkled over the tops.

237 Dal Makhani

PREPARATION TIME 20 minutes, plus at least 10 hours soaking and making the bread and chutney **COOKING TIME** 1 hour 5 minutes **SERVES** 4

⅔ cup dried whole black lentils
3 tbsp. butter
1 onion, finely chopped
3 garlic cloves, crushed
2 tsp. peeled and finely grated
  gingerroot
1 green chili, split in half lengthwise
2 tsp. cumin seeds
1 tsp. ground coriander
1 tsp. turmeric
1 tsp. paprika, plus extra for
  sprinkling

7oz. canned red kidney beans,
  drained and rinsed
1 large handful cilantro leaves,
  chopped
4 tbsp. light cream
salt
1 recipe quantity Naan
  (see page 190), to serve
1 recipe quantity Spiced Tomato
  Chutney (see page 210), to serve

1   Rinse and drain the lentils. Put them in a deep bowl, cover with cold water, and leave to soak 10 to 12 hours. Drain and rinse under cold water, then drain well.
2   Put the lentils in a saucepan and add 2 cups plus 2 tablespoons boiling water. Bring to a boil over high heat, then lower the heat to low and simmer 35 to 40 minutes until tender. Drain and set aside.
3   Melt the butter in a large saucepan over low heat. Add the onion, garlic, ginger, chili, cumin seeds, and coriander and fry, stirring occasionally, 5 to 6 minutes until the onion is soft. Add the turmeric, paprika, kidney beans, and lentils and fry 1 minute to mix well. Add 2 cups plus 2 tablespoons water and bring back to a boil, then lower the heat to low and cook, stirring frequently, 10 to 15 minutes until thick. Remove from the heat and season with salt.
4   Stir in the cilantro leaves and drizzle the cream over. Sprinkle with a little extra paprika and serve hot with warm bread and chutney.

238 Goan Vegetable Xacutti Curry

PREPARATION TIME 15 minutes, plus making the rice **COOKING TIME** 30 minutes **SERVES** 4

4 tsp. sunflower oil
2 potatoes, peeled and cut into
  1in. cubes
2 large carrots, cut into 1in. cubes
15oz. canned crushed tomatoes
1⅓ cups frozen peas
salt
rice, to serve

XACUTTI CURRY PASTE
2 tsp. sunflower oil
3 cloves
2 cinnamon sticks
2 tsp. white poppy seeds
2 tsp. whole black peppercorns
4 dried red chilies
1¼ cups shredded coconut
4 garlic cloves, coarsely chopped
2 onions, coarsely chopped

1   To make the curry paste, heat the oil in a small skillet over medium heat. Add the cloves, cinnamon, poppy seeds, peppercorns, and chilies and fry, stirring occasionally, 1 to 2 minutes until fragrant, then transfer to a blender or food processor and set aside.
2   Put the coconut in a small, dry skillet over medium-low heat and dry-roast, stirring continuously, 2 to 3 minutes until light golden. Watch carefully to make sure it does not scorch. Transfer to the blender and add the garlic and onions, then blend 2 to 3 minutes until the mixture forms a coarse paste. Set aside.
3   Heat the oil in a skillet or saucepan over low heat. Add the potatoes and carrots, cover, and leave to cook 2 minutes, then stir in the curry paste and tomatoes and season with salt. Simmer, covered, 15 to 20 minutes until the potatoes and carrots are cooked through, adding the peas in the last 5 minutes of cooking. Serve hot with rice.

239 Japanese Vegetable Curry

PREPARATION TIME 10 minutes, plus making the curry sauce, rice, and pickle
COOKING TIME 1 hour 5 minutes   SERVES 4

4 tbsp. olive oil
1 Japanese eggplant, trimmed and
   cut ¼in.-thick rounds
2 yellow bell peppers, seeded and
   cut into bite-size pieces
1 small onion, sliced
1 garlic clove, finely chopped
1 carrot, cut into bite-size pieces

1¾ cups Japanese Curry Sauce
   (see page 12)
salt and freshly ground black pepper
Japanese rice, to serve
1 recipe quantity Japanese Wasabi
   Pickled Cucumbers (see page 202),
   to serve

1 Heat half the oil in medium skillet over low heat. Add the eggplant and yellow peppers and fry, stirring occasionally, 8 to 10 minutes until tender. Season with salt and pepper, then set aside and cover to keep warm.
2 Heat the remaining oil in large saucepan over low heat. Add the onion and garlic, lower the heat to low, and fry, stirring occasionally, 10 to 12 minutes until the onion is soft and translucent. Add the carrot and cook 1 minute, then stir in 1 cup plus 2 tablespoons water and simmer over low heat 15 minutes until the carrot is tender. Add the curry sauce and simmer, stirring occasionally, 10 to 12 minutes.
3 Stir in the eggplant and peppers and cook 10 to 12 minutes longer until just warmed through. Serve hot with rice and pickle

240 Jungle Curry with Lychees and Sweet Potato

PREPARATION TIME 15 minutes, plus making the curry paste and rice
COOKING TIME 15 minutes   SERVES 4

1 tbsp. sunflower oil
3 tbsp. Thai Red Curry Paste
   (see page 15)
1 tsp. peeled and grated gingerroot
finely grated zest of 1 lime
1¾ cups vegetable stock
15oz. canned lychees in syrup,
   drained and syrup reserved

2 sweet potatoes, peeled and cut
   into bite-size pieces
2 tbsp. soy sauce
2 tbsp. kaffir lime leaves,
   thinly sliced
1 red chili, seeded and thinly sliced
jasmine rice, to serve

1 Heat the oil in a wok or skillet over low heat. Add the curry paste, ginger, and lime zest and cook, stirring, 1 minute, or until fragrant. Stir in the stock, then bring to a boil and add the lychees and sweet potatoes.
2 Cook over low heat 8 to 10 minutes until tender. Stir in 4 to 5 tablespoons of the lychee syrup and the soy sauce, then remove from the heat, sprinkle with the lime leaves and chili, and serve hot with rice.

241 Lebanese Zucchini Curry

PREPARATION TIME 5 minutes, plus making the bread   COOKING TIME 45 minutes   SERVES 4

2 tbsp. olive oil
1 large onion, finely chopped
4 zucchini, cut into ½in. cubes
1lb. 12oz. canned peeled whole
   tomatoes with juice
2 garlic cloves, crushed

½ tsp. cayenne pepper
¼ tsp. turmeric
1 tsp. dried mint
salt and freshly ground black pepper
1 recipe quantity Turkish Pide Bread
   (see page 190), to serve

1 Heat the oil in a large saucepan over low heat. Add the onion and cook, stirring occasionally, 10 to 12 minutes until soft. Add the zucchini and cook, stirring occasionally, 5 to 6 minutes longer. Add the tomatoes and garlic.
2 Cook over low heat 20 minutes. Stir in the remaining ingredients and cook 4 to 5 minutes, then season with salt and pepper and serve with bread.

242 Malaysian Cabbage with Eggs

PREPARATION TIME 10 minutes, plus making the crêpes **COOKING TIME** 12 minutes **SERVES** 4

1 tbsp. sunflower oil
1 garlic clove, crushed
1 red bell pepper, seeded and thinly
  sliced
6 cups finely shredded white
  or green cabbage

2 eggs, lightly beaten
salt and freshly ground black pepper
1 recipe quantity Malaysian Roti Jala
  (see page 194), to serve

1 Heat the oil in a large skillet over medium-high heat. Add the garlic and red pepper
   and fry, stirring occasionally, 3 to 4 minutes. Add the cabbage, season with salt and
   pepper, and stir-fry 5 minutes until it is cooked but still a little crunchy.
2 Stir in the eggs and continue stirring 1 to 2 minutes longer until the eggs are just
   scrambled and mixed well with the cabbage. Serve immediately with crêpes.

243 Curried Mushrooms

PREPARATION TIME 15 minutes, plus making the curry powder and bread
COOKING TIME 13 minutes **SERVES** 4

4 garlic cloves, finely chopped
2 tsp. peeled and finely chopped
  gingerroot
1 onion, finely chopped
1 tbsp. Curry Powder (see page 11)
5 tbsp. sunflower oil
7 cups halved or thickly sliced large
  button or morel mushrooms

scant ½ cup heavy cream
2 tomatoes, finely chopped
6 tbsp. finely chopped cilantro leaves
salt and freshly ground black pepper
1 recipe quantity Roomali Roti
  (see page 194), to serve

1 Put the garlic, ginger, onion, curry powder, and 3 tablespoons water in a blender
   or food processor and blend 2 to 3 minutes until smooth.
2 Heat 3 tablespoons of the oil in a large, nonstick wok or skillet over high heat.
   Add the mushrooms and stir-fry 4 to 5 minutes, then transfer to a bowl and wipe
   out the wok with paper towels.
3 Heat the remaining 2 tablespoons of the oil in the wok over low heat. Add the
   onion mixture and fry, stirring occasionally, 3 to 4 minutes. Add the mushrooms
   (and any juices), cream, and tomatoes. Fry, stirring occasionally, 3 to 4 minutes
   until hot. Season well with salt and pepper, then remove from the heat and stir
   in the cilantro leaves. Serve hot with bread.

244 Papaya in Coconut Milk

PREPARATION TIME 15 minutes, plus making the rice **COOKING TIME** 35 minutes **SERVES** 4

2 tbsp. sunflower oil
8 to 10 garlic cloves, finely chopped
1¾in. piece gingerroot, peeled and
  thinly sliced
10 whole black peppercorns
1 green papaya, peeled, seeded,
  and thinly sliced

1¼ cups coconut milk
scant 1 cup coconut cream
salt
1 recipe quantity Tomato & Cilantro
  Rice (see page 186), to serve

1 Heat the oil in a large wok or saucepan over low heat. Add the garlic and
   cook, stirring occasionally, 2 to 3 minutes until light golden. Add the ginger and
   peppercorns and cook, stirring, 3 to 4 minutes longer. Add the papaya and cook,
   stirring occasionally, 4 to 5 minutes until soft. Stir in the coconut milk, season well
   with salt, and bring to a boil.
2 Lower the heat to low and simmer, covered, 10 to 15 minutes until the papaya
   is translucent. Add the coconut cream and simmer for 5 minutes until thick.
   Serve hot with rice.

245 Punjabi Cabbage

PREPARATION TIME 15 minutes, plus making the curry powder, bread and chutney
COOKING TIME 15 minutes **SERVES** 4

3 tbsp. sunflower oil
4 shallots, finely chopped
2 tsp. peeled and finely grated
   gingerroot
2 tsp. finely grated garlic
2 long green chilies, split in half
   lengthwise
2 tsp. cumin seeds
1 tsp. turmeric
1 tsp. crushed coriander seeds

1lb. coarsely chopped or shredded
   white or green cabbage
1 tbsp. Curry Powder (see page 11)
1 tbsp. ghee or butter
salt and freshly ground black pepper
1 recipe quantity Wholewheat
   Paratha (see page 193), to serve
1 recipe quantity Mint Chutney
   (see page 204), to serve

1   Heat the oil in a large, nonstick wok or skillet over low heat. Add the shallots, ginger, garlic, and chilies and cook, stirring occasionally, 2 to 3 minutes until the shallots are soft. Add the cumin seeds, turmeric, and coriander seeds and cook, stirring, 1 minute, or until fragrant.
2   Increase the heat to high and add the cabbage, tossing well to coat in the spice mixture. Add the curry powder and season well with salt and pepper. Cook, covered, over medium-low heat 10 minutes, stirring occasionally. Stir in the ghee and serve hot with bread and chutney.

246 Spiced Red Kidney Beans

PREPARATION TIME 10 minutes, plus overnight soaking and making the curry powder, rice, and chutney **COOKING TIME** 1 hour 5 minutes **SERVES** 4

1 cup dried red kidney beans
2 tbsp. sunflower oil
1 onion, finely chopped
2in. piece of cinnamon stick
   or cassia bark
2 dried bay leaves
4 garlic cloves, minced
2 tsp. peeled and finely grated
   gingerroot
1 tsp. ground coriander

2 tsp. ground cumin
2 tbsp. Curry Powder (see page 11)
15oz. canned crushed tomatoes
4 tbsp. plain yogurt, whisked
salt and freshly ground black pepper
chopped cilantro leaves, to serve
1 recipe quantity Mushroom Pilau
   (see page 183), to serve
1 recipe quantity Mint & Cilantro
   Chutney (see page 201), to serve

1   Put the beans in a large, deep bowl, cover with cold water, and leave to soak overnight, then drain and rinse well.
2   Put the beans and 4¼ cups water in a large saucepan and bring to a boil over high heat. Boil 10 minutes, then lower the heat to medium-low and simmer 40 minutes, or until the beans are tender, then drain.
3   Shortly before the beans finish cooking, heat the oil in a large, heavy-bottomed saucepan over low heat. Add the onion, cinnamon, bay leaves, garlic, and ginger and fry, stirring occasionally, 4 to 5 minutes until fragrant. Add the coriander, cumin, and curry powder and mix well.
4   Add the beans, tomatoes, and 1 cup plus 2 tablespoons boiling water and bring to a boil over high heat, then lower the heat to medium-low and simmer, stirring frequently, 10 minutes, or until thick. Remove from the heat and season with salt and pepper. Swirl in the yogurt just before serving, then sprinkle with cilantro leaves and serve with rice and chutney.

247 Red Lentil Curry with Mustard Seeds & Tamarind

PREPARATION TIME 10 minutes, plus making the curry powder, bread, and chutney
COOKING TIME 50 minutes   **SERVES** 4

1¼ cups dried red lentils, rinsed
  and drained
1 tsp. turmeric
2 tbsp. sunflower oil
1 tsp. black mustard seeds
1 tbsp. Curry Powder
  (see page 11)
4 dried red chilies
1 bay leaf

2 tsp. tamarind paste
1 tbsp. sugar
salt
1 recipe quantity Saag Roti
  (see page 192), to serve
1 recipe quantity Apple & Mango
  Chutney (see page 198),
  to serve

1   Put the lentils and turmeric in a medium saucepan and mix well. Add 4½ cups water and bring to a boil over medium-high heat. Lower the heat to low and simmer, stirring frequently, 40 minutes until tender, then whisk until fairly smooth.
2   Heat the oil in a large wok or skillet over medium-high heat. When it is hot, add the mustard seeds. As soon as they begin to pop after a few seconds, add the cayenne, chilies, and bay leaf and fry, stirring occasionally, 5 to 6 seconds until the chilies darken in color.
3   Add the lentils and ⅔ cup water and season with salt. Mix well, then add the tamarind paste and sugar and bring to a boil. Lower the heat to low and simmer 8 to 10 minutes until thick. Serve hot with bread and chutney.

248 Saag Dal

PREPARATION TIME 15 minutes, plus at least 5 hours soaking and making the bread and chutney
COOKING TIME 40 minutes   **SERVES** 4

1 cup moong dal (split dried mung
  beans), rinsed and drained
1 tsp. turmeric
3 cups coarsely chopped baby
  leaf spinach
12 to 15 cherry tomatoes
1 small handful finely chopped
  cilantro leaves
2 tbsp. ghee or butter
2 tsp. cumin seeds
2 tsp. black mustard seeds

2 green chilies, seeded and
  thinly sliced
1 tbsp. ground coriander
1 tbsp. ground cumin
2 tbsp. finely chopped garlic
2 tbsp. peeled and finely chopped
  gingerroot
salt
1 recipe quantity Naan (see page 190)
1 recipe quantity Indian Red Cabbage
  Chutney (see page 202), to serve

1   Put the dal in a deep bowl, cover with cold water, and leave to soak 5 to 6 hours, or overnight, then rinse under cold running water and drain.
2   Put the dal, turmeric, and 6 cups water in a heavy-bottomed medium saucepan and bring to a boil over high heat. Boil 10 minutes, then lower the heat to low and simmer, stirring frequently, 10 to 15 minutes until thick, skimming off any scum that rises to the surface.
3   Carefully whisk the mixture until fairly smooth. Mix in the spinach, then add the tomatoes and cook, stirring frequently, over low heat 10 to 12 minutes until smooth. Remove from the heat and stir in the cilantro leaves.
4   Melt the ghee in a small skillet over high heat. When it is hot, add the cumin and mustard seeds, chilies, coriander, cumin, garlic, and ginger and cook, stirring, 30 to 40 seconds until fragrant. Stir the mixture into the dal and season with salt. Serve hot with bread and chutney.

249 Bhindi Masala

PREPARATION TIME 20 minutes, plus making the curry powder, bread, and raita
COOKING TIME 20 minutes **SERVES** 4

3 tbsp. freshly grated or
  shredded coconut
2 tbsp. sunflower oil
6 to 8 curry leaves
2 tsp. black mustard seeds
1 onion, finely chopped
2 tsp. ground cumin
1 tsp. ground coriander
2 tsp. Curry Powder (see page 11)
1 tsp. turmeric

3 garlic cloves, finely chopped
5 cups trimmed okra cut diagonally
  into 1in. pieces
2 tomatoes, finely chopped
salt and freshly ground black pepper
1 recipe quantity Besan Roti
  (see page 193), to serve
1 recipe quantity Corn Raita
  (see page 212), to serve

1   If using shredded coconut, soak it in warm water for 20 minutes, then drain.
2   Heat the oil in a large, nonstick wok or skillet over low heat. Add the curry leaves, mustard seeds, and onion and fry, stirring, 3 to 4 minutes until the onion begins to become soft. Add the cumin, coriander, curry powder, and turmeric and fry, stirring, 1 to 2 minutes longer until fragrant. Add the garlic and okra, increase the heat to high, and stir-fry 2 to 3 minutes until fragrant.
3   Add the tomatoes and season well with salt and pepper. Cover, lower the heat to low, and cook, stirring occasionally, 10 to 12 minutes until the okra is just tender. Sprinkle with the coconut and serve hot with bread and raita.

250 Shredded Cabbage Curry

PREPARATION TIME 20 minutes, plus making the rice and chutney **COOKING TIME** 15 minutes
SERVES 4

½ cup freshly grated or shredded
  coconut
2¾ cups very finely shredded
  cabbage, washed and drained
1 onion, finely chopped
2 green chilies, seeded and chopped
½ tsp. turmeric

1 tsp. black mustard seeds
1 recipe quantity Pilau Rice
  (see page 180), to serve
1 recipe quantity Sweet Mango
  Chutney (see page 213),
  to serve

1 If using shredded coconut, soak it in warm water for 20 minutes, then drain.
2 Put the cabbage in a large saucepan. Add the onion, chilies, turmeric, and
   mustard seeds and cook, covered, over medium-low heat 12 to 15 minutes,
   stirring occasionally, until the cabbage is soft but still a little crunch.
3 Stir in the coconut and serve hot with rice and chutney.

251 Spiced Chickpea Curry with Spinach

PREPARATION TIME 20 minutes, plus making the curry powder and bread
COOKING TIME 45 minutes   **SERVES** 4

2 tbsp. sunflower oil
2 onions, halved and thinly sliced
1 tbsp. Curry Powder (see page 11)
2 tsp. ground coriander
2 tsp. ground cumin
1 tsp. cayenne pepper
½ tsp. turmeric
15oz. canned crushed tomatoes

15oz. canned chickpeas, rinsed
  and drained
2 tbsp. chopped mint leaves
3oz. baby leaf spinach
½ cup plain yogurt
salt and freshly ground black pepper
1 recipe quantity Puri (see page 191),
  to serve

1 Heat the oil in a skillet over low heat. Add the onions and cook, stirring
   occasionally, 15 minutes, or until light golden. Add the curry powder, coriander,
   cumin, cayenne, and turmeric and cook, stirring, 1 to 2 minutes until fragrant.
   Add the tomatoes and 7 tablespoons water.
2 Bring to a boil over high heat, then cover, lower the heat to medium-low,
   and simmer 15 minutes, or until thick. Add the chickpeas, season with salt and
   pepper, and simmer 10 minutes, then stir in the mint. Divide the spinach onto
   plates. Top with the curry, drizzle the yogurt over, and serve with bread.

252 Spiced Eggplant Dal

PREPARATION TIME 15 minutes, plus making the curry powder and rice
COOKING TIME 45 minutes   **SERVES** 4

3 tbsp. sunflower oil
2 onions, finely chopped
4 garlic cloves, finely chopped
1 tsp. peeled and grated gingerroot
2 tbsp. Curry Powder (see page 11)
1 tbsp. cumin seeds
1 tbsp. black mustard seeds

scant 1 cup split yellow lentils,
  rinsed and drained
1 eggplant, cut into bite-size cubes
8 cherry tomatoes
1 handful cilantro leaves, chopped
salt
basmati rice, to serve

1 Heat the oil in a medium saucepan over high heat. Add the onions and stir-fry
   6 to 8 minutes until starting to color. Lower the heat to low, stir in the garlic,
   ginger, curry powder, and cumin and mustard seeds and cook 1 to 2 minutes.
   Add the lentils and 2½ cups plus 2 tablespoons water and bring to a boil.
2 Add the eggplant and tomatoes, then lower the heat to low. Simmer, covered,
   25 to 30 minutes, stirring occasionally, until thick. Season with salt, stir in the
   cilantro leaves, and serve hot with rice.

253 South Indian Vegetable Stew

PREPARATION TIME 15 minutes, plus making the idlis and accompaniment
COOKING TIME 25 minutes **SERVES** 4

2 tbsp. sunflower oil
6 shallots, halved and thinly sliced
2 tsp. black mustard seeds
8 to 10 curry leaves
1 green chili, thinly sliced
2 tsp. peeled and finely grated
 gingerroot
1 tsp. turmeric
2 tsp. ground cumin
6 whole black peppercorns
7oz. green beans, trimmed
2 carrots, cut into
 ½in.-thick batons

1 zucchini, cut into
 ½in.-thick batons
8oz. potatoes, peeled and
 cut into ½in.-thick batons
1¼ cups coconut milk
½ cup vegetable stock or water
juice of ½ lemon
salt and freshly ground black pepper
1 recipe quantity Idlis (see page 179),
 to serve
1 recipe quantity Spicy Yogurt
 Pachadi (see page 202), to serve

1 Heat the oil in a large, heavy-bottomed skillet with a tight-fitting lid over low
 heat. Add the shallots and fry, stirring occasionally, 4 to 5 minutes until soft. Add
 the mustard seeds, curry leaves, chili, ginger, turmeric, cumin, and peppercorns
 and cook, stirring, 1 to 2 minutes longer until fragrant.
2 Add the green beans, carrots, zucchini, potatoes, coconut milk, and stock and
 bring to a boil. Lower the heat to low and simmer, covered, 12 to 15 minutes
 until the vegetables are tender, then season with salt and pepper. Just before
 serving, squeeze the lemon juice over and serve hot with idlis and pachadi.

254 South Indian Mango & Yogurt Curry

PREPARATION TIME 20 minutes, plus making the rice and chutney
COOKING TIME 17 minutes **SERVES** 4

2 cups freshly grated or
 shredded coconut
3 firm ripe mangoes, peeled, pitted,
 and cut into small bite-size pieces
1 tsp. turmeric
1 tsp. cayenne pepper
3 or 4 green chilies, coarsely chopped
1 tbsp. cumin seeds
1¼ cups plain yogurt, lightly whisked

4 tbsp. sunflower oil
2 tsp. black mustard seeds
3 or 4 hot dried red chilies
10 to 12 fresh curry leaves
1 recipe quantity Curry Leaf
 & Coconut Rice (see page 186),
 to serve
1 recipe quantity Sweet Mango
 Chutney (see page 213), to serve

1 If using shredded coconut, soak it in warm water 20 minutes, then drain.
2 Put the mangoes, turmeric, cayenne, and 1 cup plus 2 tablespoons water
 in a heavy-bottomed saucepan. Bring to a boil over high heat, then remove
 immediately from the heat.
3 Meanwhile, put the coconut, green chilies, cumin seeds, and 1 cup plus
 2 tablespoons water in a blender or food processor and blend 2 to 3 minutes
 until the mixture forms a fine paste.
4 Stir the paste into the mango mixture and cook, covered, over low heat
 10 to 12 minutes, stirring occasionally, until thick. Add the yogurt and cook,
 stirring, 1 to 2 minutes until just warmed through. Make sure the mixture does
 not come to a boil. Remove from the heat and set aside.
5 Heat the oil in a small pan over medium-high heat. Add the mustard seeds and,
 when they begin to pop after a few seconds, add the dried chilies and curry
 leaves. Cook, stirring, for a few seconds until the chilies darken, then pour the
 mixture into the mango curry and serve hot with rice and chutney.

255 Thai Pumpkin Curry

PREPARATION TIME 20 minutes, plus making the curry paste and rice
COOKING TIME 30 minutes SERVES 4

2 tbsp. sunflower oil
1 red onion, halved and thinly sliced
2 garlic cloves, minced
1 tsp. peeled and grated gingerroot
3 tbsp. Thai Red Curry Paste
   (see page 15)
5¾ cups pumpkin, cut into bite-size
   cubes
1¾ cups coconut milk
6 kaffir lime leaves

2 tsp. grated palm sugar
3 lemongrass stalks, lightly crushed
1 handful Thai basil leaves
¼ cup skinless roasted peanuts,
   coarsely chopped
salt and freshly ground black pepper
1 recipe quantity
   Aromatic Sticky Rice
   (see page 178), to serve

1   Heat the oil in a large, nonstick wok or skillet over low heat. Add the onion,
    garlic, and ginger and fry, stirring occasionally, 3 to 4 minutes until soft. Stir in the
    curry paste and pumpkin and continue cooking, stirring, 3 to 4 minutes. Add the
    coconut milk, lime leaves, palm sugar, lemongrass, and scant 1 cup water. Bring
    to a boil, then lower the heat to low.
2   Cook, stirring occasionally, 20 minutes, or until the pumpkin is tender. Season
    with salt and pepper, sprinkle the basil and peanuts over, and serve hot with rice.

256 Singapore Spicy Long Beans

PREPARATION TIME 15 minutes, plus making the rice   COOKING TIME 10 minutes   SERVES 4

5oz. yard-long (snake) beans, cut
   into 1¾in. pieces
2 red chilies, coarsely chopped
4 shallots, coarsely chopped
1 garlic clove, coarsely chopped

2 tbsp. sunflower oil
½ tsp. turmeric
salt
1 recipe quantity Nonya Fried Rice
   (see page 175), to serve

1   Bring a saucepan of lightly salted water to a boil. Add the beans and cook
    3 to 4 minutes until soft but still crisp, then drain and set aside. Meanwhile, put
    the chilies, shallots, and garlic in a blender and blend 2 to 3 minutes until smooth,
    adding a little water if the mixture is too thick.
2   Heat the oil in a wok or skillet over low heat. Stir in the chili paste and cook,
    stirring, 2 to 3 minutes until fragrant. Add the beans and turmeric, season with
    salt, and cook, stirring, 2 to 3 minutes until well coated. Serve hot with rice.

257 Spiced Coconut & Okra Curry

PREPARATION TIME 20 minutes, plus making the idlis   COOKING TIME 11 minutes   SERVES 4

⅔ cup freshly grated or
   shredded coconut
4 tbsp. sunflower oil
1 onion, finely chopped
1 tbsp. black mustard seeds
1 tbsp. cumin seeds
2 or 3 dried red chilies

10 to 12 curry leaves
6 cups okra, cut diagonally into
   ¾in.-long pieces
½ tsp. turmeric
salt and freshly ground black pepper
1 recipe quantity Idlis (see page 179),
   to serve

1   If using shredded coconut, soak it in warm water 20 minutes, then drain.
2   Heat the oil in a wok or skillet over low heat. Add the onion and cook, stirring,
    5 minutes, or until soft. Add the mustard and cumin seeds, chilies, and curry
    leaves and stir-fry over high heat 2 minutes until fragrant.
3   Stir in the okra and turmeric and continue stir-frying 3 to 4 minutes until soft.
    Remove from the heat, sprinkle the coconut over, and season with salt and
    pepper. Serve hot with idlis.

258 Spiced Watermelon Curry

PREPARATION TIME 15 minutes   **COOKING TIME** 9 minutes   **SERVES** 4

1 tbsp. pumpkin seeds
2 tbsp. sunflower oil
2 large garlic cloves, minced
2 tsp. fennel seeds
1 tsp. nigella seeds
1 tsp. paprika

1 tsp. turmeric
1lb. 7oz. watermelon,
  cut into chunks
juice of 1 lime
1 tbsp. chopped mint leaves
poppadoms, to serve

1   Put the pumpkin seeds in a small skillet and dry-roast over low heat 2 to 3 minutes, stirring frequently, until lightly toasted and golden. Remove from the heat and leave to cool.

2   Heat the oil in a large pan over low heat. Add the garlic, fennel and nigella seeds, paprika, and turmeric and cook, stirring, 1 minute until fragrant. Add the watermelon and cook, stirring occasionally, 4 to 5 minutes until the juices are released. Remove from the heat and stir in the lime juice. Sprinkle with the pumpkin seeds and mint and serve immediately with poppadoms.

259 Sweet Potato Curry

PREPARATION TIME 15 minutes, plus making the rice **COOKING TIME** 30 minutes **SERVES** 4

1 onion, chopped
3 garlic cloves, minced
2 red chilies, finely chopped
1 tsp. turmeric
1 tsp. peeled and finely grated
   gingerroot
1 tbsp. light soy sauce

1 cup plus 2 tbsp. coconut milk
1½ cups vegetable stock
1 tbsp. lemon juice
1lb. sweet potatoes, peeled and
   cut into ¾in. cubes
basmati rice, to serve

1　Put all of the ingredients, except the sweet potatoes, in a large saucepan.
　　Bring to a boil, stirring, then lower the heat to low and simmer 5 to 8 minutes.
2　Mix in the sweet potatoes and simmer 15 to 20 minutes longer until they are
　　tender but not mushy. Serve hot with rice.

260 Saag Paneer

PREPARATION TIME 20 minutes, plus making the bread **COOKING TIME** 20 minutes **SERVES** 4

1lb. 2oz. frozen spinach
4 tbsp. ghee or butter
2 tsp. cumin seeds
1 onion, very finely chopped
2 tomatoes, finely chopped
2 tsp. finely grated garlic
1 tbsp. peeled and grated gingerroot
1 tsp. cayenne pepper
1 tsp. ground coriander

9oz. paneer, cut into bite-size pieces
2 tbsp. heavy cream
1 tsp. lemon juice
2 tbsp. finely chopped cilantro leaves
salt and freshly ground black pepper
1 recipe quantity Wholewheat
   Paratha (see page 193),
   to serve

1　Bring a large saucepan of water to a boil. Add the spinach, bring back to a boil,
　　and cook 2 to 3 minutes until it wilts. Drain well, transfer to a food processor and
　　blend 2 to 3 minutes until smooth.
2　Melt the ghee in a large, heavy-bottomed skillet over medium-low heat. Add the
　　cumin seeds and onion and cook, stirring occasionally, 6 to 8 minutes until the
　　onion is light golden. Add the tomatoes, garlic, ginger, cayenne, and coriander.
　　Season well with salt and pepper, mix well, and cook 2 to 3 minutes.
3　Increase the heat to high, add the paneer, and stir-fry 30 to 40 seconds. Add the
　　spinach puree and stir-fry 4 to 5 minutes until well mixed. Remove from the heat
　　and stir in the cream, lemon juice, and cilantro leaves. Serve hot with bread.

261 Sri Lankan Coconut Dal

PREPARATION TIME 15 minutes, plus making the rice **COOKING TIME** 30 minutes **SERVES** 4

heaped 1 cup dried red lentils, rinsed
   and drained
2 shallots, finely chopped
1¾ cups coconut milk
2 tomatoes, chopped
2 green chilies, sliced
1 tsp. turmeric

4 tbsp. sunflower oil
1 onion, thinly sliced
8 to 10 curry leaves
2 tsp. black mustard seeds
salt and freshly ground black pepper
basmati rice, to serve

1　Put the lentils, shallots, coconut milk, tomatoes, chilies, turmeric, and 1¼ cups
　　water in a saucepan. Season with salt and pepper, then bring to a boil over high
　　heat. Lower the heat to medium-low and simmer, stirring occasionally, 15 to 20
　　minutes until the lentils are tender.
2　Heat the oil in a large skillet over low heat. Add the onion and fry 6 to 8 minutes
　　until light brown, then add the curry leaves and mustard seeds and cook, stirring,
　　1 to 2 minutes until fragrant. Stir the mixture into the lentils and serve with rice.

262 Sri Lankan Green Bean Curry

PREPARATION TIME 10 minutes, plus making the curry powder and rice
COOKING TIME 20 minutes   SERVES 4

1 tbsp. sunflower oil
1 onion, sliced
1 or 2 green chilies, sliced
1 garlic clove, very finely chopped
5 or 6 curry leaves
1 tbsp. Curry Powder
 (see page 11)
¼ tsp. turmeric

½ tsp. fenugreek seeds
1lb. green beans, trimmed and halved
½ cup coconut milk
squeeze of lime juice
salt and freshly ground black pepper
1 recipe quantity Lemon Rice
 (see page 182), to serve

1   Heat the oil in a saucepan over low heat. Add the onion, chilies, garlic, and curry
    leaves and cook, stirring occasionally, 6 to 8 minutes until the onions are golden
    brown. Sprinkle the curry powder, turmeric, and fenugreek seeds over and season
    well with salt and pepper. Cook, stirring, 2 to 3 minutes until fragrant.
2   Add the green beans and cook, stirring, 3 to 4 minutes until beginning to soften.
    Lower the heat to low, add the coconut milk, and cook 3 to 4 minutes longer.
    Remove from the heat, add a squeeze of lime juice and serve hot with rice.

263 Steamed Baby Eggplants with Chilies & Herbs

PREPARATION TIME 20 minutes, plus making the rice   COOKING TIME 35 minutes   SERVES 4

1lb. 2oz. baby eggplants,
 halved lengthwise
5 tbsp. sunflower oil
6 garlic cloves, very finely chopped
1 tbsp. peeled and very finely
 chopped gingerroot
8 scallions, cut diagonally into
 1¼in. pieces
2 red chilies, seeded and
 thinly sliced
3 tbsp. light soy sauce

1 tbsp. Chinese rice wine
1 tbsp. palm sugar or soft light sugar
1 small handful mint leaves
1 small handful cilantro leaves,
 coarsely chopped
3oz. canned water chestnuts, drained,
 rinsed, and coarsely chopped
⅓ cup roasted skinless peanuts,
 coarsely chopped
1 recipe quantity Classic Egg-Fried
 Rice (see page 178), to serve

1   Place a trivet or steamer rack in a wok or saucepan. Fill the wok with 2 inches
    of water and bring the water to a boil over high heat. Put the eggplants on
    a heatproof plate and carefully lower it onto the trivet. Lower the heat to low
    and steam, covered, 25 to 30 minutes until the eggplants are cooked through
    and soft to the touch. Top up the water as needed to prevent the wok from
    drying out. Remove from the wok, transfer the eggplants to a serving bowl,
    and set aside to cool.
2   Heat the oil in a nonstick skillet over low heat. Add the garlic, ginger, scallions,
    and chilies and fry, stirring occasionally, 2 to 3 minutes until fragrant. Remove
    from the heat and carefully add the soy sauce, rice wine, and sugar, stirring
    until the sugar dissolves.
3   Toss the mint, cilantro leaves, and water chestnuts with the eggplants and pour
    the garlic–ginger mixture evenly over the top. Gently toss in the peanuts and
    serve hot with rice.

264 Tarka Dal

PREPARATION TIME 15 minutes, plus making the rice and pickle   **COOKING TIME** 40 minutes
SERVES 4

heaped 1 cup split red lentils, rinsed
  and drained
1 tsp. turmeric
4 tomatoes, coarsely chopped
scant ½ cup finely chopped
  cilantro leaves
salt and freshly ground black pepper
1 recipe quantity Curry Leaf
  & Coconut Rice (see page 186),
  to serve
1 recipe quantity Beet Pickle
  (see page 199), to serve

TARKA (SPICED OIL)
4 tbsp. sunflower oil
2 tsp. black mustard seeds
3 tsp. cumin seeds
2 garlic cloves, very thinly sliced
2 tsp. peeled and minced gingerroot
6 to 8 curry leaves
1 dried red chili
2 tsp. ground cumin
2 tsp. ground coriander

1   Put the lentils and 4 cups water in a heavy-bottomed saucepan and bring to
    a boil over high heat. Boil 8 to 10 minutes, skimming off any scum that rises
    to the surface. Lower the heat to medium and simmer, stirring occasionally,
    20 to 25 minutes until the lentils are soft.

2   Remove from the heat and, using an immersion blender or electric whisk, blend
    until smooth. Return to the heat and stir in the turmeric and tomatoes. Bring to
    a boil, season with salt and pepper, and stir in the cilantro leaves.

3   To make the tarka, heat the oil in a large skillet over medium-high heat. When
    it is hot, add all of the remaining ingredients for the tarka and cook, stirring,
    1 to 2 minutes until fragrant. Remove from the heat and stir the mixture into
    the dal. Serve hot with rice and pickle.

265 Vietnamese Tofu with Green Beans & Lemongrass

PREPARATION TIME 20 minutes, plus making the rice and pickle   **COOKING TIME** 15 minutes
SERVES 4

2 tbsp. canola oil
1lb. extra-firm tofu, patted dry and
  cut into ½in. cubes
3 garlic cloves, finely chopped
1 tbsp. peeled and finely grated
  gingerroot
2 tbsp. finely chopped lemongrass
1 red chili, finely chopped

1lb. green beans, trimmed
1 tsp. light soy sauce
salt and freshly ground black pepper
1 recipe quantity Aromatic Sticky Rice
  (see page 178), to serve
1 recipe quantity Vietnamese Carrot
  & Radish Pickle (see page 208),
  to serve

1   Heat half of the oil in a large wok or skillet over high heat. Add the tofu and fry
    3 to 4 minutes, stirring occasionally, until crisp and lightly golden. Remove from
    the wok, drain on paper towels, and season with salt and pepper.

2   Add the remaining oil and the garlic, ginger, lemongrass, and chili to the wok.
    Stir-fry 30 seconds until fragrant. Add the green beans, toss well, and continue
    cooking, stirring occasionally, 4 to 5 minutes, or until the beans are soft but still
    crunchy and starting to brown in spots. Add 4 tablespoons water, cover the wok,
    and leave to steam 3 to 4 minutes until tender.

3   Return the tofu to the wok and add the soy sauce. Season again with salt and
    pepper, if necessary, mix well and serve hot with rice and pickle.

266 Vegetable & Tofu Pho

PREPARATION TIME 40 minutes   COOKING TIME 40 minutes   SERVES 4

9oz. dried rice noodles
4 cups coarsely chopped Swiss
    chard leaves
1⅓ cups broccoli florets
2 scallions, thinly sliced
2oz. bean sprouts
1 tsp. cayenne pepper
1 tbsp. sesame oil
9oz. fried tofu, sliced or diced
2 tbsp. finely chopped mint leaves
2 tbsp. finely chopped
    cilantro leaves
1 tbsp. sesame seeds
1 lime, cut into wedges

VEGETABLE PHO STOCK
4 cups vegetable stock
1 small onion, chopped
6 garlic cloves, peeled but left whole
1in. piece gingerroot, peeled and
    roughly sliced
3 cinnamon sticks
1 bay leaf
1 tsp. Sichuan peppercorns

1   Put all of the ingredients for the stock in a large saucepan and bring to a boil over high heat. Lower the heat to low and simmer, covered, 30 minutes, or until slightly thickened. Meanwhile, put the noodles in a heatproof bowl, cover with hot water, and leave to soak 15 to 20 minutes until soft. Refresh in a bowl of cold water, then drain and set aside.
2   Strain the stock into a clean pan and discard the solids. Return the stock to low heat and add the chard, broccoli, scallions, bean sprouts, cayenne, and sesame oil, then cook 10 to 12 minutes.
3   To serve, divide the rice noodles into four bowls and top with the tofu. Ladle the stock and vegetable mixture over, sprinkle over the mint and cilantro leaves and sesame seeds, and serve with lime wedges for squeezing over.

267 Vegetable Samosas

PREPARATION TIME 20 minutes, plus making the curry powder and chutney
COOKING TIME 25 minutes   MAKES 20

1 large potato, cut into ½in. cubes
1 carrot cut into ½in. cubes
2 tbsp. sunflower oil
1 onion, chopped
1 tbsp. Curry Powder (see page 11)
⅓ cup frozen peas
4 tbsp. chopped cilantro leaves

4 tbsp. chopped mint leaves
5 large sheets of phyllo pastry dough
1 egg, beaten
salt and freshly ground black pepper
1 recipe quantity Coconut & Cilantro
    Chutney (see page 201), to serve

1   Bring a saucepan of lightly salted water to a boil. Add the potato and carrot and boil 8 to 10 minutes until tender, then drain.
2   Meanwhile, heat the oil in a large skillet over low heat. Add the onion and curry powder, season with salt and pepper, and cook, stirring occasionally, 10 minutes, or until the onion is soft and just starting to color. Add the carrots, potatoes, and peas and mix well. Remove from the heat and mix in the cilantro and mint leaves. Set aside to cool.
3   Put the phyllo dough on a clean work surface. Cut it in half lengthwise, then in half once more widthwise, so you have 4 rectangles from each sheet. Cover with a clean, barely damp tea towel to prevent them drying out while you work.
4   Preheat the oven to 425°F. Put one phyllo rectangle on a work surface with one of the short edges closest to you. Put 2 teaspoons of the vegetable mixture on the end closest to you, leaving a small gap between the filling and the edge of the dough. Fold the dough over the filling to form a triangle and continue folding to form a triangular package. Brush the edge with a little of the beaten egg to seal, then put the samosa on a baking tray and brush again with the egg. Repeat with the remaining dough and filling to make 20 samosas.
5   Bake 10 to 12 minutes until golden brown. Serve hot with chutney.

Spiced Beet Curry

PREPARATION TIME 15 minutes, plus making the rice   **COOKING TIME** 30 minutes   **SERVES** 4

2 tbsp. sunflower oil
1 tsp. black mustard seeds
1 onion, chopped
2 garlic cloves, chopped
2 red chilies, seeded and
    finely chopped
8 curry leaves
1 tsp. turmeric
1 tsp. cumin seeds
1 cinnamon stick

1lb. 4oz. raw beets, peeled and
    cut into batons
7oz. canned crushed tomatoes
salt
½ cup coconut milk
juice of 1 lime, plus 1 lime, cut into
    wedges, to serve (optional)
2 tbsp. chopped cilantro leaves
1 recipe quantity Saffron Rice
    (see page 180), to serve

1   Heat the oil in a wok or saucepan over low heat. Add the mustard seeds
    and, as soon as they begin to pop after a few seconds, add the onion, garlic,
    and chilies and fry, stirring occasionally, 5 minutes, or until the onion is soft.

2   Add the curry leaves, turmeric, cumin seeds, cinnamon, and beets and fry,
    stirring, 1 to 2 minutes longer until fragrant, then add the tomatoes and 1 cup
    plus 2 tablespoons water and season with salt. Simmer, stirring occasionally,
    15 to 20 minutes until the beets are tender.

3   Stir in the coconut milk and simmer 1 to 2 minutes longer until the sauce
    thickens. Stir in the lime juice and season again with salt if necessary. Sprinkle
    with the cilantro leaves and serve hot with rice and extra lime wedges, if desired.

269 West Indian Vegetable Curry

PREPARATION TIME 15 minutes, plus making the curry powder and bread
COOKING TIME 35 minutes   **SERVES** 4

1 tbsp. sunflower oil
2 onions, finely chopped
1 red pepper, seeded and
   finely chopped
6 scallions, finely chopped
3 garlic cloves, minced
1 tbsp. finely chopped thyme leaves,
   plus thyme sprigs to serve
2 tsp. Curry Powder (see page 11)
2 cups plus 2 tbsp. vegetable stock

2 carrots, cut into bite-size cubes
1lb. pumpkin, peeled, seeded,
   and cut into small wedges
15oz. canned crushed tomatoes
2 zucchini, halved lengthwise
   and sliced
1 Scotch bonnet or habanero chili
1 recipe quantity Trinidadian Roti
   Paratha (see page 189), to serve

1   Heat the oil in a large flameproof casserole over medium-high heat. Add the onions,
    red pepper, scallions, garlic, thyme, and curry powder. Fry, stirring occasionally,
    5 minutes, or until the vegetables are tender. Add the stock and bring to a boil.
2   Add the carrots, pumpkin, tomatoes, zucchini, and chili and bring back to a boil.
    Lower the heat to low and simmer 10 minutes, or until thick. Discard the chili and
    simmer 15 minutes longer, or until the vegetables are just tender. Top with thyme
    sprigs and serve hot with bread.

270 Kali Dal

PREPARATION TIME 20 minutes, plus at least 10 hours soaking and making the bread
COOKING TIME 1 hour 5 minutes   SERVES 4

heaped ½ cup dried whole black
    lentils, rinsed and drained
3 tbsp. butter
1 onion, finely chopped
3 garlic cloves, crushed
2 tsp. peeled and finely grated
    gingerroot
2 green chilies, split in half
    lengthwise
1 tsp. turmeric
1 tsp. paprika, plus extra for
    sprinkling

1 tbsp. ground coriander
1 tbsp. ground cumin
7oz. canned red kidney beans,
    drained and rinsed
7oz. baby leaf spinach
1 large handful cilantro leaves,
    chopped
⅔ cup heavy cream
salt
1 recipe quantity Naan
    (see page 190), to serve

1   Put the lentils in a deep bowl, cover with cold water, and leave to soak 10 to
    12 hours. Transfer to a colander and rinse under cold running water, then drain.
2   Put the lentils and 2 cups plus 2 tablespoons boiling water in a saucepan. Bring
    to a boil over high heat, then lower the heat to low and simmer, stirring
    occasionally, 35 to 40 minutes until tender. Drain and set aside.
3   Melt the butter in a large saucepan over low heat. Add the onion, garlic, ginger,
    and chilies and fry, stirring occasionally, 5 to 6 minutes until the onion is soft.
    Add the turmeric, paprika, coriander, cumin, kidney beans, and lentils and mix
    well. Add 2 cups plus 2 tablespoons water and bring back to a boil over high
    heat. Lower the heat to low and stir in the spinach. Simmer, stirring frequently,
    10 to 15 minutes. Remove from the heat and season with salt. Stir in the cilantro
    leaves and drizzle the cream over. Sprinkle with paprika and serve hot with bread

271 Tofu & Mixed Vegetable Curry

PREPARATION TIME 20 minutes, plus making the rice   COOKING TIME 25 minutes   SERVES 4

2 tbsp. sunflower oil
2 tsp. peeled and finely grated
    gingerroot
8 garlic cloves, coarsely chopped
8 Thai or small shallots, finely
    chopped
2 red chilies, seeded and coarsely
    chopped
4 tbsp. very finely chopped
    lemongrass
1 tsp. turmeric
1¾ cups coconut milk
scant 1 cup vegetable stock

7oz. snow peas, trimmed
12 baby corn cobs, trimmed
14oz. firm tofu, cut into bite-size
    cubes
1 tbsp. dark soy sauce
1 tbsp. lime juice, plus extra if needed
1 small handful coarsely chopped
    cilantro leaves
salt
Thai basil leaves, to serve
sliced red chilies, to serve
1 recipe quantity Classic Egg-Fried
    Rice (see page 178), to serve

1   Put the oil, ginger, garlic, shallots, chilies, lemongrass, turmeric, and half
    the coconut milk in a blender or food processor. Blend 2 to 3 minutes until
    fairly smooth.
2   Heat a large, nonstick wok or skillet over high heat. Add the coconut milk
    mixture and cook, stirring occasionally, 3 to 4 minutes until thick, then add
    the remaining coconut milk and the stock. Bring to a boil, lower the heat
    to low, and simmer slowly, uncovered, 10 minutes, or until thick.
3   Add the snow peas and corn cobs and continue simmering 6 to 7 minutes
    until starting to turn tender. Stir in the tofu, soy sauce, and lime juice. Check
    the seasoning and season again with salt and lime juice if necessary. Simmer
    1 to 2 minutes longer until hot. Remove from the heat, and stir in the cilantro
    leaves. Divide into four bowls, sprinkle with basil leaves and chilies, and serve
    with rice.

CHAPTER 6

RICE & BREADS

The fragrant, nutty aroma of rice cooking in the kitchen always takes me back to my childhood in India. Simple preparations such as Pilau Rice and Lemon Rice were an everyday staple of our diet, served as an accompaniment to meat, chicken and vegetable curries. They're here for you to try, too, along with other everyday favorites from all over the world, including Cucumber & Shrimp Nasi Goreng and Chinese Mixed Fried Rice. Options abound for festive or special occasions, too, such as Aromatic Shrimp Pilaf, Fava Bean Pilaf, served with Pomegranate Seeds, or Spicy Spinach Biryani with Cauliflower.

Hot steaming flatbreads straight off the fire are another vivid memory of my Indian kitchen. Naan, roti, and paratha were cooked daily and served with different lentil dishes and curries. These breads are also ideal accompaniments to broiled and grilled kebabs and spiced fish or poultry recipes. Steamed breads like Idlis (made with rice flour) are the perfect foil to a spicy South Indian curry.

All of these recipes are easy to make, too. So dive in and discover how much they add to any meal.

LAMB BIRYANI (*SEE PAGE 168*)

272 Lamb Biryani

PREPARATION TIME 20 minutes, plus at least 4 hours marinating, 30 minutes resting, and making the raita **COOKING TIME** 1 hour 35 minutes **SERVES** 4

1lb. 2oz. boned leg of lamb,
  cut into bite-size pieces
4 garlic cloves, very finely chopped
1 tsp. peeled and finely grated
  gingerroot
⅔ cup plain yogurt
⅓ cup finely chopped cilantro leaves
4 tbsp. sunflower oil
1 onion, finely chopped
1 tbsp. ground coriander
1 tsp. ground cumin
1 tsp. cayenne pepper
1 tsp. turmeric
7oz. canned crushed tomatoes
butter, for greasing
salt and freshly ground black pepper

poppadoms, to serve
1 recipe quantity Raita
  (see page 204), to serve

RICE
4 tbsp. sunflower oil
1 onion, halved and thinly sliced
2 tsp. cumin seeds
6 cloves
10 whole black peppercorns
4 green cardamom pods
1 cinnamon stick
heaped 1 cup basmati rice
1 tsp. saffron threads
3 tbsp. warm milk

1 Put the lamb in a glass or ceramic dish. Mix together the garlic, ginger, yogurt, and cilantro leaves and rub this mixture into the lamb. Cover and leave to marinate in the refrigerator 4 to 6 hours.

2 Heat the oil in a heavy-bottomed saucepan over low heat. Add the onion and fry, stirring occasionally, 12 to 15 minutes until light golden. Add the lamb and cook over high heat, stirring frequently, 15 minutes, or until well brown. Stir in the coriander, cumin, cayenne, turmeric, and tomatoes and season well with salt and pepper. Bring to a boil, then lower the heat to low and simmer 30 minutes, or until the lamb is tender and most of the liquid is absorbed.

3 Meanwhile, make the rice. Heat the oil in another heavy-bottomed pan with a tight-fitting lid over low heat. Add the onion, cumin seeds, cloves, peppercorns, cardamom, and cinnamon and cook, stirring, 6 to 8 minutes until light brown. Add the rice and cook, stirring, for 2 minutes longer, or until well coated. Add 1¾ cups water and bring to a boil. Cover tightly, lower the heat to low, and simmer 6 to 7 minutes. Remove from the heat and keep covered. In a small bowl, mix together the saffron and warm milk and set aside to infuse.

4 Preheat the oven to 350°F and lightly butter a medium ovenproof casserole with a tight-fitting lid. Spread a thin layer of the meat mixture over the bottom and cover evenly with half of the rice. Drizzle half of the saffron mixture over, then layer again. Cover the dish with foil, then with the lid, and bake 30 minutes. Remove from the oven and leave to rest, covered, 30 minutes before serving with poppadoms and raita.

273 Azerbaijani Dill Pilaf

PREPARATION TIME 20 minutes **COOKING TIME** 25 minutes **SERVES** 4

scant 1 cup long-grain white rice
3 tbsp. butter
2 cups green beans trimmed and cut
  into bite-size pieces

2½ cups plus 2 tbsp. chicken stock
½ to ⅔ cup finely chopped dill
salt and freshly ground black pepper

1 Put the rice and butter in a heavy saucepan over low heat. Cook, stirring, 2 to 3 minutes until the grains are well coated, then add the green beans and stock. Bring to a boil. Season well with salt and pepper, then lower the heat to low and cook, covered, 15 to 20 minutes until the rice is cooked through.

2 Remove from the heat and leave to stand, covered, 10 minutes. Fluff up the rice with a fork, stir in the dill, and serve hot.

Chinese Mixed Fried Rice

PREPARATION TIME 15 minutes, plus making the rice   **COOKING TIME** 20 minutes   **SERVES** 4

5 tbsp. canola oil

1oz. pork tenderloin, cut into
  small cubes

12 raw jumbo shrimp, shelled
  and deveined

1 cooked boneless, skinless, chicken
  breast half or thigh, cut into cubes

⅔ cup frozen peas

1oz. canned water chestnuts, drained
  and roughly diced

1oz. canned bamboo shoots, drained
  and diced

2 tsp. Chinese rice wine

scant 1 cup chicken stock

1 large egg, lightly beaten

2¾ cups cooked long-grain white rice

⅔ cup thickly sliced shiitake
  mushrooms

3 scallions, thinly sliced

1 tbsp. sesame oil

2 tbsp. light soy sauce

salt and freshly ground black pepper

1 red chili, thinly sliced, to serve

1   Heat 2 tablespoons of the oil in a wok over high heat. Add the pork and shrimp
    and stir-fry 3 to 4 minutes. Add the chicken, peas, water chestnuts, and bamboo
    shoots and continue stir-frying 1 to 2 minutes longer, or until the mixture is
    sizzling and cooked through. Add the rice wine and stock and bring to a boil.
    Cook 2 to 3 minutes, then season with salt, transfer to a bowl, and set aside.

2   Return the wok to the heat and add the remaining 3 tablespoons of the oil.
    Season the egg with salt and pepper, add it to the wok and swirl it around the
    bottom. Cook 1 to 2 minutes until the egg is half-cooked, then add the rice.
    Stir-fry 4 to 5 minutes until hot. Add the stir-fried meat and vegetables and stir
    well, then add the scallions, sesame oil, and soy sauce, and stir-fry 30 seconds
    longer, or until well mixed. Serve hot topped with red chili.

275 Japanese Mushroom Rice

PREPARATION TIME 20 minutes, plus at least 30 minutes soaking   **COOKING TIME** 20 minutes
SERVES 4

1 tbsp. instant dashi powder
2oz. dried shiitake mushrooms
1½ cups Japanese short-grain
   white rice
3 thin slices of peeled gingerroot
3 cups light chicken stock
3 tbsp. brown rice vinegar
1 tbsp. sesame oil

1 tbsp. sunflower oil
20 baby button mushrooms,
   left whole and stems trimmed
2 tbsp. light soy sauce
2 tbsp. mirin
1 tbsp. toasted sesame seeds
2 scallions, sliced

1   Dissolve the dashi powder in 2½ cups plus 2 tablespoons hot water. Add the
    shiitake mushrooms and leave to soak at least 30 minutes.
2   Put the rice, ginger, and stock in a heavy-bottomed saucepan with a tight-fitting
    lid and bring to a boil over high heat. Boil 2 to 3 minutes, then lower the heat to
    low, cover the pan tightly, and cook 7 to 8 minutes longer. Remove from the heat
    and leave to stand, covered, 10 minutes. Drizzle the rice vinegar over the rice and
    fluff up with a fork, then set aside.
3   Drain the shiitake mushrooms and slice thinly. Heat the oils in a large skillet over
    low heat. Add the shiitake and button mushrooms and fry, stirring occasionally,
    5 to 6 minutes until light brown. Stir in the soy sauce and mirin and remove from
    the heat. Divide the rice into bowls and top with the mushrooms. Sprinkle the
    sesame seeds and scallions over and serve hot.

276 Turkish Vermicelli & Rice Pilaf

PREPARATION TIME 25 minutes **COOKING TIME** 25 minutes **SERVES** 4 to 6

4 tbsp. butter
2 tbsp. olive oil
7oz. rice vermicelli, broken
    into 1in. pieces
1¼ cups long-grain
    white rice

3¾ cups hot chicken stock
½ tsp. cinnamon
½ tsp. ground cardamom
¼ tsp. ground cloves
salt and freshly ground black pepper

1 Heat the butter and oil in a heavy-bottomed saucepan with a tight-fitting lid over low heat. When the butter melts, add the vermicelli and cook, stirring, 2 to 3 minutes until golden brown. Add the rice and cook, stirring, 1 minute until well coated. Slowly add the stock, season with salt and pepper, and boil 1 minute.
2 Cover the pan tightly, lower the heat to low, and simmer 18 to 20 minutes until the liquid is absorbed. Remove from the heat and leave to stand, covered, 12 to 15 minutes. Fluff up the rice with a fork, sprinkle with the cinnamon, cardamom, and cloves, and serve hot.

277 Curried Chicken Fried Rice

PREPARATION TIME 15 minutes, plus making the curry powder and the rice
COOKING TIME 10 minutes **SERVES** 4

1 large egg
2 tsp. sesame oil
3 tbsp. canola oil
1 red chili, finely chopped
1 garlic clove, crushed
1 tsp. peeled and finely chopped
    gingerroot
1 tsp. Chinese five-spice powder
1 tbsp. Curry Powder (see page 11)
2½ cups cold cooked long-grain
    white rice

2¾ cups cooked boneless, skinless
    chicken breasts, shredded
2oz. bean sprouts
1 carrot, finely grated
1 red bell pepper, seeded and cut
    into thin strips
1 yellow bell pepper, seeded and
    cut into thin strips
2 bok choy, coarsely chopped
8 scallions, finely chopped
3 tbsp. light soy sauce
freshly ground black pepper

1 Whisk together the egg and sesame oil and set aside. Heat the canola oil in a large wok or skillet over medium-high heat. When it is hot and almost smoking, add the chili, garlic, ginger, five-spice powder, curry powder, and rice and stir-fry 3 to 4 minutes until completely heated through.
2 Add the chicken, bean sprouts, carrot, peppers, bok choy, and scallions and stir-fry 3 to 4 minutes. Add the soy sauce and season well with pepper, then push the mixture to one side of the wok.
3 Pour the egg mixture into the empty side of the wok and leave 10 seconds to begin to set. Using a chopstick, briskly swirl the egg around to break it up, then toss it into the rice. Stir-fry 1 minute longer and serve hot.

278 Vietnamese Chicken Rice

PREPARATION TIME 25 minutes, plus making the dipping sauce   **COOKING TIME** 2 hours
SERVES 4

1¾ cups long-grain white rice, rinsed
   and drained
2 or 3 shallots, halved and sliced
1 small handful mint leaves,
thinly sliced
4 scallions, thinly sliced
1 recipe quantity Nuoc Cham Dipping
   Sauce (see page 204),
   to serve

CHICKEN STOCK
4 chicken legs
1 onion, quartered
1¾in. piece gingerroot, peeled
   and coarsely chopped
1 tbsp. fish sauce
4 or 5 whole black peppercorns
1 small handful mint, leaves picked

1 Put all of the ingredients for the stock in a deep saucepan. Add 4⅓ cups water and bring to a boil over high heat. Skim off any foam, then lower the heat to low and simmer, covered, 1 hour.

2 Increase the heat to medium and simmer, uncovered, 30 minutes longer, until the stock reduces slightly. Skim off any fat, then strain the stock into a clean pan (reserving the chicken legs), season with salt, and set aside. Discard the skin from the chicken and shred the meat, then set aside.

3 Put the rice and 3¼ cups of the stock in a heavy-bottomed pan with a tight-fitting lid. When the rice settles, check that the stock covers the rice by 1 inch; if not, top it up. Bring to a boil over high heat, then cover the pan tightly, lower the heat to low, and cook 25 minutes, or until all of the liquid is absorbed.

4 Remove the pan from the heat and, using a fork, stir in the shredded chicken, shallots, and most of the mint. Cover the pan and leave to stand 10 minutes, then serve warm, sprinkled with the remaining mint and the scallions, and with the nuoc cham as an accompaniment in small bowls for dipping.

279 Lebanese-Style Chicken Pilaf

PREPARATION TIME 20 minutes   **COOKING TIME** 40 minutes   **SERVES** 4

2 tbsp. ghee or butter
1 onion, chopped
10oz. ground chicken
1 cinnamon stick
8 green cardamom pods,
   lightly crushed

3 tbsp. golden raisins
1 cup basmati rice
a large pinch of saffron threads
2 cups plus 2 tbsp. chicken stock
⅔ cup pine nuts
salt and freshly ground black pepper

1 Melt the ghee in a heavy-bottomed saucepan with a tight-fitting lid over medium-low heat. Add the onion and fry, stirring occasionally, 10 to 15 minutes until golden brown and starting to caramelize. Transfer to a plate, using a slotted spoon, and set aside.

2 Put the ground chicken in the same pan and stir-fry over high heat 4 to 5 minutes. Add the cinnamon, cardamom, golden raisins, rice and saffron, season well with salt and pepper, and stir-fry 2 to 3 minutes.

3 Return the onion to the pan and add the stock. Bring to a boil, then cover the pan tightly, lower the heat to low, and simmer for 12 to 15 minutes until the rice is cooked and all of the stock is absorbed. Remove the pan from the heat and leave to stand, covered, 10 minutes.

4 Meanwhile, put the pine nuts in a small skillet and dry-roast over low heat, stirring frequently, 2 to 3 minutes until lightly toasted and golden. Remove from the heat.

5 Sprinkle the rice with the pine nuts and serve warm.

Cucumber & Shrimp Nasi Goreng

PREPARATION TIME 10 minutes, plus making the curry powder and rice
COOKING TIME 18 minutes   **SERVES** 4

3 large eggs, lightly beaten
3 to 4 tbsp. canola oil, plus extra
   for frying the shallots
6 shallots, sliced
3 tbsp. Curry Powder (see page 11)
2½ cups cold cooked long-grain
   white rice

10oz. shelled and deveined cooked
   small shrimp
½ cucumber, seeded and finely
   chopped
1 small handful cilantro leaves,
   chopped
salt and freshly ground black pepper

1   Season the eggs with salt and pepper. Heat 1 teaspoon of the oil in a large
    wok or deep, wide nonstick skillet over low heat. Add half of the eggs in a thin
    layer and cook 2 to 3 minutes until set and golden. Carefully remove the omelet
    from the pan, roll it into a log, and set aside to cool. Repeat with the remaining
    eggs and another 1 teaspoon of the oil. Cut the cooled omelets into thin slices
    and set aside.

2   Carefully wipe out the wok with paper towels and add fresh oil to a depth
    of ½ inch. Heat the oil over high heat, then add the shallots and fry, stirring
    occasionally, 5 minutes, or until crisp and golden. Remove with a slotted spoon
    and leave to drain on paper towels.

3   Discard the oil and wipe the wok clean again. Add another 2 tablespoons of the
    oil to the wok and heat it over low heat. Add the curry powder and cook, stirring,
    1 minute, or until fragrant. Add the rice and stir-fry 2 minutes, then add the
    shrimp and stir-fry 1 minute longer. Stir the omelet strips and shallots into the
    rice, then add the cucumber and cilantro and stir 2 to 3 minutes until heated
    through. Serve hot.

281 Aromatic Shrimp Pilaf

PREPARATION TIME 15 minutes, plus making the curry powder   COOKING TIME 35 minutes
SERVES 4

2 tbsp. sunflower oil
1 large onion, finely chopped
2 garlic cloves, finely chopped
1 tbsp. Curry Powder
  (see page 11)
1¼ cups basmati rice
2½ cups plus 2 tbsp. fish stock

finely grated zest and juice
  of 1 large lime
⅓ cup cilantro leaves, finely chopped
10oz. shelled and deveined
  cooked shrimp
salt and freshly ground black pepper

1   Heat the oil in a heavy-bottomed saucepan over low heat. Add the onion and
    fry, stirring occasionally, 4 to 5 minutes until beginning to color. Add the garlic
    and curry powder and cook, stirring, 1 to 2 minutes until fragrant. Add the rice
    and mix well, then add the stock and lime zest. Season well with salt and pepper.
2   Simmer, covered, 15 to 20 minutes until the stock is absorbed and the rice
    is tender. Stir in the lime juice, cilantro, and shrimp and cook, stirring, 4 to 5
    minutes longer until the shrimp are warmed through. Serve hot.

282 Mauritian Pilaf

PREPARATION TIME 25 minutes   COOKING TIME 45 minutes   SERVES 4 to 6

4 tbsp. sunflower oil
10oz. beef, such as sirloin or
  tenderloin, cut into bite-size pieces
10oz. boneless, skinless chicken breast
  or thigh, cut into bite-size pieces
1 onion, chopped
1 tsp. minced garlic
1 tsp. peeled and finely grated
  gingerroot

1 tbsp. turmeric
4 curry leaves
2 tbsp. finely chopped cilantro leaves
2 tbsp. chopped thyme leaves
3 cloves
1 teaspoon whole black peppercorns
1½ cups basmati rice
salt

1   Heat the oil in a wide, heavy-bottomed saucepan with a tight-fitting lid over
    medium-low heat. Add the beef and chicken and cook, stirring occasionally,
    6 to 8 minutes until golden brown. Transfer to a plate, using a slotted spoon,
    then set aside.
2   Add the onion, garlic, and ginger to the pan and cook, stirring occasionally,
    8 to 10 minutes until the onion is soft and translucent.
3   Return the beef and chicken to the pan and add the turmeric, curry leaves,
    cilantro, thyme, cloves, and peppercorns. Mix well, then add the rice and cook,
    stirring, 2 to 3 minutes longer until the grains are well coated.
4   Add 3¾ cups water and bring to a boil. Season well with salt, cover tightly,
    and lower the heat to low. Cook 20 minutes, or until the rice is tender. Remove
    from the heat and leave to stand, covered, 10 minutes. Fluff up the rice with
    a fork and serve hot.

283 Nonya Fried Rice

PREPARATION TIME 5 minutes, plus making the rice   **COOKING TIME** 12 minutes   **SERVES** 4

4 tbsp. sunflower oil
3 large eggs, lightly beaten
1 large onion, halved and sliced
4 tbsp. dried shrimp

2½ cups cold cooked long-grain
  white rice
1¼ cups fresh or frozen peas

1   Heat half of the oil in a wok or skillet over low heat. Add the eggs and cook, stirring, 2 to 3 minutes until just scrambled. Transfer to a plate and set aside. Add the remaining oil to the wok and when it is hot, add the onion and dried shrimp. Cook, stirring, 3 to 4 minutes until light brown.
2   Return the eggs to the wok and add the rice and peas. Stir-fry 3 to 4 minutes until the rice is hot. Remove from the heat and serve hot.

284 Indonesian-Style Quick Fried Rice

PREPARATION TIME 15 minutes, plus making the curry powder and rice
COOKING TIME 13 minutes   **SERVES** 4

1 zucchini, cut into 2 x ½in. batons
1 carrot, cut into matchsticks
1½ cups trimmed and halved
  green beans
2 tbsp. sunflower oil, plus extra
  for greasing
6 scallions, thinly sliced diagonally
3 garlic cloves, thinly sliced
1 tsp. ground coriander
1 tsp. Curry Powder (see page 11)

1 red bell pepper, seeded and cut
  into thin strips
2½ cups cooked long-grain white rice
2 tbsp. light soy sauce
2 extra-large eggs
1 tbsp. finely chopped cilantro leaves,
  plus extra whole leaves,
  to serve
salt and freshly ground black pepper
mint leaves, to serve

1   Bring a large saucepan of water to a boil. Add the zucchini, carrot, and green beans and cook 2 minutes, then drain and set aside.
2   Heat the oil in a large wok or skillet with a tight-fitting lid over low heat. Add the scallions, garlic, coriander, and curry powder and stir-fry 2 to 3 minutes, then add the red pepper and stir-fry 1 minute longer. Add the rice, zucchini, carrot, and beans and stir-fry 3 to 4 minutes, then stir in the soy sauce. Toss to mix well, then season with salt and pepper. Remove from the heat, cover, and set aside.
3   Lightly grease a medium nonstick skillet with oil and put it over low heat. In a bowl, whisk together the eggs, chopped cilantro leaves, and 1 tablespoon water. Pour the mixture into the pan and swirl the pan around so the egg evenly covers the bottom of the pan. Cook 1 to 2 minutes until the bottom of the omelet is set, then carefully turn it over and cook for 1 minute longer. Turn the omelet out onto a clean work surface or plate, roll it into a log, and cut it into thin strips.
4   Divide the fried rice onto four plates and top with the omelette strips. Sprinkle with mint and cilantro leaves and serve immediately.

285 Persian Pilaf with Sour Cherries

PREPARATION TIME 35 minutes, plus 20 minutes draining and soaking
COOKING TIME 35 minutes   **SERVES** 4 to 6

1⅓ cups dried sour cherries
  or dried barberries
2 cups basmati rice
1 tsp. saffron threads
3 tsp. cinnamon

3 tbsp. sunflower oil
5 tbsp. butter
6 tbsp. pistachio nuts,
  coarsely chopped
salt

1 Put the cherries in a bowl, cover with cold water, and leave to soak 15 minutes, then drain. Meanwhile, put the rice in a bowl, cover with warm water, and stir the rice around with your hand to clean, then drain through a sieve and rinse well under cold running water and set aside to drain well. Put the saffron and 1 tablespoon hot water in a small bowl and set aside.

2 Bring a heavy-bottomed saucepan with a tight-fitting lid of salted water to a boil and add the rice, cinnamon, and oil. Cook, uncovered, 10 to 12 minutes until the rice is almost cooked but retains a little bite. Drain and set aside. Rinse out the saucepan.

3 Melt 2 tablespoons of the butter in the saucepan over medium-high heat, then stir in the saffron and soaking liquid. Add a ladleful of rice and mix well, then spread this mixture over the bottom of the pan. Sprinkle a layer of the cherries over, then spread another layer of rice over. Continue layering, finishing with a layer of rice on top. Melt the remaining butter in a small pan and drizzle it over the rice.

4 Cover tightly and cook over very low heat 15 to 20 minutes until the rice is tender. Spoon it onto a platter, scraping the crispy rice layer from the bottom of the pan over the rice. Sprinkle with the pistachio nuts and serve hot.

286 Thai Green Curry Vegetable Fried Rice

PREPARATION TIME 20 minutes, plus making the curry paste and rice
COOKING TIME 20 minutes   **SERVES 4**

3 tbsp. light soy sauce
2 tsp. Thai Green Curry Paste
   (see page 15)
5 tbsp. sunflower oil
4 large eggs
2 garlic cloves, finely chopped
4 shallots, thinly sliced
1 small red chili, thinly sliced
1 carrot, cut into matchsticks
⅔ cup trimmed fine green beans,
   cut into ¾in. pieces

½ cup corn kernels
1 red bell pepper, seeded and
   cut into ½in. dice
1½ cups thinly sliced shiitake
   mushrooms
2½ cups cooked long-grain white rice
crisp green salad leaves,
   to serve
1 lime, cut into wedges, to serve

1   In a small bowl, mix together the soy sauce and curry paste and set aside.
2   Heat 3 tablespoons of the oil in a nonstick skillet over medium-high heat until
    hot. Crack the eggs into the pan and cook 4 to 5 minutes until the edges are
    crisp and golden, then remove from the heat and set aside.
3   Meanwhile, heat the remaining oil in a wok or skillet over high heat. Add the
    garlic, shallots, and chili and stir-fry 1 to 2 minutes, then add the carrot, green
    beans, corn, red pepper, and mushrooms and stir-fry 3 to 4 minutes until slightly
    soft. Add the rice, stir-fry 4 to 5 minutes, then add the soy sauce mixture. Stir-fry
    2 to 3 minutes longer until hot.
4   Divide the rice into four bowls and top with the fried eggs. Serve hot with salad
    leaves and lime wedges for squeezing over.

287 Turkish Carrot & Pea Pilaf

PREPARATION TIME 40 minutes, plus 20 minutes soaking   **COOKING TIME** 17 minutes
SERVES 4

scant 1½ cups basmati rice
4 tbsp. sunflower oil
2 tsp. cumin seeds
8 whole black peppercorns
4 green cardamom pods,
   lightly crushed

2 cloves
1 cinnamon stick
1 large carrot, coarsely grated
1½ cups frozen peas
salt and freshly ground black pepper

1   Rinse and drain the rice, then put it in a bowl, cover with cold water, and leave
    to soak 20 minutes, then drain well.
2   Heat the oil in a heavy-bottomed saucepan with a tight-fitting lid over low heat.
    Add the cumin seeds, peppercorns, cardamom, cloves, and cinnamon and cook,
    stirring, 2 to 3 minutes until fragrant. Add the carrot and peas and cook, stirring,
    2 to 3 minutes longer, then stir in the rice.
3   Slowly add 2½ cups plus 2 tablespoons hot water. Season well with salt and
    pepper and bring to a boil over high heat. Cover the pan tightly, lower the heat
    to low, and cook 8 to 10 minutes until tender. Remove from the heat and leave
    to stand, covered, 10 minutes. Fluff up the rice with a fork and serve hot.

288 Aromatic Sticky Rice

PREPARATION TIME 20 minutes   COOKING TIME 14 minutes   SERVES 4

1½ cups jasmine rice
3 leeks, thinly sliced
3 star anise
6 whole black peppercorns

2 garlic cloves, peeled but left whole
1 cinnamon stick
salt and freshly ground black pepper

1   Put the rice in a sieve and rinse well under cold running water, then drain well. Transfer the rice to a large saucepan with a tight-fitting lid and add the leeks, star anise, peppercorns, garlic, cinnamon, and 3¾ cups cold water.
2   Bring to a boil over high heat, then lower the heat to low, cover the pan tightly, and simmer 10 to 12 minutes until the rice is cooked and the leeks are tender. Do not remove the lid during cooking. Remove from the heat and leave to stand, covered, 10 minutes.
3   Fluff up the rice with a fork, discarding the garlic, star anise, and cinnamon. Season well with salt and pepper and serve hot.

289 Classic Egg Fried Rice

PREPARATION TIME 5 minutes, plus making the rice   COOKING TIME 9 minutes   SERVES 4

2 extra-large eggs
2 tsp. sesame oil
2 tbsp. canola oil
2½ cups cold cooked long-grain
   white rice

2 scallions, finely chopped
⅔ cup fresh or frozen peas
salt and freshly ground black pepper

1   Put the eggs and sesame oil in a small bowl and beat with a fork. Season well with salt and pepper and set aside.
2   Heat a large wok or skillet over high heat. Add the canola oil and, when it is very hot and slightly smoking, add the rice. Stir-fry 3 minutes, or until heated through, then drizzle in the egg mixture and continue stir-frying 2 to 3 minutes until the eggs set and the mixture is dry.
3   Toss in the scallions and peas and cook, stirring, 2 to 3 minutes until the peas are just cooked and the mixture is hot. Serve hot.

290 Lebanese Herbed Rice with Chickpeas

PREPARATION TIME 35 minutes   COOKING TIME 14 minutes   SERVES 4

1¼ cups basmati rice
2 tbsp. sunflower oil
15oz. canned chickpeas, rinsed and
   drained

4 tbsp. chopped chives
4 tbsp. chopped dill
salt and freshly ground black pepper

1   Wash the rice in several changes of cold water, then cover with fresh cold water and leave to soak 15 minutes. Drain well.
2   Heat the oil in a heavy-bottomed saucepan over low heat. Add the rice and cook, stirring, 30 seconds until the grains are well coated, then add the chickpeas and 2¾ cups plus 1 tablespoon hot water. Season well with salt and pepper, mix well, and bring to a boil over high heat. Lower the heat to low, cover tightly, and cook 10 to 12 minutes until the rice is tender.
3   Remove from the heat and leave to stand, covered, 15 minutes. Fluff up the rice with a fork and stir in the chives and dill. Serve warm or at room temperature.

291 Idlis

PREPARATION TIME 15 minutes, plus at least 16 hours soaking and fermenting and making the sambhar and chutney   **COOKING TIME** 10 minutes   **SERVES** 4 to 6

1¼ cups urad dal (split black lentils),
  rinsed and drained
2½ cups long-grain rice, rinsed
  and drained
2 tbsp. salt
1 tsp. baking soda

sunflower oil, for greasing
1 recipe quantity Sambhar
  (see page 209), to serve
1 recipe quantity South Indian
  Coconut Chutney (see page 209),
  to serve

1   Put the urad dal in a bowl, cover with cold water, and leave to soak at least
    8 hours, or overnight. Drain, transfer to a blender and blend 2 to 3 minutes
    until smooth, then transfer to a large bowl. Put the rice in the blender and blend
    3 to 4 minutes until coarsely ground. Mix the rice into the lentils, then stir in the
    salt and baking soda. Leave to stand, covered, in a warm place 8 hours, or
    overnight to ferment. The batter will start to bubble gently.
2   When ready to cook, generously grease three or four four-hole idli molds with oil
    and fill each one three-quarters full with the batter to make 12 to 16 idlis. Fill the
    bottom of the idli pan with water, put the molds in the pan, cover, and steam
    over low heat 10 minutes, or until the idlis are springy to the touch and dry.
    Serve warm with sambhar and chutney.

292 Jamaican Plantain Rice

PREPARATION TIME 25 minutes   **COOKING TIME** 25 minutes   **SERVES** 4

1¼ cups long-grain white rice, well
  rinsed and drained
1 cup plus 2 tbsp. coconut milk
1 tbsp. all-purpose flour
1 tsp. cayenne pepper
1 plantain, peeled and thickly sliced

3 tbsp. sunflower oil
1 red chili, thinly sliced
1 small handful cilantro leaves,
  chopped
salt and freshly ground black pepper

1   Put the rice, coconut milk, and 3 cups water in a heavy-bottomed saucepan
    and season with salt. Bring to a boil over high heat, then cover the pan tightly
    and lower the heat to low. Cook 12 to 15 minutes until the rice is tender and
    the liquid is absorbed. Remove from the heat and leave to stand, covered,
    10 minutes.
2   Sprinkle the flour and cayenne on a plate and season generously with salt
    and pepper. Roll the plantain slices in the flour to coat.
3   Heat the oil in a skillet over medium-high heat. Add the plantain and fry
    3 to 4 minutes on each side until crisp and golden brown. Remove from the
    pan and drain on paper towels.
4   Fluff up the rice with a fork, stir in the plantain, chili, and cilantro, and serve.

293　Turmeric Rice with Chickpeas

PREPARATION TIME 15 minutes   COOKING TIME 35 minutes   SERVES 4

2 tbsp. sunflower oil
1 onion, finely chopped
1 red bell pepper, seeded and sliced
   into strips
1 garlic clove, finely chopped
1¼ cups white basmati rice
2 tsp. turmeric

scant 2½ cups vegetable stock
15oz. canned chickpeas, rinsed
   and drained
3oz. green beans, trimmed
   and halved
salt and freshly ground black pepper

1　Heat the oil in a large, heavy-bottomed saucepan with a tight-fitting lid over low heat. Add the onion and fry, stirring occasionally, 5 minutes, or until soft and translucent. Add the red pepper and garlic and continue frying 2 minutes longer.

2　Add the rice and cook, stirring, 1 minute, or until the grains are well coated. Add the turmeric and stock and bring to a boil over high heat, then cover the pan tightly, lower the heat to low, and simmer 15 minutes.

3　Stir in the chickpeas and green beans, then simmer, covered, 5 to 10 minutes longer until all of the liquid is absorbed and the rice and vegetables are tender. Season with salt and pepper and serve hot.

294　Saffron Rice

PREPARATION TIME 30 minutes   COOKING TIME 15 minutes   SERVES 4

2 tsp. saffron threads
3 tbsp. warm milk
1 tbsp. ghee or butter
2 cinnamon sticks
2 green cardamom pods

2 or 3 cloves
¼ tsp. turmeric
scant 1¼ cups basmati rice,
   well rinsed and drained
salt

1　Put the saffron and milk in a small bowl and leave to soak 5 minutes.

2　Melt the ghee in a nonstick saucepan with a tight-fitting lid over low heat. When it is hot, add the cinnamon, cardamom, cloves, turmeric, and saffron and soaking liquid. Cook, stirring, 20 to 30 seconds until fragrant, then add the rice and cook, stirring, 2 minutes until the grains are well coated.

3　Slowly add 2 cups plus 2 tablespoons boiling water, then season with salt and bring to a boil over high heat. Cover the pan tightly, lower the heat to low, and cook 10 to 12 minutes until the liquid is absorbed and the rice is tender. Remove from the heat and leave to stand, covered, 10 minutes. Fluff up the rice with a fork and serve hot.

295　Pilau Rice

PREPARATION TIME 30 minutes, plus 30 minutes soaking   COOKING TIME 25 minutes   SERVES 4

1¾ cups basmati rice
1 tbsp. ghee or butter
1 onion, finely chopped
4 cardamom pods

8 cloves
1 cinnamon stick or cassia bark
2 tsp. saffron threads
2 dried bay leaves

1　Wash the rice under cold running water, drain, and then soak in fresh cold water 30 minutes, if time permits, and drain well.

2　Melt the ghee in a heavy-bottomed saucepan with a tight-fitting lid over low heat. Add the onion and cook, stirring occasionally, 6 to 8 minutes until soft. Add all of the remaining ingredients and cook, stirring, 1 to 2 minutes until fragrant. Add the rice and stir until the grains are coated, then stir in 2½ cups water.

3　Bring to a boil over high heat, then cover tightly, lower the heat to low, and cook 12 to 15 minutes until tender and the water is absorbed. Remove from the heat and leave to stand, covered, 12 to 15 minutes. Fluff up the rice with a fork and serve immediately.

296 Kitcheree

PREPARATION TIME 25 minutes, plus making the pickles   **COOKING TIME** 25 minutes
SERVES 4

3 tbsp. sunflower oil
1 onion, finely chopped
1 tsp. turmeric
1 tbsp. cumin seeds
1 dried red chili
1 cinnamon stick
3 cloves
½ tsp. crushed cardamom seeds
heaped ½ cup split red lentils, rinsed,
  and thoroughly drained
heaped 1 cup basmati rice, well
  rinsed and drained

2½ cups plus 2 tbsp. vegetable stock
⅓ cup finely chopped cilantro leaves
salt and freshly ground black pepper
1 recipe quantity Pickled Green
  Chilies (see page 208), to serve
1 recipe quantity
  Sri Lankan Lemon & Date Pickle
  (see page 213), to serve
poppadoms, to serve
plain yogurt, to serve

1   Heat the oil in a heavy-bottomed saucepan with a tight-fitting lid over low
heat. Add the onion and cook, stirring occasionally, 6 to 8 minutes until very
soft. Add the turmeric, cumin seeds, chili, cinnamon, cloves, and cardamom
and cook, stirring, 2 to 3 minutes until fragrant, then add the lentils and rice
and cook 2 to 3 minutes longer.

2   Add the stock and cilantro, season well with salt and pepper, and bring to
a boil over high heat. Lower the heat to low, cover the pan tightly, and cook
10 minutes. Remove from the heat and leave to stand, covered, 10 minutes.
Serve immediately with pickles, poppadoms, and yogurt.

297 Afghan Fried Brown Rice

PREPARATION TIME 25 minutes   **COOKING TIME** 45 minutes   **SERVES** 4

scant 1½ cups long-grain white rice
2 tbsp. ghee or butter
2 onions, thinly sliced
1 cinnamon stick
1 bay leaf

6 cloves
1 mace blade
1 tsp. sugar
salt

1   Put the rice in a bowl, cover with cold water, and leave to soak 15 minutes.
Drain and rinse well, then set aside.

2   Melt the ghee in a heavy-bottomed saucepan with a tight-fitting lid over low
heat. Add the onions and fry, stirring occasionally, 12 to 15 minutes until light
brown and starting to caramelize. Add the cinnamon, bay leaf, cloves, and mace
and cook 5 minutes longer. Sprinkle the sugar over and continue cooking, stirring
frequently, 2 to 3 minutes until the mixture is a rich golden brown.

3   Add the rice and cook, stirring, 2 to 3 minutes until the grains are well coated.
Season with salt and slowly add 2½ cups plus 2 tablespoons boiling water.
Simmer, covered, 12 to 15 minutes until the rice is cooked through. Remove
the pan from the heat and serve the rice hot.

298 Lemon Rice

PREPARATION TIME 25 minutes   **COOKING TIME** 15 minutes   **SERVES** 4

1 tbsp. olive oil
12 to 14 curry leaves
1 dried red chili
2 pieces of cassia bark
   or 2 cinnamon sticks
2 or 3 cloves
4 to 6 green cardamom pods, crushed

2 tsp. cumin seeds
¼ tsp. turmeric
scant 1¼ cups basmati rice,
   well rinsed and drained
juice of 1 large lemon
salt and freshly ground black pepper
chopped cilantro leaves, to serve

1 Heat the oil in a nonstick saucepan with over low heat. Add the curry leaves, chili, cassia bark, cloves, cardamom, cumin seeds, and turmeric and cook, stirring, 20 to 30 seconds until fragrant. Add the rice and cook, stirring, 2 minutes until the grains are well coated, then add the lemon juice and slowly pour in 2 cups plus 2 tablespoons boiling water and season well with salt and pepper.
2 Bring to a boil over high heat, then cover the pan tightly, lower the heat to low, and cook 10 to 12 minutes until the rice is tender. Remove from the heat and leave to stand, covered, 10 to 15 minutes.
3 Fluff up the rice with a fork and season with more salt and pepper, if necessary. Serve hot, sprinkled with cilantro.

299 Mushroom Pulao

PREPARATION TIME 45 minutes   **COOKING TIME** 30 minutes   **SERVES** 4

scant 1½ cups basmati rice, rinsed and
  drained
4 tbsp. sunflower oil
3 cups sliced mushrooms
2 tsp. cumin seeds
8 whole black peppercorns
4 green cardamom pods,
  lightly crushed

2 cloves
1 cinnamon stick
4 tbsp. crisp-fried onions
  or shallots
1¼ cups frozen peas
3 cups vegetable stock
salt and freshly ground black pepper

1   Put the rice in a bowl, cover with cold water, and leave to soak 20 minutes,
    then drain well.
2   Heat the oil in a heavy-bottomed saucepan with a tight-fitting lid over high
    heat. Add the mushrooms and stir-fry 6 to 8 minutes until starting to color.
    Add the cumin seeds, peppercorns, cardamom, cloves, cinnamon and
    onions, and stir-fry 2 to 3 minutes until fragrant. Add the peas and stir-fry
    2 to 3 minutes longer. Add the rice and stir 1 minute until the grains are
    well coated.
3   Add the stock, season well with salt and pepper, and bring to a boil over
    high heat. Cover the pan tightly, lower the heat to low, and cook 10 to 12
    minutes until the rice is tender. Remove from the heat and leave to stand,
    covered, 10 to 15 minutes. Fluff up the rice with a fork and serve hot.

300 Nasi Goreng

PREPARATION TIME 25 minutes, plus making the rice   **COOKING TIME** 20 minutes   **SERVES** 4

2 eggs
¼ tsp. turmeric
2 tbsp. sunflower oil
1 onion, halved and thinly sliced
6 scallions, sliced diagonally into
  ¾in. pieces
2 garlic cloves, very finely chopped
1 tsp. peeled and finely grated
  gingerroot

1 red bell pepper, seeded
  and thinly sliced
2oz. bean sprouts
2½ cups cold cooked long-grain
  white rice
1 tbsp. kecap manis
1 tbsp. sambal oelek
chopped cilantro and mint leaves,
  to serve

1   Put the eggs and turmeric in a bowl and beat together lightly. Heat 1½ teaspoons
    of the oil in a nonstick skillet over low heat and add half of the egg mixture,
    swirling it around the bottom of the pan to cover. Cook 2 to 3 minutes until just
    set, then remove the omelet from the pan, roll it into a log, and set aside. Repeat
    with another 1½ teaspoons of the oil and the remaining egg mixture. Cut the
    rolled omelets into thin strips and set aside.
2   Heat the remaining 1 tablespoon of the oil in a large, nonstick wok or skillet over
    high heat. Add the onion, scallions, garlic, and ginger and stir-fry 4 to 5 minutes
    until the onion begins to color.
3   Add the red pepper and bean sprouts and stir-fry 3 to 4 minutes longer, then
    stir in the rice, kecap manis, sambal oelek, and omelet strips. Stir-fry 3 to 4
    minutes until the rice is hot. Remove from the heat and serve hot, sprinkled
    with cilantro and mint.

301 Bamboo Steamed Sticky Rice

PREPARATION TIME 5 minutes, plus at least 6 hours soaking   **COOKING TIME** 25 minutes
SERVES 4

1¼ cups jasmine rice

1   Put the rice in a bowl, cover with cold water, and leave to soak for at least
    6 hours. Drain, rinse thoroughly, then drain again.
2   Fill a wok or heavy saucepan one-third full with water and put a bamboo
    steamer, with the lid on, over the wok or pan, making sure the bottom of
    the steamer does not touch the water. Bring the water to a boil over high heat.
3   Uncover the steamer and line the basket with a damp piece of cheesecloth or
    muslin. Put the rice in the middle and spread it out a little. Fold the cloth over
    the rice, cover with the lid, and steam 25 minutes, or until the rice is tender
    but firm. Serve hot.

302 North Indian Green Bean & Carrot Pulao

PREPARATION TIME 25 minutes, plus 30 minutes soaking and making the garam masala
COOKING TIME 30 minutes   **SERVES** 4

scant 1½ cups basmati rice
3 tbsp. ghee or butter
2 tsp. mustard seeds
1 red chili, finely chopped
1 potato, peeled and cut into small
   bite-size cubes
2 large carrots, cut into small cubes

1½ cups green beans cut into small
   bite-size pieces
1 tsp. turmeric
1 tsp. Garam Masala (see page 11)
1 tbsp. peeled and finely grated
   gingerroot
salt

1   Wash the rice in several changes of cold water and drain. Put it in a bowl,
    cover with fresh cold water, and leave to soak 30 minutes, then drain well.
2   Melt the ghee in a heavy-bottomed saucepan with a tight-fitting lid over
    medium-high heat. When it is hot, add the mustard seeds. After a few seconds
    they will begin to pop. Immediately add the chili, potato, carrots, green beans,
    turmeric, garam masala, and ginger and stir-fry 1 minute until well mixed.
3   Lower the heat to medium-low, add the rice, and season with salt. Cook, stirring,
    2 minutes, then add 2¾ cups plus 1 tablespoon water and bring to a boil over
    high heat. Cover the pan tightly, lower the heat to low, and cook 25 minutes, or
    until the rice and vegetables are tender. Remove from the heat and leave to stand,
    covered, 10 to 12 minutes. Fluff up the rice with a fork and serve hot.

303 Burmese-Style Coconut Spiced Rice

PREPARATION TIME 10 minutes, plus making the rice   **COOKING TIME** 17 minutes   **SERVES** 4

1 tbsp. canola oil
2 onions, finely chopped
2¾ cups cold cooked long-grain
   white rice
4 tbsp. freshly grated or
   shredded coconut

3 bay leaves
1 tsp. cinnamon
1 tsp. curry powder
¼ tsp. turmeric
¼ tsp. ground cloves

1   Put the oil, onions, and 2 tablespoons water in large nonstick skillet. Cook over
    high heat, stirring occasionally, 10 to 12 minutes until the water evaporates and
    the onions start to brown.
2   Add all of the remaining ingredients, lower the heat to low, and cook, stirring
    continuously, 4 to 5 minutes until the rice is hot. Serve warm.

304 Burmese Golden Rice

PREPARATION TIME 20 minutes   **COOKING TIME** 30 minutes   **SERVES** 4

4 tbsp. sunflower oil
8 garlic cloves, thinly sliced
6 shallots, halved and thinly sliced
1¼ cups long-grain white rice

2 tsp. turmeric
1 tsp. saffron threads
salt

1   Heat the oil in a nonstick skillet over medium-low heat. Add the garlic and shallots and fry, stirring occasionally, 5 to 6 minutes until light brown and crisp. Remove from the pan, using a slotted spoon, and drain on paper towels.
2   Put the rice and scant 3 cups water into a large heavy-bottomed saucepan with a tight-fitting lid and season with salt. Stir in the turmeric and saffron, then bring to a boil over high heat. Lower the heat to low, cover tightly and cook 15 to 20 minutes until tender. Remove the pan from the heat and leave to stand, covered, 10 to 12 minutes.
3   Fluff up the rice with a fork and serve hot sprinkled with the garlic and shallots.

305 Spicy Spinach Biryani with Cauliflower

PREPARATION TIME 15 minutes, plus making the masala paste   **COOKING TIME** 35 minutes
SERVES 4

1¼ cups white basmati rice
6 to 8 green cardamom pods,
   lightly crushed
1 large pinch of saffron threads,
   crumbled
½ cup slivered almonds
4 tbsp. ghee or butter

1 large onion, thinly sliced
1 cauliflower, cut into small florets
4 tbsp. Green Masala Paste
   (see page 14)
7oz. baby spinach leaves
salt

1   Put the rice, cardamom, and 2 cups plus 2 tablespoons cold water in a large saucepan with a tight-fitting lid and bring to a boil over high heat. Lower the heat to low, cover the pan tightly, and cook 8 minutes, or until the rice is almost tender and the water is absorbed. Gently stir the saffron into the rice, then cover, and set aside.
2   While the rice is cooking, put the almonds in a large skillet with a tight-fitting lid over low heat and cook, stirring continuously, 2 to 3 minutes until lightly toasted. Watch closely so they do not burn. Transfer to a bowl and set aside.
3   Melt the ghee in the skillet over low heat. Add the onion and cauliflower and fry, stirring frequently, 5 minutes, or until just starting to color. Add the masala paste, half of the almonds, and scant 1 cup cold water and cook, covered, over low heat 10 minutes, or until most of the liquid is absorbed.
4   Add the onion mixture to the rice, then add the spinach, and season with salt. Stir gently to mix, then cover tightly and cook 10 minutes longer until the spinach just wilts. Remove from the heat, sprinkle with the remaining almonds, and serve hot.

306 Zucchini & Tamarind Rice

PREPARATION TIME 10 minutes, plus making the rice   COOKING TIME 20 minutes
SERVES 4

1 tbsp. sunflower oil
1 large onion, thinly sliced
2 zucchini, coarsely grated
1 red chili, seeded and
 finely chopped

1 tbsp. tamarind paste
2½ cups cold cooked basmati rice
½ cup coarsely chopped mint leaves
salt and freshly ground black pepper

1   Heat the oil in a large skillet over low heat. Add the onion and cook, stirring
    occasionally, 10 minutes, or until light brown.
2   Increase the heat to high and add the zucchini, chili, and tamarind paste.
    Stir-fry 5 minutes, then add the rice and mint. Continue stir-frying 5 to 6 minutes
    longer until hot. Remove from the heat, season well with salt and pepper, and
    serve hot.

307 Curry Leaf & Coconut Rice

PREPARATION TIME 35 minutes   COOKING TIME 12 minutes   SERVES 4

heaped 1 cup basmati rice
2 tbsp. ghee or butter
2 tsp. black mustard seeds
2 tsp. cumin seeds

2 dried red chilies, coarsely chopped
10 curry leaves
⅓ cup coconut cream

1   Wash the rice in several changes of water. Put it in a bowl, cover with cold
    water, and leave to soak 15 minutes, then drain well.
2   Melt the ghee in a heavy-bottomed saucepan with a tight-fitting lid over low
    heat. Add the mustard and cumin seeds, chilies, and curry leaves and cook,
    stirring, 30 seconds, then slowly add scant 2½ cups water and the coconut
    cream and mix well.
3   Bring to a boil over high heat, then lower the heat to low, cover tightly, and
    cook 10 minutes, or until the rice is cooked. Remove from the heat and leave
    to stand, covered, 10 minutes. Serve warm.

308 Tomato & Cilantro Rice

PREPARATION TIME 40 minutes   COOKING TIME 20 minutes   SERVES 4

scant 1½ cups basmati rice
3 tbsp. sunflower oil
4 shallots, finely chopped
2 garlic cloves, finely chopped
2 tsp. cumin seeds

4 tomatoes, skinned, seeded, and
 finely chopped
2 tbsp. finely chopped cilantro leaves
salt and freshly ground black pepper

1   Wash the rice in several changes of water. Put it in a bowl, cover with cold water,
    and leave to soak 20 minutes, then drain well.
2   Heat the oil in a heavy-bottomed saucepan with a tight-fitting lid over low heat.
    Add the shallots, garlic and cumin seeds and fry, stirring occasionally, 4 to 5
    minutes until soft and fragrant.
3   Add the tomatoes and rice and cook, stirring occasionally, 2 to 3 minutes.
    Season with salt and pepper, then slowly add 2½ cups plus 2 tablespoons water.
4   Bring to a boil over high heat. Cover the pan tightly, lower the heat to low, and
    cook 10 to 12 minutes until the rice is tender. Remove from the heat and leave
    to stand, covered, 10 minutes. Fluff up the rice with a fork, stir in the cilantro
    and serve hot.

Fava Bean Pilaf

PREPARATION TIME 20 minutes   COOKING TIME 15 minutes   SERVES 4

1¼ cups white basmati rice
1 tbsp. cumin seeds
2 cups podded fava beans
4 tbsp. butter
6 scallions, thinly sliced

⅓ cup finely chopped dill
salt and freshly ground black pepper
1 small handful pomegranate seeds,
  to serve (optional)

1 Put the rice in a bowl, cover with cold water, and stir with your hands to wash, then drain. Repeat several times until the water runs clear, then drain well.
2 Put the cumin seeds in a small skillet and dry-roast, stirring continuously, over medium-low heat 2 to 3 minutes until fragrant. Remove from the heat and leave to cool.
3 Meanwhile, bring a saucepan of water to a boil. Add the fava beans and cook 1 to 2 minutes, then drain and transfer immediately to a bowl of ice-cold water. Leave to cool, then pop the beans out of their skins, discard the skins, and set the beans aside.
4 Melt the butter in a large saucepan with a tight-fitting lid over low heat. Add the scallions and cumin seeds and cook, stirring frequently, 2 to 3 minutes. Add the rice and stir until well coated. Add 2 cups plus 2 tablespoons water, season well with salt and pepper, and bring to a boil over high heat. Stir once, then lower the heat to low, cover tightly, and cook 5 to 7 minutes until the rice is tender. Remove from the heat and leave to stand, covered, 10 to 12 minutes.
5 Stir the fava beans and dill into the rice, then pile it onto a serving plate, scraping any crispy bits from the bottom of the pan over the top of the rice. Sprinkle with the pomegranate seeds, if using, and serve hot.

310 Turkish Tomato Pilaf

PREPARATION TIME 45 minutes   **COOKING TIME** 20 minutes   **SERVES** 4 to 6

1½ cups basmati rice
1lb. 2oz. tomatoes, quartered
1 chicken or vegetable stock cube
1 cinnamon stick

2 tsp. sugar
5 tbsp. butter
salt and freshly ground black pepper

1   Put the rice in a bowl, cover with cold water, and leave to soak 20 minutes, then drain. Rinse under cold running water and drain well.
2   Put the tomatoes in a food processor and blend 2 to 3 minutes or until smooth. Transfer them to a measuring cup and top up with just enough water to make 3 cups. Pour the mixture into a saucepan.
3   Crumble in the stock cube and add the cinnamon stick and sugar, then season well with salt and pepper. Bring the mixture to a boil over high heat, then add the rice and stir well.
4   Lower the heat to low and simmer, covered, 15 to 20 minutes until the rice is tender and the liquid has been absorbed.
5   Remove from the heat, stir in the butter and serve hot.

311 Vegetable Jollof Rice

PREPARATION TIME 15 minutes   **COOKING TIME** 40 minutes   **SERVES** 4

1 tbsp. sunflower oil
1 large red onion, finely chopped
2 garlic cloves, very finely chopped
1 Scotch bonnet or habanero chili, seeded and finely chopped
2 tsp. peeled and finely grated gingerroot
15oz. canned crushed tomatoes
1½ cups white basmati rice

3 cups hot vegetable stock or water
2 yellow bell peppers, seeded and thickly sliced
2 red bell peppers, seeded and thickly sliced
2 cups okra, cut into ¾in. pieces (optional)
1 small bunch cilantro leaves, coarsely chopped

1   Heat the oil in a heavy-bottomed saucepan with a tight-fitting lid over low heat. Add the onion, garlic, chili, and ginger and fry, stirring occasionally, 5 minutes, or until the onion is soft and translucent.
2   Add the tomatoes and bring to a boil over high heat. Add the rice and stock and bring the mixture back to a boil. Lower the heat to low, cover the pan with foil and a lid (so no steam can escape), and cook 20 minutes.
3   Uncover the pan and scatter the peppers and okra, if using, over the rice. Cover again and cook 10 to 12 minutes longer until the vegetables are soft and the rice is tender. Fluff up the rice with a fork, sprinkle with the cilantro, and serve.

312   Thai Fried Rice

PREPARATION TIME 25 minutes, plus making the curry paste   COOKING TIME 16 minutes
SERVES 4

heaped 1 cup jasmine rice
2 tbsp. sunflower oil
2 scallions, finely chopped
2 tsp. finely chopped lemongrass

2 red chilies, finely chopped
1 tbsp. Thai Red Curry Paste
  (see page 15)
6 tbsp. coconut cream

1   Wash the rice in several changes of water. Put it in a bowl, cover with cold
    water, and leave to soak 15 minutes, then drain well.
2   Heat the oil in a heavy-bottomed saucepan with a tight-fitting lid over low
    heat. Add all of the ingredients, including the rice, and cook, stirring, 2 to 3
    minutes until fragrant and the grains are evenly coated. Slowly add 2 cups
    plus 2 tablespoons water and mix well, then bring to a boil over high heat.
3   Lower the heat to low, cover the pan tightly, and cook 10 to 12 minutes
    until the rice is tender. Remove from the heat and leave to stand, covered,
    10 minutes. Fluff up the rice with a fork and serve hot.

313   Trinidadian Roti Paratha

PREPARATION TIME 35 minutes   COOKING TIME 8 minutes   MAKES 4

4 cups all-purpose flour, plus extra
  for kneading and rolling
1 tsp. baking powder

1 tsp. salt
sunflower oil, for brushing

1   Sift the flour, baking powder, and salt together into a large bowl. Make a well
    in the center, pour in 1½ cups plus 2 tablespoons water, and mix until the dough
    just comes together into a ball. Knead well on a floured work surface 8 to 10
    minutes until smooth and fairly soft.
2   Divide the dough into 4 equal pieces. On a floured work surface, roll out each
    piece into an 8- x 4-inch oval. Brush the top of each one with oil and sprinkle
    with a little flour. Using a sharp knife, make a cut from the center to the edge
    of each paratha and roll it into a cone shape. Press the point of the cone into the
    center and flatten slightly into a thick circle. Leave to rest, covered, 20 minutes
    on the floured work surface.
3   On the lightly floured work surface, roll out each paratha into a ¼-inch-thick
    circle. Grease a large skillet with a little oil and heat it over low heat, then put
    1 paratha in the pan and cook 1 minute or until it starts to bubble. Brush the top
    with oil, then flip it over and cook 1 minute longer. Remove from the pan and
    wrap the paratha in a clean, dry dish towel to keep warm while you cook the
    remaining parathas, greasing the pan again as needed. Serve warm.

314 Naan

PREPARATION TIME 20 minutes, plus 40 minutes resting   **COOKING TIME** 16 minutes   **MAKES** 8

3⅔ cups self-rising flour, plus extra
   for kneading and rolling
2 tsp. sugar
1 tsp. salt
1 tsp. baking powder

4 tbsp. melted ghee or butter,
   plus extra for brushing
1 cup warm milk
2 tbsp. nigella seeds

1   Sift the flour, sugar, salt, and baking powder together into a large bowl. Add the melted butter and rub it into the flour mixture with your fingertips. Gradually add the warm milk and mix until the ingredients come together into a soft dough.

2   Transfer the dough to a lightly floured work surface and knead 6 to 8 minutes until smooth. Return the dough to the bowl, cover with plastic wrap, and leave to rest 20 to 25 minutes.

3   Divide the dough into 8 equal pieces. Shape each piece into a ball and flatten each one into a thick circle. Put the naans on a plate, cover with a clean, damp dish towel, and leave to rest 10 to 15 minutes.

4   Preheat the broiler to medium-high. On a lightly floured work surface, roll out each naan into a 9-inch-wide circle. Brush the top of each one with melted butter and sprinkle with the nigella seeds. Working in batches, put the breads side by side on a lightly greased broiler rack and broil 1 to 2 minutes on each side until puffed up and lightly brown in spots. Wrap in a clean, dry dish towel to keep warm and soft while you cook the remaining naans. Serve warm.

315 Turkish Pide Bread

PREPARATION TIME 20 minutes, plus 2½ hours rising   **COOKING TIME** 40 minutes
MAKES 1 large loaf

1oz. active dry yeast
1 tsp. sugar
¾ cup milk
4 tbsp. butter
5 cups white bread flour, plus extra
   for kneading

2 tsp. salt
sunflower oil, for greasing
1 egg, lightly beaten
2 tbsp. sesame seeds
2 tbsp. fennel seeds

1   Put the yeast, sugar, and 1 cup plus 2 tablespoons warm water in a small bowl and leave to stand 5 to 10 minutes until the yeast dissolves. Meanwhile, put the milk and butter in a small saucepan and heat over a medium-low heat until the milk is warm and the butter melts. Do not bring to a boil.

2   Sift the flour and salt together into a large bowl, make a well in the center, and add the yeast and milk mixtures. Gradually incorporate the flour, mixing until the ingredients come together to form a dough. Remove from the bowl and knead on a lightly floured work surface 8 to 10 minutes until the dough is smooth and elastic. Put the dough in a lightly greased bowl and cover with plastic wrap or a clean, damp dish towel. Leave to rise in a warm place 2 hours, or until it doubles in size.

3   Punch down the dough and shape it to fit in either a lightly greased 12-inch round pan or a lightly greased baking sheet. Cover again with the damp dish towel and leave to rise again for another 30 minutes.

4   Preheat the oven to 375°F. Generously brush the pide with the beaten egg, then gently press your fingertips into the dough to make rows of indentations across the top of the dough, leaving a border of about 2 inches around the edge. Be careful not to poke all of the way through the dough. Sprinkle the sesame and fennel seeds over the top and bake 40 minutes, or until light golden. Serve warm.

316 Burmese Paratha

PREPARATION TIME 25 minutes, plus 1 hour resting **COOKING TIME** 50 minutes **MAKES** 8

3¼ cups all-purpose flour
1 tsp. salt
1 tsp. sugar
2 tbsp. butter

1 egg, beaten
4 tbsp. milk
½ cup peanut oil, for frying,
    plus extra for greasing

1   Sift the flour into a large bowl. Add the salt, sugar, and butter and, using your fingertips, rub in the butter until the mixture resembles bread crumbs. Make a well in the center and add the egg and milk. Gradually add ⅔ cup water and mix by hand until the ingredients come together into a sticky dough.
2   Turn out the dough onto a well-greased work surface and knead 10 minutes, or until soft and elastic. Divide the dough into 8 equal pieces and roll them into balls with well-greased hands. Put the dough balls on a plate, cover with plastic wrap, and leave to rest at least 1 hour.
3   Grease the work surface and your hands again with oil. Flatten 1 dough ball with the palm of your hand and then stretch it into a thin circle. Make sure the dough is as thin as possible, almost see-through, then brush the top with oil and set aside on the work surface. Repeat with the remaining dough, spreading the parathas out in a single layer on the work surface.
4   To create the paratha's characteristic layers, fold two opposite ends of each circle over into the middle to form an elongated shape, then fold over the other two sides to create a rectangle.
5   Heat 1 tablespoon of the oil in a nonstick skillet over low heat. Working with one paratha at a time, fry each one 2 to 3 minutes until the underside is golden brown. Brush the top with a little more oil, then flip the paratha over, and cook 2 to 3 minutes longer until the underside is lightly brown. Serve hot.

317 Puri

PREPARATION TIME 15 minutes, plus 30 minutes chilling **COOKING TIME** 20 minutes
MAKES 20

2 cups wholewheat flour, plus extra
    for rolling
a pinch of salt

2 tbsp. ghee or butter, melted
3 cups canola oil, for deep-frying,
    or more as needed

1   Sift the flour and salt together into a large bowl. Add the ghee and 4 tablespoons cold water and mix together to make a stiff dough. If necessary, add an additional 3 to 4 teaspoons water to bring the ingredients together, taking care not to add too much. Cover with a clean, damp dish towel and chill 30 minutes.
2   Divide the dough into 20 equal pieces, shape each one into a ball and then flatten each ball with the palm of your hand. On a floured work surface, roll out each puri into a 14-inch circle.
3   Put the oil in a large wok or deep saucepan over medium-high heat and heat it to 350°F, or until a small piece of bread dropped into the oil browns in 15 seconds. Working in batches to avoid overcrowding the wok, carefully add the puris and deep-fry 1 to 2 minutes on each side until puffed up and golden. Remove from the oil, using a slotted spoon, and drain well on paper towels. Serve immediately.

318 Saag Roti

PREPARATION TIME 20 minutes, plus 30 minutes resting **COOKING TIME** 25 minutes
MAKES 20

7oz. baby spinach leaves, coarsely
   chopped
1 tbsp. cumin seeds
4 cups chapati flour, plus extra
   for kneading and rolling

¼ tsp. salt
1 red chili, finely chopped, plus
   extra to serve
4 tbsp. ghee or butter, melted
chopped cilantro leaves, to serve

1 Bring a large saucepan of water to a boil. Add the spinach and cook 1 to 2
   minutes until it just wilts, then drain well in a colander, squeeze out any extra
   liquid, and set aside. Meanwhile, put the cumin seeds in a small skillet and
   dry-roast over medium-low heat, stirring continuously, 2 to 3 minutes until
   fragrant and lightly toasted. Remove from the heat and leave to cool.

2 Sift the flour into a large bowl and add the salt. Stir in the cumin seeds, chili,
   and spinach and make a well in the center. Stir in the ghee and 1 cup plus
   2 tablespoons lukewarm water and mix until the ingredients come together in
   a soft, pliable dough. Knead on a lightly floured work surface 4 to 5 minutes until
   smooth and elastic, then put it in a lightly greased bowl, cover with a clean, damp
   dish towel, and leave to rest 30 minutes.

3 Divide the dough into 20 equal pieces and roll them into balls. On a lightly floured
   work surface, roll out each ball into a very thin 4- to 5-inch-wide circle.

4 Heat a flat griddle or a large, heavy-bottomed skillet over high heat until hot.
   Lightly brush the rotis with ghee and, working in batches, cook 1 to 2 minutes
   on each side until lightly blistered and cooked through. Remove from the pan
   and cover with a clean, dry dish towel to keep warm while you cook the
   remaining roti. Sprinkle with chili and cilantro and serve warm.

319 Besan Roti

PREPARATION TIME 30 minutes   **COOKING TIME** 16 minutes   **MAKES** 8

heaped ¾ cup wholewheat flour,
    plus extra for kneading
    and rolling
1 cup gram flour
1 tsp. salt
2 tbsp. finely chopped
    cilantro leaves

1 red chili, finely chopped
2 tsp. cumin seeds
1 tsp. crushed coriander seeds
1 tsp. turmeric
⅓ cup melted ghee or butter,
    plus extra for brushing

1   Sift the flours and salt together into a large bowl. Add all of the remaining
    ingredients and mix together. Gradually add scant 1 cup water until the
    mixture comes together in a soft, pliable dough. Knead on a lightly floured
    work surface 1 to 2 minutes, then cover with a clean, damp dish towel and
    leave to rest 10 minutes.
2   Divide the mixture into 8 equal pieces and roll them into balls. On a lightly
    floured work surface, roll out each ball into a 15- to 6-inch circle. Brush the
    top of each one with a little melted ghee.
3   Heat a nonstick griddle or heavy-bottomed skillet over high heat. When it
    is hot, cook the roti, one at a time, 35 to 40 seconds on each side, pressing
    down with a metal spatula for even cooking.
4   Remove the roti from the pan and wrap it in foil to keep warm while you cook
    the remaining rotis. Serve warm.

320 Wholewheat Paratha

PREPARATION TIME 35 minutes   **COOKING TIME** 25 minutes   **MAKES** 12

1¾ cups wholewheat flour
1 cup all-purpose flour, plus extra for
    kneading, rolling and dusting
1 tsp. ground cardamom

2 tsp. salt
1 cup plus 2 tbsp. warm buttermilk
⅔ cup melted ghee or butter,
    plus extra for greasing

1   Sift the flours together into a large bowl, then add the cardamom and salt. Make
    a well in the center and pour in the buttermilk and 2 tablespoons of the ghee.
    Mix together until the ingredients come together in a soft dough. Knead on
    a lightly floured work surface 10 minutes, or until smooth and elastic, then shape
    the dough into a ball. Grease a clean bowl with melted ghee, put the dough in
    it, and cover with a clean, damp dish towel, then leave to rest 20 minutes.
2   Divide the dough into 12 equal pieces and roll them into balls. On a lightly
    floured work surface, roll out each ball into a 6-inch circle. Brush each one with
    a little of the remaining ghee, then fold in half and brush again. Fold in half once
    more to form a triangle, dust with a little flour, and roll out into a 6-inch triangle.
3   Heat a flat, nonstick cast-iron griddle or heavy skillet over low heat. Put 1 paratha
    in the pan and cook 1 minute, pressing down with a spatula for even cooking.
    Brush the top with a little more ghee, then flip it over and cook 1 minute longer.
    Remove from the pan and wrap in foil to keep warm while you cook the
    remaining parathas. Serve warm.

321 Roomali Roti

PREPARATION TIME 25 minutes, plus 45 minutes resting   COOKING TIME 12 minutes
MAKES 6

scant 2¼ cups all-purpose flour,
   plus extra for kneading
   and rolling

2 tsp. salt
3 tbsp. ghee or butter, melted

1   Sift the flour and salt together in a large bowl, then add the ghee, and mix
    with a fork until crumbly. Make a well in the center and add ⅔ cup water in
    a steady stream. Mix in the flour with your other hand until the dough just comes
    together into a ball. Knead the dough on a lightly floured work surface 8 minutes,
    or until smooth and elastic. Cover with a clean, damp dish towel and leave to rest
    45 minutes.
2   On a lightly floured work surface, knead the dough 8 to 10 minutes until
    smooth, then divide it into 6 equal pieces and roll them into balls. On a lightly
    floured work surface, flatten each one into a circle using the palm of your hand,
    then roll them out as thinly as possible, dusting with flour to keep them from
    sticking to the work surface.
3   Heat a large, heavy cast-iron pan or flat griddle over high heat. Cook the rotis,
    one at a time, 40 to 50 seconds until the top starts to bubble and tiny dark brown
    spots appear on the underside. Flip it over and cook on the other side 40 to 50
    seconds longer. Remove from the pan and keep warm under a clean, dry dish
    towel while you cook the remaining rotis. Fold each roti in half and serve hot.

322 Malaysian Roti Jala

PREPARATION TIME 10 minutes   COOKING TIME 1 hour 15 minutes   MAKES 12

2 eggs
2½ cups coconut milk
3¼ cups all-purpose flour
1 tbsp. salt

1 tsp. turmeric
4 tbsp. sunflower oil, for frying,
   plus extra as needed

1   In a large bowl, whisk the eggs well. Add the coconut milk and mix until smooth.
2   Sift the flour, salt, and turmeric together into a separate large bowl and make
    a well in the center. Add the coconut mixture in a steady stream and mix with
    a wooden spoon, then beat until the batter is smooth.
3   Preheat the oven to 200°F. Heat a heavy-bottomed skillet or flat cast-iron
    griddle over low heat (or use a tawa if you have one) and lightly grease it with
    a wad of paper towels dipped in oil. Using a ladle, pour some batter into the pan,
    moving the ladle back and forth over the surface of the batter so the crêpe will
    have a perforated appearance. Cook 2 to 3 minutes until set and pale golden
    underneath, then flip it over and cook 2 to 3 minutes longer. Transfer the roti
    to a plate, cover with a clean, damp dish towel and keep warm in the oven
    while you cook the remaining crêpes, adding more oil to the pan as needed.
    Serve warm.

Spice-Filled Naan

PREPARATION TIME 20 minutes, plus 1 hour 45 minutes rising   **COOKING TIME** 30 minutes
MAKES 4

6 tbsp. ghee or butter,
  plus extra for greasing
1 tsp. honey
2¼ cups all-purpose flour, plus
  extra for kneading and dusting
2 tsp. salt
2 tsp. active dry yeast

NAAN SPICE FILLING
4 tbsp. ghee or butter
1 onion, finely chopped
2 tsp. finely chopped garlic
2 tsp. peeled and finely chopped
  gingerroot
1 tsp. ground coriander
1 tsp. ground cumin
1 tsp. cayenne pepper
½ tsp. cinnamon

1   Melt the ghee in a small pan over low heat. Remove from the heat, add the
    honey, and stir until it dissolves. Sift the flour, salt, and yeast together into a large
    bowl and mix well. Make a well in the center and add the ghee mixture, then
    add ¾ cup water and mix until the ingredients come together into a dough.
    Knead on a lightly floured work surface 8 minutes until smooth and elastic, then
    put it in a lightly greased bowl, cover with a clean, damp dish towel, and leave
    to rise in a warm place 1 to 1½ hours, or until doubled in size.
2   Meanwhile, prepare the filling. Melt the ghee in a skillet over medium-low heat,
    then stir in all of the remaining ingredients and 2 tablespoons water. Cook,
    stirring occasionally, 10 to 15 minutes until the onion is soft. Set aside to cool.
3   Dust two baking sheets with flour. Punch down the dough and divide it into
    4 equal pieces. On a lightly floured work surface, roll out 1 piece into an 8-inch
    circle. Spoon one-quarter of the filling into the middle, then fold two opposite
    edges of the dough over the filling and pinch to seal. Carefully roll into an 8-inch
    oval and put it on the baking sheet. Repeat with the remaining dough, arranging
    the naans side by side on the baking sheets. Cover with clean, damp dish towels
    and leave to rise 15 minutes.
4   Put two more large baking sheets in the oven and preheat it to 450°F. Carefully
    transfer the naans to the heated baking sheets, arranging them side by side, and
    bake 10 to 12 minutes until puffed and golden. Serve warm.

CHAPTER 7

ACCOMPANIMENTS

Chutneys, relishes, pickles, and sauces are all essential companions

to any curry. These extras enrich, temper, and spice up a meal—

and they add a vibrant splash of color to your plate, too.

To begin, match regional dishes for the best fit: serve Sri Lankan

Coconut Relish with Black Pork Curry, for example, or Jamaican Peach

Chutney with West Indian Vegetable Curry. Think about texture,

too. If you're serving a dry curry, such as Tandoori Lamb Chops, or

a broiled kebab dish, complement it with a "saucy" accompaniment,

such as Coconut & Cilantro Chutney or Burmese Tomato Chutney.

To counter the sharp kick pickles give to a meal, serve them

with soothing accompaniments, such as cooling Raita, sweet Apple

& Mango Chutney, or refreshing Kachumber.

For me, a perfect meal is basmati rice and Tarka Dal with

a selection of pickles, such as Beet Pickle, Malaysian Onion Pickle,

and Singapore Mango Pickle. Once you're familiar with the basics,

experiment with new combinations. You'll soon develop a sense

for which ones make your meal complete.

FROM TOP: SPICED CARROT PICKLE (SEE PAGE *212*), CORN RAITA (SEE PAGE *212*), SPROUTED BEAN SAMBOL (*SEE PAGE 199*)

324 Malaysian Pickled Vegetables

PREPARATION TIME 15 minutes, plus at least 24 hours chilling   **COOKING TIME** 16 minutes
SERVES 4 to 6

1 cup plus 2 tbsp.
  white wine vinegar
5 tbsp. sugar
1 tbsp. finely chopped lemongrass
1 tbsp. peeled and
  finely chopped galangal
  or gingerroot
3 garlic cloves
1 tsp. sesame seeds

1 tsp. turmeric
1 tsp. cayenne pepper
1 carrot, cut into matchsticks
3oz. cauliflower florets
½ cucumber, peeled, seeded and
  cut into matchsticks
6 Thai or small shallots, peeled
  but left whole

1   Put the vinegar, sugar, lemongrass, galangal, garlic, sesame seeds, turmeric, and cayenne in a stainless steel or other nonreactive saucepan. Add ½ cup water and bring to a boil. Lower the heat to low and simmer slowly 6 to 8 minutes. Add the carrots and cauliflower and simmer 4 to 5 minutes, then add the cucumber and shallots and simmer 2 to 3 minutes longer. Remove from the heat and leave to cool completely.

2   Pack the vegetables into hot, sterilized glass jars (see page 10) and cover with the pickling liquid. Chill 24 to 48 hours before using. To serve, drain the vegetables from the pickling liquid and serve in little bowls as an appetizer. Store in a cool, dark place 2 to 3 weeks before using and refrigerate once opened. The pickle will keep up to 1 month.

325 Apple & Mango Chutney

PREPARATION TIME 10 minutes, plus 1 week pickling   **COOKING TIME** 1 hour 15 minutes
SERVES 4 to 6

1 tbsp. sunflower oil
1 onion, halved and thinly sliced
1 tsp. peeled and finely grated
  gingerroot
1 cinnamon stick
¼ tsp. cardamom seeds, crushed
¼ tsp. coriander seeds, lightly crushed
¼ tsp. nigella seeds
1 tsp. turmeric

1 apple, peeled, cored, and
  coarsely chopped
2½ cups mango flesh, cut into small
  bite-size cubes
1 red chili, finely chopped
⅔ cup white wine vinegar
⅔ cup sugar
salt

1   Heat the oil in a large, deep stainless-steel skillet over low heat. Add the onion and fry 3 to 4 minutes until starting to soften. Stir in the ginger and cook 8 to 10 minutes longer, stirring frequently, until the onion is golden. Stir in the cinnamon and the cardamom, coriander, and nigella seeds and cook, stirring frequently, 1 to 2 minutes, then stir in the turmeric.

2   Add the apple and scant 1 cup water and cook, covered, 6 to 8 minutes. Stir in the mango and chili and cook, covered, 20 minutes longer, or until the apple breaks down and the mango is tender.

3   Add the vinegar and sugar and heat until the sugar dissolves. Season with salt, then leave to simmer, uncovered, 30 minutes, stirring often, until the mixture is thick. Spoon into hot, sterilized glass jars (see page 10), cover with vinegar-proof seals, and leave to cool on a wire rack. Store in a cool, dark place 1 week before using and refrigerate once opened. The chutney will keep for up to 1 month.

326 Asian-Style Cucumber Pickle

PREPARATION TIME 5 minutes, plus at least 2 hours chilling   **SERVES** 4 to 6

4 tbsp. rice vinegar
4 tsp. sugar
1 tsp. soy sauce
1 tsp. fish sauce

1 tsp. dried chili flakes
2 small cucumbers, cut into
   ¼in.-thick slices

1   In a large bowl, whisk together the rice vinegar, sugar, soy sauce, fish sauce, and crushed red chili. Add the cucumbers and toss well.
2   Cover and chill 2 to 3 hours, tossing the mixture occasionally. The pickle will keep in the refrigerator up to 3 weeks.

327 Sprouted Bean Sambol

PREPARATION TIME 40 minutes, plus 30 minutes standing   **SERVES** 4

3 tbsp. freshly grated or shredded
   coconut
4oz. sprouted beans, washed and
   drained

3 green chilies, seeded and sliced
1 small onion, thinly sliced
juice of 1 lemon
salt

1   If using shredded coconut, soak it in warm water 20 minutes, then drain.
2   In a bowl, mix together all of the ingredients, season with salt, and leave to stand at room temperature 30 minutes. The sambol will keep in the refrigerator up to 4 days.

328 Beet Pickle

PREPARATION TIME 15 minutes, plus 1 week pickling   **COOKING TIME** 3 minutes   **SERVES** 4 to 6

3 raw beets, peeled and cut into
   ½in. cubes
5 green chilies, slit in half lengthwise
2 tbsp. salt
2 tbsp. white wine vinegar

4 tbsp. sunflower oil
2 tsp. black mustard seeds
1 tsp. fenugreek seeds
1 tbsp. asafetida powder
1 tbsp. cayenne pepper

1   Put the beets and chilies in a stainless steel or other nonreactive mixing bowl. Sprinkle the salt and vinegar over and toss well, then set aside.
2   Heat the oil in a small skillet over low heat. Add the mustard and fenugreek seeds and fry 2 to 3 minutes until the mustard seeds start to pop. Remove from the heat and pour the mixture over the beets.
3   Sprinkle the asafetida and cayenne pepper over and stir to mix well. Transfer the mixture to hot, sterilized glass jars with tight-fitting lids (see page 10). Store in a cool, dark place 1 week before using and refrigerate once opened. The pickle will keep up to 1 month after opening.

329 Malaysian Star Fruit Sambal

PREPARATION TIME 10 minutes, plus at least 3 hours standing   **COOKING TIME** 1 minute   **SERVES** 4 to 6

1 tbsp. shrimp paste
3 red chilies, finely chopped
1 tbsp. sugar

3 star fruit, sliced
salt

1   Put the shrimp paste in a small nonstick skillet over high heat and cook, stirring, 1 minute, or until fragrant. Transfer to a mortar, add the chilies and sugar, and pound with a pestle until fine, then season with salt.
2   Put the chili mixture and star fruit in a bowl and mix well, mashing the fruit slightly. Cover and leave to stand at room temperature 3 to 4 hours.

330 Kachumber

PREPARATION TIME 30 minutes   **SERVES** 4

1 red onion, finely chopped
4 tomatoes, finely chopped
1 cucumber, finely chopped
1 red chili, seeded and finely chopped
juice of 1 large lemon

1 small handful cilantro leaves,
  finely chopped
¼ cup coarsely chopped skinless
  roasted peanuts
salt and freshly ground black pepper

1   Put the onion, tomatoes, cucumber, chili, lemon juice, and cilantro in a bowl,
    and mix well. Season well with salt and pepper, then cover and leave to stand
    at room temperature 10 to 15 minutes.
2   Before serving, mix well and sprinkle the chopped nuts over.

331 Burmese Tomato Chutney

PREPARATION TIME 5 minutes   **COOKING TIME** 15 minutes   **SERVES** 4 to 6

2 tbsp. peanut oil
¼ tsp. turmeric
½ tsp. paprika
1 onion, thinly sliced
1 garlic clove, thinly sliced
1 tbsp. shrimp paste

1 tbsp. fish sauce
2 large tomatoes, coarsely chopped
1 red chili, seeded and chopped
2 scallions, finely chopped
2 tbsp. chopped cilantro leaves
salt

1   Heat the oil in a large skillet over low heat. Add the turmeric, paprika, onion, and garlic and cook, stirring occasionally, 6 to 8 minutes until the onion is golden. Add the shrimp paste and cook, stirring, 2 minutes, then add the fish sauce, tomatoes, and 2 tablespoons water. Stir-fry over high heat 5 minutes.
2   Stir in the chili, scallions, and cilantro leaves, remove from the heat, and season with salt. Serve at room temperature. Store in a cool, dark place and refrigerate once opened. The chutney will keep up to 4 days.

332 Coconut & Cilantro Chutney

PREPARATION TIME 20 minutes   **SERVES** 4 to 6

1 cup freshly grated or
   shredded coconut
3 cups coarsely chopped cilantro
   leaves and stems
1 cup coarsely chopped mint leaves
1 small onion, coarsely chopped
1in. piece gingerroot, peeled and
   coarsely chopped
2 garlic cloves, coarsely chopped

1 or 2 red chilies, seeded
   and chopped
juice of 2 limes
1 tsp. coriander seeds
2 cloves
¼ tsp. cinnamon
1 tsp. sugar
salt

1   If using shredded coconut, soak it in warm water 20 minutes, then drain.
2   Put the coconut, cilantro, mint, onion, ginger, garlic, chilies, and lime juice in a food processor. Blend 1 to 2 minutes until the mixture forms a thick, coarse paste. Add a little water if necessary.
3   Put the coriander seeds, cloves, and cinnamon in a clean spice grinder and grind 1 to 2 minutes until the mixture forms a fine powder. Mix the spices and sugar into the coconut mixture, then season with salt. Mix well and use immediately or store in an airtight container in the refrigerator up to 4 days.

333 Mint & Cilantro Chutney

PREPARATION TIME 15 minutes   **SERVES** 4 to 6

2 cups finely chopped mint leaves
2 cups finely chopped cilantro leaves
½ cup thick Greek-style yogurt
2 green chilies, seeded and chopped
1 tbsp. peeled and finely grated
   gingerroot

1 tsp. ground cumin
1 tsp. cayenne pepper
1 tsp. sugar
juice of 2 limes
salt

1   Put the mint, cilantro, yogurt, chilies, ginger, cumin, cayenne, sugar, and lime juice in a blender or small food processor and blend 1 to 2 minutes until smooth, adding 1 to 2 tablespoons water if necessary.
2   Season with salt and transfer to a bowl. Cover and chill until ready to use. The chutney will keep in the refrigerator up to 3 days.

334 Indian Red Cabbage Chutney

PREPARATION TIME 15 minutes   **COOKING TIME** 40 minutes   **SERVES** 6 to 8

1lb. finely shredded red
  cabbage
8oz. apples, peeled, cored, and
  finely chopped
1 tbsp. peeled and finely chopped
  gingerroot
3 garlic cloves, finely chopped

2 tsp. cayenne pepper
1 tsp. turmeric
1 cinnamon stick
1⅓ cups firmly packed light
  brown sugar
scant 1 cup red wine vinegar

1   Put all of the ingredients in a large, heavy-bottomed stainless steel or other
    nonreactive saucepan and bring to a boil over high heat, stirring until the
    sugar dissolves. Lower the heat to low and simmer 35 to 40 minutes, stirring
    frequently, until thick.
2   Transfer the chutney to hot, sterilized glass jars (see page 10), cover with
    vinegar-proof seals, and leave to cool on a wire rack. Store in a cool, dark
    place 1 week before using. The chutney will keep in the refrigerator up to
    1 month after opening.

335 Spicy Yogurt Pachadi

PREPARATION TIME 15 minutes   **COOKING TIME** 40 seconds   **SERVES** 4

1 large cucumber, peeled and
  finely diced
2 tomatoes, finely chopped
2 tsp. sugar
5 tbsp. finely chopped
  cilantro leaves
1½ cups plain yogurt

1 tbsp. sunflower oil
1 tsp. black mustard seeds
1 tsp. cumin seeds
1 tbsp. coarsely chopped skinless
  roasted peanuts
2 tbsp. pomegranate seeds
salt

1   Put the cucumber, tomatoes, sugar, and cilantro leaves in a bowl, season
    with salt, and toss well.
2   In a separate bowl, whisk the yogurt until smooth, then pour it over the
    cucumber mixture and toss to coat well. Transfer to a shallow serving bowl.
3   Heat the oil in a small skillet over high heat. Add the mustard and cumin
    seeds and stir-fry 30 to 40 seconds until the mustard seeds begin to pop.
    Remove from the heat and drizzle the spices over the cucumber mixture,
    then sprinkle with the nuts and pomegranate seeds. Store in the
    refrigerator up to 3 days.

336 Japanese Wasabi Pickled Cucumbers

PREPARATION TIME 10 minutes, plus 48 hours pickling   **SERVES** 4

4 small cucumbers
1 tbsp. wasabi powder

4 tbsp. sugar
4 tbsp. salt

1   Put the cucumbers in a sealable plastic food bag. In a small bowl, mix together
    the wasabi powder, sugar, and salt. Add this mixture to the bag and shake to
    coat the cucumbers well. Seal the bag and put it in the refrigerator for 48 hours.
2   Remove the cucumbers from the bag, and rinse them under cold water. Cut them
    into thin diagonal slices and serve. Store in the refrigerator up to 3 months.

337 Turkish Spiced Walnut Dip

PREPARATION TIME 15 minutes, plus at least 2 hours chilling and making the curry powder
SERVES 4 to 6

2 cups chopped walnuts
1 red bell pepper, seeded and
  finely chopped
1 red onion, finely chopped
3 garlic cloves, crushed
3 green chilies, finely chopped

1 tsp. molasses
¼ tsp. Curry Powder (see page 11)
1 tbsp. ground cumin
⅓ cup olive oil
salt and freshly ground black pepper

1 Put the walnuts, red pepper, onion, garlic, chilies, molasses, curry powder,
   cumin, and olive oil in a food processor and blend until the mixture forms
   a fairly smooth puree. Season with salt and pepper, then transfer to a bowl.
2 Chill, covered, 2 to 3 hours. The dip can be stored in an airtight jar in the
   refrigerator for up to 1 week.

338 Burmese Cucumber Pickle

PREPARATION TIME 10 minutes   **COOKING TIME** 16 minutes   **SERVES** 4 to 6

½ cup malt vinegar or cider vinegar
1 tsp. salt
2 large cucumbers, halved
  lengthwise, seeded and cut
  into 2in. batons

4 tbsp. peanut oil
2 tbsp. sesame oil
8 garlic cloves, thinly sliced
1 onion, thinly sliced
2 tbsp. sesame seeds

1 Put the vinegar, salt, and 2 cups plus 2 tablespoons water in a saucepan and bring
   to a boil over high heat. Add the cucumbers and boil 3 to 4 minutes until they are
   just transparent; do not overcook. Drain immediately and set aside to cool.
2 In a skillet, heat the peanut and sesame oils over low heat, add the garlic and fry
   2 to 3 minutes, stirring occasionally, until light golden. Remove with a slotted
   spoon and drain on paper towels.
3 Add the onion to the same pan and fry 6 to 8 minutes until light brown.
4 Meanwhile, put the sesame seeds in a dry skillet and heat over medium-low heat
   4 to 5 minutes, stirring constantly, until they are evenly golden brown. Watch
   carefully so they do not burn.
5 Put the cucumber in a shallow bowl. Add the oil from the skillet along with the
   garlic, onion, and sesame seeds and toss well. Store in a cool, dark place and
   refrigerate once opened. The pickle will keep up to 1 week.

339 Malaysian Red Chili Sambal

PREPARATION TIME 10 minutes, plus 30 minutes soaking   **COOKING TIME** 15 minutes
SERVES 4 to 6

8 to 10 dried red chilies
3 large onions, finely chopped
6 garlic cloves, chopped
2 to 3 tbsp. shrimp paste
scant 1 cup sunflower oil

1 tbsp. sugar
1 tsp. salt
2 tbsp. tomato paste
juice of 2 limes

1 Put the chilies in a bowl, cover with hot water, and leave to soak 30 minutes, then
   drain. Transfer to a small food processor, add the onions, garlic, and shrimp paste
   and blend 2 to 3 minutes until the mixture forms a fairly smooth paste.
2 Heat the oil in a wok or saucepan over low heat. Add the chili paste and cook,
   stirring occasionally, 15 minutes until thick. Stir in the sugar, salt, tomato paste,
   and lime juice, then remove from the heat and leave to cool. Store in an airtight
   jar in the refrigerator up to 1 week. Serve at room temperature.

340 Onion Pickle

PREPARATION TIME 10 minutes, plus at least 2 hours standing   **SERVES** 4 to 6

2 onions, halved and very thinly sliced
6 bird's-eye chilies, thinly sliced
2 or 3 kaffir lime leaves,
   finely shredded

1 tbsp. peeled and finely grated
   gingerroot
1 tbsp. salt
2 tbsp. sugar
juice of 2 limes

1   Put all of the ingredients in a medium bowl and mix together well.
2   Cover and leave to stand at room temperature 2 to 3 hours. The pickle will keep in the refrigerator up to 1 month.

341 Mint Chutney

PREPARATION TIME 10 minutes   **SERVES** 4 to 6

2 cups finely chopped
   mint leaves
juice of 3 limes
2 green chilies,
   seeded and chopped
2 tbsp. sugar

1 tbsp. peeled and finely grated
   gingerroot
1 tsp. ground cumin
1 tsp. ground coriander
salt

1   Put the mint, lime juice, chilies, sugar, ginger, cumin, and coriander in a blender or small food processor and blend until smooth, adding 1 to 2 tablespoons water if necessary. Season with salt, then transfer to a bowl.
2   Use immediately or store in an airtight container in the refrigerator up to 3 days.

342 Nuoc Cham Dipping Sauce

PREPARATION TIME 15 minutes   **SERVES** 4 to 6

2 garlic cloves, peeled but left whole
1 red chili, slit lengthwise and seeded
juice and pulp of 1 lime

4 tbsp. fish sauce
2 tbsp. sugar

1   Put the garlic and chili in a food processor (or use a mortar and pestle) and blend 2 to 3 minutes until the mixture forms a paste. Add the lime juice and pulp and blend well. Transfer the mixture to a small bowl. Add the fish sauce, sugar, and 2 to 4 tablespoons water, to taste, and mix until the sugar dissolves.
2   Use immediately or store in an airtight container in the refrigerator up to 1 week.

343 Raita

PREPARATION TIME 10 minutes   **COOKING TIME** 4 minutes   **SERVES** 4

1½ cups plain yogurt, whisked
1 small cucumber, peeled and
   coarsely grated
5 tbsp. finely chopped mint leaves

1 to 2 tsp. cumin seeds
pinch of cayenne (optional)
salt and freshly ground black pepper

1   Put the yogurt in a bowl. Squeeze out all of the excess liquid from the grated cucumber, then stir the cucumber and mint into the yogurt. Season well with salt and pepper, cover, and chill until ready to serve.
2   Put the cumin seeds in a small skillet and dry-roast over low heat 3 to 4 minutes until fragrant. Remove from the heat and leave to cool.
3   Transfer the raita to a serving bowl and sprinkle the cumin seeds and cayenne over, if using. The raita will keep in the refrigerator up to 4 days.

344 Kimchi

PREPARATION TIME 15 minutes, plus at least 3 hours standing and 24 hours pickling
SERVES 4 to 6

1lb. coarsely chopped Chinese
  cabbage,
1 tbsp. salt
2 scallions, finely chopped
4 garlic cloves, crushed
1 tbsp. cayenne pepper

2 tsp. peeled and finely chopped
  gingerroot
7 tbsp. light soy sauce
7 tbsp. white wine vinegar
1 tbsp. sugar
sesame oil, to serve

1 Put the cabbage in a stainless steel or other nonreactive bowl. Sprinkle with
the salt, toss well, and leave to stand 3 to 4 hours (the cabbage will wilt).
2 Drain off the excess liquid and return the cabbage to the bowl. Add the
scallions, garlic, cayenne, ginger, soy sauce, vinegar, and sugar and toss
together until well mixed.
3 Transfer to a large glass jar, seal, and chill at least 24 hours before using.
Sprinkle with a few drops of sesame oil before using. The kimchi will keep
up to 1 week in the refrigerator.

345 Garlic Pickled in Miso

PREPARATION TIME 10 minutes, plus at least 3 months pickling   **COOKING TIME** 3 minutes
SERVES 4 to 6

16 garlic cloves, peeled but left whole
⅔ cup red miso paste

1 Put the garlic in a small saucepan of boiling water and boil 3 minutes,
then drain. Pat the garlic dry with paper towels, then cut each clove
in half lengthwise.
2 Put the miso in a small, sterilized glass jar with a tight-fitting lid (see page 10).
Push the garlic into the miso, making certain it is completely covered. Cover
the jar or container and refrigerate at least 3 months.
3 After 3 months, begin removing the pickled garlic from the miso as needed,
leaving the rest to continue pickling. Rinse the cloves and pat dry with paper
towels before serving. Once you have eaten all of the pickled garlic, you can
use the pickling miso to make miso soup.

346 Mauritian Mayonnaise

PREPARATION TIME 15 minutes, plus making the curry powder **SERVES** 4 to 6

2 extra-large egg yolks, at room
  temperature
1 tsp. minced garlic
1 teaspoon Dijon mustard
1 tsp. Curry Powder (see page 11)

1 tsp. salt
½ tsp. freshly ground black pepper
scant 1¼ cups sunflower oil
2 to 3 tsp. white wine vinegar

1 Put the egg yolks in a large bowl. Add the garlic, mustard, curry powder,
salt, and pepper. Using an immersion blender or whisk, blend until smooth
and well combined.
2 Gradually add the oil in a thin, steady stream, whisking vigorously all of the time,
until the mixture is thick and fluffy, then whisk in the vinegar until the mixture
is smooth and thick. Check the seasoning and adjust to taste. The mayonnaise
is best served as soon as possible, so serve immediately or store in the refrigerator
up to 3 days.

347 Spiced Beet & Apple Chutney

PREPARATION TIME 10 minutes   **COOKING TIME** 40 minutes   **SERVES** 8 to 10

2½ cups chopped onions
2 cups plus 2 tbsp. white wine vinegar
2lb. 4oz. cooked (but not pickled)
  beets, finely chopped
2 firm cooking apples, peeled, cored,
  and finely chopped

2½ cups firmly packed light
  brown sugar
1 tbsp. crushed coriander seeds
1 tbsp. crushed cumin seeds
2 tsp. salt

1 Put all of the ingredients, except the salt, in a large saucepan. Bring to a boil over high heat and boil 10 minutes, stirring continuously, until the sugar dissolves. Stir in the salt, then lower the heat to low and simmer 25 to 30 minutes, stirring often, until thick.

2 Pour into hot, sterilized glass jars (see page 10), cover tightly with vinegar-proof lids, and leave to cool on a wire rack. Serve at room temperature or store in the refrigerator up to 2 weeks.

348   Nuoc Mau (Vietnamese Caramel Sauce)

PREPARATION TIME 5 minutes, plus 2 weeks pickling   **COOKING TIME** 25 minutes   **SERVES** 4 to 6

1 cup sugar

1   Put a medium heavy-bottomed saucepan in the sink and fill the sink with enough water to come halfway up the side of the pan. Leave the water in the sink and put the pan on the stovetop. Put the sugar and 4 tablespoons water in the pan and cook over medium-low heat, stirring, 2 to 3 minutes until the sugar dissolves.

2   As the syrup heats, it will turn from opaque to clear and small bubbles will form at the edge of the pan and gradually grow larger, moving toward the center until they eventually cover the entire surface. Continue cooking, without stirring, 15 minutes longer, or until the sugar caramelizes and turns a dark golden brown color similar to dark tea. When the syrup starts to smoke, remove the pan from the heat and slowly swirl the syrup around. Watch closely, as it will turn darker by the second. When it is very dark, like the color of black coffee or dark molasses, carefully immerse the pan in the sink of cold water to stop the cooking process. Be careful, because the hot pan and cold water will create a lot of steam.

3   When any bubbles subside, add another ½ cup water and return the pan to the stovetop. Cook over low heat 6 to 8 minutes, stirring continuously, until the caramel dissolves into the water. The result will be a slightly viscous, bittersweet caramel sauce. Pour the sauce into a hot sterilized glass jar with a tight-fitting lid (see page 10), seal, and leave to cool. The sauce will keep up to 2 weeks, covered, in a cool, dark place at room temperature.

349   Pickled Ginger

PREPARATION TIME 10 minutes, plus 1 hour standing and 3 weeks pickling
COOKING TIME 5 minutes   **SERVES** 4 to 6

1lb. gingerroot, peeled and very
  thinly sliced
2 tsp. salt

2 cups rice vinegar
1 cup superfine sugar

1   Put the ginger in a medium bowl, sprinkle the salt over, and toss well. Leave to stand 1 hour, then remove it from the bowl and pat dry with paper towels. Pack the slices in a large, sterilized jar with a tight-fitting lid (see page 10).

2   Put the rice vinegar and sugar in a stainless steel or other nonreactive saucepan and stir well. Bring to a boil over high heat and boil, stirring continuously, 5 minutes, or until the sugar dissolves. Carefully pour the hot mixture over the ginger and leave to cool on a wire rack. Once cooled, seal the jar and store in the refrigerator 3 weeks before opening.

350   Vietnamese Shallot Sauce

PREPARATION TIME 5 minutes   **COOKING TIME** 13 minutes   **SERVES** 4 to 6

heaped ⅓ cup sugar
4 tbsp. fish sauce
6 Thai or small shallots, thinly sliced

1 tsp. freshly ground black pepper,
  or to taste

1   Put the sugar in a small, heavy-bottomed saucepan over low heat and cook 8 to 10 minutes, swirling the pan constantly, until the sugar browns and starts to smoke slightly. Immediately remove the pan from the heat and slowly stir in the fish sauce. Be extra careful to avoid spattering—the mixture will bubble vigorously. Return the mixture to low heat and cook 3 minutes, swirling the pan occasionally, until the sugar completely dissolves.

2   Stir in the shallots and pepper, then remove from the heat and use immediately.

351 Pickled Green Chilies

PREPARATION TIME 10 minutes, plus at least 4 days pickling   **SERVES** 4 to 6

10oz. green chilies, sliced into thin
  rings
½ cup white wine vinegar

1 tbsp. salt
5 tbsp. sugar

1 Pack the chilies in a sterilized glass jar with a tight-fitting vinegar-proof lid (see page 10).
2 Put the vinegar, salt, sugar, and 1 cup plus 2 tablespoons water In a small bowl and mix together until the sugar dissolves.
3 Pour the pickling liquid over the chilies to cover them completely. Seal and store in the refrigerator 4 to 5 days before using. The chilies will keep in the refrigerator up to 1 month.

352 Pickled Papaya

PREPARATION TIME 15 minutes, plus 1 hour standing and at least 2 hours marinating
COOKING TIME 20 minutes   **SERVES** 4 to 6

1 green (unripe) papaya, peeled,
  halved lengthwise,
  and seeded
1 tbsp. salt

1 cup white wine vinegar
heaped 1 cup sugar
5 or 6 bird's-eye chilies

1 Thinly slice the papaya and put it in a clean, stainless steel or other nonreactive bowl. Sprinkle the salt over, toss well, and then cover and leave to stand 1 hour until the papaya softens. Transfer the papaya to a large sieve and squeeze out the excess liquid. Set aside.
2 Meanwhile, put the vinegar, sugar, and 1 cup plus 2 tablespoons water in a heavy-bottomed saucepan and bring it to a gentle simmer over medium-low heat. Simmer 4 to 5 minutes, stirring continuously, until the sugar dissolves. Continue simmering 10 to 15 minutes longer until slightly thickened. Remove the pan from the heat and set aside to cool completely.
3 Pack the drained papaya slices and the chilies in a hot sterilized glass jar with a tight-fitting lid (see page 10), then pour the cooled vinegar syrup over to cover. When cool, seal and leave to marinate 2 to 3 hours before serving. The pickle will keep in the refrigerator up to 1 week.

353 Vietnamese Carrot & Radish Pickle

PREPARATION TIME 35 minutes, plus at least 2 hours marinating   **SERVES** 4 to 6

1½ cups finely grated daikon
  (white radish)
1⅓ cups finely grated carrots
2 tbsp. salt

2 tbsp. sugar
7 tbsp. rice vinegar or
  white wine vinegar

1 Put the daikon and carrots in a bowl, sprinkle the salt over, and toss together lightly. Leave to stand at least 20 minutes.
2 Transfer the daikon and carrot mixture to a sieve and rinse off the salt under cold running water. Drain thoroughly, then use your hands to gently squeeze as much of the liquid from the vegetable mixture as possible.
3 Transfer the vegetables to a small stainless steel or other nonreactive bowl, add the sugar and vinegar, and toss well. Cover and leave to marinate in the refrigerator at least 2 hours. Store any leftovers in a hot sterilized glass jar with a tight-fitting lid (see page 10). The pickle will keep in the refrigerator up to 1 month.

354 Sambhar

PREPARATION TIME 35 minutes, plus making the idlis COOKING TIME 50 minutes
SERVES 4 to 6

4 tbsp. tamarind paste
1¼ cups split red lentils, rinsed
   and drained
1 tsp. turmeric
4 tbsp. sunflower oil
2 dried red chilies
8 curry leaves
1 tsp. black mustard seeds
½ tsp. fenugreek seeds
1 onion, finely chopped
¼ tsp. asafetida powder
8oz. green beans,
   trimmed and cut into
   bite-size pieces

2 carrots, chopped
1 large tomato, finely chopped
1 recipe quantity Idlis (see page 179),
   to serve

SAMBHAR POWDER
1 tsp. ground coriander
1 tsp. cayenne pepper
1 tsp. ground cumin
1 tsp. ground black pepper
½ tsp. black mustard seeds
a pinch of cinnamon
a pinch of ground cloves

1   In a small bowl, mix together all of the ingredients for the sambhar powder.
2   Put the tamarind paste in a medium bowl, cover with scant 1 cup hot water
    and leave to stand 15 minutes, then press the mixture through a sieve into
    a clean bowl, extracting as much of the tamarind as possible.
3   Put the lentils in a large, heavy-bottomed saucepan with 3¾ cups water. Add the
    turmeric and 2 tablespoons of the oil. Bring to a boil over high heat and skim off
    any scum that rises to the surface. Boil 25 to 30 minutes until the lentils are soft,
    then whisk 1 to 2 minutes to break up the lentils into a coarse mixture.
4   Meanwhile, in a separate pan, heat the remaining 2 tablespoons of the oil over
    medium heat. When the oil is hot, add the chilies, curry leaves, and mustard and
    fenugreek seeds and fry 2 minutes, or until fragrant and the mustard seeds start
    to pop. Add the onion and continue frying 5 minutes longer, or until the onion is
    light brown. Add the tamarind mixture, lower the heat to low, and leave to cook
    10 minutes until the onions are completely soft and translucent.
5   Add the onion mixture to the lentils and stir in the asafetida, green beans, carrots,
    tomato, and sambhar powder. Leave to simmer over low heat 15 to 20 minutes
    until slightly thickened. Serve immediately with idlis.

355 South Indian Coconut Chutney

PREPARATION TIME 20 minutes, plus at least 2 hours soaking COOKING TIME 5 minutes
SERVES 4

2 tsp. split yellow lentils, rinsed
   and drained
1⅓ cups freshly grated or shredded
   coconut
2 green chilies, seeded and finely
   chopped
1 tsp. salt

2 tbsp. sunflower oil
2 tsp. black mustard seeds
6 to 8 curry leaves
1 dried red chili, slit lengthwise
   and seeded
1 tsp. tamarind paste

1   Soak the lentils in cold water 2 to 3 hours; drain and set aside. If using shredded
    coconut, soak it in warm water 20 minutes, then drain.
2   Put the coconut, green chilies, and salt in a food processor and blend 1 minute,
    or until smooth. Add a little water if the mixture is too thick. Transfer to a bowl.
3   Heat the oil in a small skillet over low heat. Add the mustard seeds and the lentils
    and cook, covered, 3 to 4 minutes until you hear the mustard seeds begin to pop.
    Add the curry leaves and dried chili and cook, stirring, 1 minute.
4   Pour the lentil mixture into the coconut mixture, add the tamarind paste, and mix
    well. Serve immediately, or store, covered, in the refrigerator up to 4 days
    until ready to use.

356 Tobago Tamarind Chutney

PREPARATION TIME 5 minutes   **COOKING TIME** 11 minutes   **SERVES** 4 to 6

1 cup tamarind paste
¾ cup sugar
4 garlic cloves, finely chopped

1 Scotch bonnet or habanero chili,
   seeded and finely chopped
1 tsp. ground cumin
2 tsp. cornstarch

1 Put the tamarind paste, sugar, garlic, chili, cumin, and scant 1 cup water
   in a saucepan. Bring to a boil over high heat, then lower the heat to low and
   simmer, stirring occasionally, 6 to 8 minutes.
2 Dissolve the cornstarch in 3 tablespoons cold water and stir in 1 tablespoon
   of the tamarind mixture until smooth. Pour this mixture into the pan and cook,
   stirring, 2 to 3 minutes until the chutney is thick enough to coat the back of a
   spoon. If it is too thick, add 1 tablespoon water to thin it slightly. Use immediately
   or store in the refrigerator up to 3 days. Serve warm or at room temperature.

357 Singapore Mango Pickle

PREPARATION TIME 10 minutes, plus 1 hour standing and 2 days pickling
COOKING TIME 5 minutes   **SERVES** 4 to 6

3 cups, peeled, pitted, and thinly
   sliced green (unripe) mango

4½ tsp. salt
heaped 1 cup sugar

1 Put the mango in a large stainless steel or other nonreactive bowl, sprinkle
   the salt over, and toss well. Cover and leave to stand at least 1 hour, stirring
   occasionally. Drain the mango and rinse under cold running water. Spread in
   a single layer on paper towels to dry.
2 Meanwhile, in a small saucepan, bring the sugar and 1 cup plus 2 tablespoons
   water to a boil over high heat and cook 5 minutes, stirring frequently, until the
   sugar dissolves. Remove from the heat and leave to cool completely.
3 Pack the mango slices into a hot, sterilized jar with a tight-fitting lid (see
   page 10) and pour the syrup over to cover the mango completely. Seal and
   leave the pickle to mature 2 days before eating. It will keep in the refrigerator
   up to 1 month.

358 Spiced Tomato Chutney

PREPARATION TIME 10 minutes   **COOKING TIME** 35 minutes   **SERVES** 4 to 6

4 tbsp. sunflower oil
1 onion, halved and thinly sliced
3 garlic cloves, thinly sliced
1 tsp. peeled and finely grated
   gingerroot
3 tsp. dried chili flakes

2 tsp. black mustard seeds
2 tsp. cumin seeds
1 tsp. crushed coriander seeds
15oz. crushed tomatoes
1 cup sugar
salt and freshly ground black pepper

1 Heat the oil in a skillet over low heat. Add the onion and fry 6 to 7 minutes
   until light brown. Stir in the garlic, ginger, chilies, mustard, and cumin and
   coriander seeds and cook 2 to 3 minutes.
2 Stir in the tomatoes and sugar and cook, stirring occasionally, 20 to 25 minutes.
   Season well with salt and pepper, then remove from the heat.
3 Pour the chutney into a hot, sterilized glass jar with a tight-fitting lid (see page
   10) and leave to cool on a wire rack. Use immediately or seal well and store in
   the refrigerator up to 1 week. Serve at room temperature.

359 Jamaican Peach Chutney

PREPARATION TIME 10 minutes   **COOKING TIME** 10 minutes   **SERVES** 4 to 6

1 tbsp. butter
1 onion, finely chopped
2 large peaches, halved, pitted, and
    finely chopped

3 tbsp. light brown sugar
3 tbsp. white wine vinegar
1 tsp. jerk seasoning

1   Melt the butter in a small skillet over low heat. Add the onion, and cook
    5 to 6 minutes, stirring frequently, until soft and translucent.
2   Add the peaches, sugar, vinegar, and jerk seasoning and cook 2 to 3 minutes,
    stirring often, until the sugar dissolves and the chutney is thoroughly heated
    through. Serve immediately. The chutney will keep in the refrigerator up to 1 week.

360 Corn Raita

PREPARATION TIME 10 minutes, plus cooling time   COOKING TIME 7 minutes   SERVES 4

4 tbsp. sunflower oil
1 tsp. black mustard seeds
1 tsp. finely chopped garlic
1 tsp. peeled and finely chopped
  gingerroot
1 red chili, seeded and
  finely chopped

2 cups fresh or canned corn kernels
½ red bell pepper, seeded and
  finely chopped
heaped 1 cup plain yogurt
2 tbsp. finely chopped cilantro leaves
salt

1   Heat the oil in a large, nonstick skillet over low heat. Add the mustard seeds, garlic, ginger, and chili and cook, stirring occasionally, 2 to 3 minutes until the mixture is fragrant.
2   Stir in the corn, pepper, and 2 to 3 tablespoons water and continue stirring 3 to 4 minutes until the pepper is slightly softer. Season with salt, remove from the heat, and leave to cool.
3   Put the yogurt in a bowl and whisk until smooth. Stir in the corn mixture and cilantro and serve immediately or store in the refrigerator up to 4 days.

361 Papaya & Chili Raita

PREPARATION TIME 5 minutes   SERVES 4

1lb. 8oz. papaya, halved lengthwise
  and seeded
2 red chilies, seeded and finely
  chopped

⅔ cup plain yogurt
2 tsp. roasted cumin seeds, crushed
1 tsp. cayenne pepper
salt

1   Peel the papaya and cut the flesh into ½-inch cubes. Put them in a bowl and gently toss in the chilies.
2   Put the yogurt in a separate bowl and stir in the cumin seeds. Season well with salt, then add this mixture to the papaya. Stir to coat evenly, then sprinkle over the cayenne.
3   Serve immediately or store in the refrigerator up to 2 days.

362 Spiced Carrot Pickle

PREPARATION TIME 15 minutes, plus 2 weeks pickling   COOKING TIME 5 minutes
MAKES about 3¼ cups

1lb. carrots, cut into 2in. batons
7oz. Thai or small shallots, peeled
  but left whole
6 to 8 green chilies
⅔ cup white wine vinegar
½ tsp. turmeric
1 tsp. salt

PICKLING PASTE
⅔ cup white wine vinegar
4 garlic cloves, minced
2 tsp. peeled and finely grated
  gingerroot
1 tbsp. black mustard seeds
2 tsp. cayenne pepper
1 tbsp. sugar
salt

1   Put the carrots, shallots, chilies, vinegar, and 1¼ cups water in a saucepan, then sprinkle the turmeric and salt over. Bring to a boil over high heat and cook 3 to 4 minutes, then drain and set aside while you make the pickling paste.
2   Put all of the ingredients for the pickling paste in a small food processor and blend until fairly smooth. Season with salt, blend again briefly, and transfer to a bowl. Add the drained vegetables and toss to coat evenly.
3   Pack the pickle mixture in a hot, sterilized glass jar (see page 10) and seal with a vinegar-proof lid. Store in a cool, dark place 2 weeks before eating and refrigerate once opened. The pickle will keep in the refrigerator for up to 1 month.

363 Sri Lankan Lemon & Date Pickle

PREPARATION TIME 20 minutes, plus 24 hours soaking and 1 month pickling
COOKING TIME 50 minutes **SERVES** 4 to 6

10 dried red chilies, stems removed
and seeded
1 tbsp. black mustard seeds
2 cups plus 2 tbsp. white wine vinegar
2 tbsp. peeled and finely grated
gingerroot
20 garlic cloves, coarsely chopped

2 cups sugar
2¾ cups pitted dried dates,
halved
6 preserved or pickled lemons,
coarsely chopped
1⅔ cups golden raisins

1 Put the chilies, mustard seeds, and vinegar in a stainless steel or other nonreactive
bowl and leave to soak 24 hours.
2 Transfer the mixture to a blender, add the ginger and garlic, and blend 1 to 2
minutes until fairly smooth. Transfer the mixture to a large saucepan and add
the sugar. Bring to a boil over high heat, then lower the heat to low and simmer
slowly 20 to 30 minutes until thick.
3 Add the dates, lemons, and golden raisins and bring the mixture back to a boil.
Lower the heat to low again and simmer 15 to 20 minutes longer, stirring
frequently. Remove from the heat, spoon the pickle into hot, sterilized glass jars
(see page 10), seal with vinegar-proof lids, and leave to cool on a wire rack. Store
in a cool, dark place 1 month before using and up to 3 months total. Refrigerate
once opened and use within 1 month of opening.

364 Sweet Mango Chutney

PREPARATION TIME 20 minutes **COOKING TIME** 55 minutes **MAKES** about 2 cups

1 tbsp. sunflower oil
1 tsp. peeled and finely grated
gingerroot
2 garlic cloves, crushed
5 cloves
1 star anise
2 cassia bark or cinnamon sticks
5 whole black peppercorns

1 to 2 tbsp. nigella seeds
½ tsp. cayenne pepper
1lb. 12oz. ripe but firm mango flesh,
coarsely chopped
1¾ cups white wine vinegar
1⅓ cups sugar
salt

1 Heat the oil in a medium saucepan over low heat. Add the ginger, garlic, cloves,
star anise, cassia bark, black peppercorns, nigella seeds, and cayenne. Cook,
stirring, 1 to 2 minutes until fragrant, then add the mango, vinegar, and sugar.
Bring to a boil and cook 4 to 5 minutes, stirring gently, until the sugar dissolves.
Lower the heat to low and simmer 45 minutes, or until the mixture thickens to
a jamlike consistency. Stir occasionally to make sure the chutney does not catch
on the bottom of the pan and burn.
2 Season with salt and pour into hot, sterilized glass jars (see page 10). Seal with
vinegar-proof lids and leave to cool completely on a wire rack before using. The
chutney will keep in the refrigerator up to 2 months after opening.

365 Sri Lankan Coconut Relish

PREPARATION TIME 5 minutes, plus 30 minutes standing **SERVES** 4 to 6

1 tbsp. grated red onion
1 garlic clove, crushed
scant ½ cup shredded coconut
1 tsp. cayenne pepper

1 tsp. paprika
1 tbsp. anchovy sauce
1 tbsp. lime juice

1 Put all of the ingredients in a small bowl and mix well.
2 Leave to stand at room temperature 30 minutes before serving. The relish
will keep in the refrigerator up to 3 days.

Index